The Fulbright Premise

The Fulbright Premise:

SENATOR J. WILLIAM FULBRIGHT'S VIEWS ON PRESIDENTIAL POWER

Naomi B. Lynn

and

Arthur F. McClure

Lewisburg
BUCKNELL UNIVERSITY PRESS

Library of Congress Cataloging in Publication Data

Lynn, Naomi B.
    The Fulbright premise.

    Bibliography: p.
    1. Executive power—United States. 2. United States—Foreign relations. 3. Fulbright, John William, 1905–   I. McClure, Arthur F., joint author. II. Title.
JK570.L93   353.03'2   72-14248
ISBN 0-8387-1358-0

To
Bob Lynn
and Judy McClure
For all the reasons—

CONTENTS

FOREWORD

As I start my second term in the House of Representatives, I am impressed by the frequency with which the political discussion turns to the question of presidential power. The subject not only emerges as a ready topic for conversation and legislation, but it also is discussed with an intensity that denotes strength of feelings that often even transcend party lines.

Although the question of the proper balance between executive and legislative power often centers on domestic issues, it is in the area of foreign policy that most of the attention has been focused. One reason for the emphasis on foreign policy is that our nation has been involved in a costly war that most Americans do not understand. Sometimes we doubt that our leaders themselves understand, when the justifications for the sacrifice are constantly changed and juggled. Peace again and again seems close—only to elude us. Both the Senate and the House too often have acted as if they were observers with only a peripheral role to play. But our Constitution calls for a balance between the executive and legislative branches.

Congress has all too often relinquished its power to the executive and then appeared to be at a loss in regaining it. Sometimes, simply out of neglect or oversight, laws are left on the books after they have fulfilled their purpose. Then, when an active executive chooses to exercise those powers, Congress finds it easier to permit this than to review the specific purposes for which the legislation was passed. As the 93rd Congress begins, however, it is apparent that the question of executive versus congressional power will be raised as an issue in a more pressing way than it

9

has been heard in recent decades. High stakes ride on the outcome of this question.

In a real sense, we have all had an equal stake in our world and nation's problems since some obstetrician swatted our respective rears and we let out our first lusty cry in protest. One thing we cannot protest: we have never been short-changed in the number and magnitude of problems, and likewise, the number and magnitude of opportunities for those of us living in the twentieth century.

I will not review either the problems or the opportunities, but it is difficult to exaggerate their immensity; let no one diminish their size by such common techniques as telling about the apparently equally great decisive problems facing our predecessors in this globe, or by pointing out that by the combination of genius and good breaks everything has always come out all right. Surely if dinosaurs conversed, similar conversations were exchanged by these magnificent creatures a few millennia ago.

In our time, there is a serious question if the human organism and our social institutions can adjust to the rapidity of change in the world in which we live. And if they cannot, obsolescence and doomsday are not the figment of a few fertile imaginations, but are a real alternative present in our midst.

It is a fact that human knowledge doubles each five to seven years. It is not an exponential change that we can easily observe, but the results as well as the implications of this fact are with us each minute. Little wonder, with this ever-accelerating rate of change, that each of our recent presidents appears to be several presidents, with several contradicting policies all in a very short span of time.

But with these potential dangers to the human race, come as well opportunities unlike any we have ever had before. Not only can presidents change like chameleons, but with modern worldwide communication, entire populations and widely held traditional wisdoms can change almost instantly. To put it conservatively, physical changes, and perhaps more importantly mental changes, which historically and only a short time ago took a decade, can now occur in less than a year, and changes which formerly took a century can occur in a decade.

The technocracy, the super-industrial state, whatever we may call it, is with us. Its meaning for human freedoms, human comforts, and even human life will predictably be decided in the balance of this century—by you and me, among others.

For the first time in human history we have the opportunities to feed, clothe, shelter, and provide medical care, and, hopefully, constructive roles for all of the people in this world—even though we are now over 3.5 billion. For the first time in human history, working together we can see the potential of the acquisition, by all of the people of this world, of human rights allocated to the people of the world—human rights properly defined as "the sum of all the rights, privileges and freedoms that every human being in society must enjoy to insure both his dignity and the full development of his personality." For the first time in human history, we must not only hope for, but we must see the more gentle, honest, and loving components of the human personality emerge and dominate, especially in the actions and attitudes of our institutions, wherein human personality traits are magnified and exaggerated many times over. Our institutions, especially our governments today, are not the *sum* of the traits, and the aspirations of the people they represent and should serve, *but* are quite the converse—the essence, the distillation of all of the negative and destructive traits of human personality—suspicion, aggressiveness, paranoia, irrationality, dishonesty, and hate. The passions of the jungle are too often the passions of our nations. And now that we no longer throw rocks and spears, or even deal with the ultimate weapons (a very few centuries ago, the crossbow), we have reached the point when war threatens not only the human rights of which mankind has so long dreamed, but the very existence of the only intelligent life known to us in this universe. To be denied the struggle of war, however, neither limits our frontiers nor lessens our challenges. The challenge of the conquest of disease, the challenge of infinity both of time and of space, and the challenge of the preservation of individual freedom vis à vis computers and information banks, are only a few of the challenges facing the imperfect and slowly mutable *homo sapiens*.

This study by Professors Lynn and McClure is a most timely one that focuses attention on the best-established area of executive-congressional conflict: the sensitive field of foreign policy. The stages Senator J. William Fulbright has gone through are both illustrative of a far broader concern and instructive for many citizens and leaders who will have to go over the same intellectual path in the near future.

We have too often been tolerant of mediocrity in our leaders, and equally contemptuous of them. It should be exactly the reverse. We should be offering leaders our real respect, and demanding absolutely that they deliver. Otherwise we will find ourselves in the predictable situation illustrated in a recent article in *Life* magazine entitled "Where Have All the Great Leaders Gone?" This illustration suggests a retelling and extension of the classic Gandhi story.

The leader is standing at the window. The people rush by. The leader exclaims, "I must hurry out and step before them, for I am their leader."

Today the leader is standing at the window. The people rush by. The leader also exclaims, "I must hurry and step before them, for I am their leader." But upon sight of the leader the people scatter.

The sequel to this is the future.

The people rush by; look up; and the window is empty.

Studies such as this will help ensure that such a situation never develops.

William R. Roy
2nd Congressional District, Kansas
U. S. House of Representatives

PREFACE

The question of the limits of presidential power, especially in foreign policy, has been with us since the founding of the Republic. In recent years it has been discussed with a new urgency that has led many to believe that it will be the central constitutional question of the 1970s. Practical politicians and scholarly observers have had to evaluate and reevaluate their own views of presidential power in light of the realities of American commitments and a debatable Vietnamese war that drains American resources. No American has wrestled with this constitutional question longer or more thoughtfully than J. William Fulbright, who has served as Chairman of the Foreign Relations Committee of the Senate longer than anyone in the nation's history. This book traces the metamorphosis in Fulbright's point of view; he began by arguing for more presidential power and ultimately became the most articulate spokesman for limiting this same power.

Naomi Lynn became interested in Senator Fulbright and his views on foreign policy while doing graduate work at the University of Kansas. Arthur McClure had done past research on the American presidency, especially Harry S. Truman's. Both contributed to the researching and writing of this book, although Professor Lynn conducted all the personal interviews.

The authors are indebted to many individuals whose cooperation made the book possible. First, to Professors Clifford Ketzel, Earl Nehring, and Roger Kanet of the University of Kansas, whose careful reading and critical comments made the initial study possible. Senator James Pearson of Kansas and Jo Kline in the Senator's Washington office made the arrangements for the interviews that contributed so much to this study. Former Vice-President Hubert Humphrey very graciously consented to an extensive interview while on a rather heavily scheduled visit to Manhattan, Kansas. Senator Mike Mansfield and Senator Albert Gore permitted interviews that proved most helpful. Congressman Dr. William Roy has written a most thought-provoking Foreword, which contributes immeasurably to this volume.

A special debt of gratitude goes to the staff in Senator J. William Fulbright's office. Their helpfulness, and their efficiency in making materials available to the authors, went beyond these writers' expectations. Sincere thanks are extended to Mr. Philip Lagerquist and the staff of the Harry S. Truman Library.

Senator Fulbright himself not only opened his files to the authors, but answered interview questions with a candor and directness that gives information and insights that go beyond those available from any other source. Moreover, he cooperated with a graciousness that made the project a real pleasure.

Beyond his cooperating with this study, we are grateful to Senator Fulbright for providing the kind of congressional leadership that we feel our nation desperately needs.

INTRODUCTION

When Senator J. William Fulbright became chairman of the Senate Foreign Relations Committee in 1959, he was fully committed to the idea that neither the committee nor its chairman should become preoccupied with, or try to interfere with short-term policies and day-to-day operations of the State Department. And the same Senator Fulbright, who at that time could state to Professor Hans Morgenthau that the experience of Senators was too limited to make their foreign policy judgments valuable as compared to those of the State Department, changed his mind a decade later.[1] Other Senators also changed their minds. As Senators in the 1970s prepared to shape a new foreign-policy role for themselves, they could take some encouragement from a similar change on the part of such respected scholars as Professor Henry Steele Commager, who went through a transition that roughly paralleled that of Senator Fulbright.[2] But just how had these basic changes of principle come about? The Fulbright story is perhaps the most intriguing.

By 1965 Fulbright was arguing for a broader policy-making role for the Senate in foreign affairs. In part this meant the exercise of a stronger negative influence; when the President acts on his own initiative the Senate has a "duty to call him to account."[3]

---

1. U. S. Congress, Senate, Committee on Foreign Relations, *What Is Wrong With Our Foreign Policy Hearings* before the Committee on Foreign Relations, Senate, 85th Cong., 1st sess., April 15, 1959.
2. Henry F. Graff, "Thinking Aloud: Participatory Foreign Policy," *The New Leader* 53 (March 2, 1970): 14. See also Commager's own testimony in *Changing American Attitudes Toward Foreign Policy, Hearings,* especially pp. 19–21.
3. U. S. Congress, Senate, Senator Fulbright and others discussing the Dominican crisis, 89th Cong., 1st sess., September 30, 1965, *Congressional Record,* 111, Part 19, p. 25623.

In Senate debate with Senator Smathers of Florida, Fulbright said:

> The Senator from Florida has too restricted a view of the Senate's role. The Constitution provides that the Senate shall advise and consent. It is the duty of the Senate, in proper cases and under proper circumstances, to advise any Executive of our views as to any past actions or, if we like as to possible future actions.[4]

The principal strength of the Senate in the foreign-relations field, according to Fulbright, lies in the area of long-range policy formulation. The Senate may not be able to handle details, but it can offer valuable advice on basics.[5]. At least one scholar, Robert A. Dahl, makes a similar point when he says that the foreign-policy role of the Congress should be that of the general, not that of the sergeant.[6]

Threads of this concept run through Fulbright's thought, and did, even during the period when he spoke strongly in favor of a relatively free foreign-policy hand for the President. The Middle East problems of 1957 led Fulbright to advocate that Congress provide through criticism a testing ground for the President's foreign-policy proposals.[7] The executive's points should be subjected to debate, not merely agreed to. By May 1964 Fulbright made this statement:

> A proper and important part of the congressional role in foreign policy is to take the lead in what ought to be a continuing national discussion and examination of the posture of the United States in the world, of our basic national interests, and of ways and means of advancing those interests.[8]

---

4. *Congressional Record,* 111, Part 19, p. 25623.
5. Quoted by Kenneth W. Grundy, "The Apprenticeship of J. William Fulbright," *Virginia Quarterly Review* 43 (Summer 1967): 383.
6. Robert A. Dahl, *Congress and Foreign Policy* (New York: W. W. Norton, 1964), p. 140.
7. E. W. Kenworth, "Fulbright Becomes a National Issue," *New York Times Magazine,* October 1, 1961, p. 74.
8. Quoted by Maurice Goldbloom, "The Fulbright Revolt," *Commentary* (September 1966), p. 65.

The Senate can discuss policy, and it can and should engage in an educational effort on foreign policy. Essentially, Fulbright's thoughts reflect the point that the Senate should engage in more advising and less consenting.

Fulbright contends that the Senate should pursue its critical discussion of the longer-range aspects of foreign policy with a clear understanding of its importance as an institution. The position of the Senate has its basis in the Constitution, but the way in which it actually functions has developed largely through tradition.[9] The upper house of the legislature in some other nations is largely ceremonial and based on honor or prestige. This is true, Senator Fulbright points out, in Japan, Great Britain, and Canada.[10] In a 1969 Senate debate Senator Hugh Scott suggested to Senator Fulbright that the House of Lords in Britain was stripped of many of its powers because it became an "obstructionist body."[11] Fulbright countered with this quotation from James Madison on the purpose of the Senate.

In order to judge of the form to be given to this institution, it will be proper to take view of the ends to be served by it. These were first to protect the people against their rulers. Secondly to protect the people against the transient impressions into which they themselves might be led.[12]

In 1967 Fulbright made a summary statement on the Senate as an institution that expresses his position:

A Senator has the obligation to defend the Senate an an institution by upholding its traditions and prerogatives. A Senator must never forget the Presidency when he is dealing with the President and he must never forget the Senate when he is talking as a Senator. A Senator is not at perfect liberty to

9. Interview with Senator J. William Fulbright, Washington, D. C., January 26, 1970.
10. U. S. Congress, Senate, Senator Fulbright and others debating the role of the Senate, 91st Cong., 1st session, January 28, 1969, *Congressional Record*, 115, No. 18, p. S 959.
11. *Congressional Record*, 115, No. 18, p. S 959.
12. *Congressional Record*, 115, No. 18, p. S 959.

think and act as an individual human being; a large part of what he says and what he does must be institutional in nature. Whoever may be President, whatever his policies, however great the confidence they may inspire, it is part of the constitutional trust of a Senator to defend and exercise the advise and consent function of the Senate. It is not his to give away.[13]

In this spirit of defending the "privileges and prerogatives" of the Senate, Fulbright in 1969 criticized the State and Defense Departments for refusing to make various documents available to the Committee on Foreign Relations.[14] Fulbright nearly a decade earlier had exchanged letters with the State Department objecting to treating the content of the Nixon-Khrushchev discussion in Russia as classified security information.[15]

As chairman of the Foreign Relations Committee Fulbright has sought to have that Committee play a significant part of the institutional role that he sees for the Senate in foreign-policy discussion. In 1967 Fulbright declared that the Committee should act as a "forum for free and wide-ranging discussion."[16] It could help prevent the occurrence of an "irretrievable mistake." It could provide a "forum for dissenters" that could keep dissent from becoming disorderly.[17] The special responsibility of the Committee Chairman was summed up in *The Arrogance of Power*:

I believe that the Chairman of the Committee on Foreign

---

13. U. S. Congress, Senate, Committee on the Judiciary, *Separation of Powers*, Part 1, *Hearings* before the Subcommittee on Separation of Powers of the Committee on the Judiciary, Senate, 90th Cong., 1st sess., July–September, 1967, p. 52.

14. U. S. Congress, Senate, Senator Fulbright speaking on privileges and prerogatives of the Senate, 91st Cong., 1st sess., August 8, 1969, *Congressional Record*, 115, No. 135, p. S 9503.

15. Correspondence between Senator J. William Fulbright and officials of the Department of State and the *New York Herald Tribune*, September 17, 1960–October 19, 1960, Fulbright files, Washington, D. C. Fulbright was especially annoyed at being denied the transcript of the "kitchen debate" because it had been made available to Earl Mazo, a reporter for the *Herald Tribune* and a Nixon biographer.

16. *Hearings* before the Subcommittee on Separation of Powers, p. 52.

17. *Hearings* before the Subcommittee on Separation of Powers, p. 52.

Relations has a special obligation to offer the best advice he
can on foreign policy; it is an obligation I believe, which is inherent in the chairmanship, which takes precedence over party
loyalty, and which has nothing to do with whether the Chairman's views are solicited or desired by the people in the executive branch.[18]

In 1959 Senator Frank Church in a Committee meeting cited
Senator Fulbright's long experience on the Committee, and then
he made this observation: "Therefore, I think the judgment you
bring there as Chairman of this committee in the foreign policy
field is entitled to every bit as much respect as the judgment of
those representatives of the State Department who often appeared before the committee."[19] Although he did not express
agreement with Senator Church's point, it seems quite likely that
Senator Fulbright has full confidence in his own ability to make
judgments that carry as much or more merit than those of the
chief executive and his spokesmen. Whether or not such confidence
is justified is certainly debatable.

If the Senate is to function effectively as an influential institution, Senator Fulbright contends that it must reassert its
power. In this contention Fulbright has widespread Senate support; even Senator Gale McGee has stated that the power of the
Senate has eroded.[20]

The problem, as Fulbright sees it, lies in the very great power
of the executive in the American system of government. The
Senator pointed this out in a 1966 Senate discussion, and he
brought up again his point about the British system's carrying
with it the possibility of the legislative branch's changing the

---

18. J. William Fulbright, *The Arrogance of Power* (New York: Viking
Books, 1966), p. 62. Senator McGee disagrees with Fulbright. He says:
". . . the chairman of important committees—Foreign Relations, Appropriations, and Armed Services—must be willing to live up to the obligations
and responsibilities that a chairmanship entails. They should accept the
fact that as chairmen they have given up some of their freedom to express their views indiscriminately." Gale W. McGee, *The Responsibilities
of World Power* (Washington, D. C.: The National Press, Inc., 1968), p. 211.
19. *What Is Wrong With Our Foreign Policy, Hearings*, p. 20.
20. *Congressional Record*, 115, No. 105, p. S 7150.

executive when they disagree with him.[21] Two points should be recognized by the Congress as it deals with the President. The first is the fact that the chief executive is not and should not be as all-powerful in foreign policy as some members of the Congress (including Senator Fulbright) have at times pictured him:

> While the President has the major responsibility for foreign affairs, he does not have all of it. The Congress has neither the authority nor the means to conduct American foreign policy, but it has ample power to implement, modify, or thwart executive proposals.[22]

Second is the point that as the Congress exercises its power to "implement, modify, or thwart" the President, it can develop the power to exact compliance from him:

> When the Executive tends to ignore congressional recommendations intruding thereby on congressional prerogative, the result is either a counterintrusion or the acceptance by the Congress of the loss of its prerogatives. Thus, for example, the persistent refusal of the Executive to comply even approximately with congressional recommendations that it limit the number of countries receiving American foreign aid has caused the Foreign Relations Committee to write numbers into its current bill, proposing thereby to make recommendations into requirements. The price of the flexibility which is valued by the Executive is, or certainly ought to be, a high degree of compliance with the intent of Congress.[23]

All this is a far cry from what Fulbright calls the "He is our President; therefore we should support him" attitude. What he terms "bitter experience" with this attitude has made him highly skeptical of it.[24]

---

21. *Congressional Record,* 112, Part 6, p. 4385.
22. J. William Fulbright, "Public Opinion and Foreign Policy," Speech at Bowling Green State University, Bowling Green, Ohio, March 9, 1963, Fulbright Files, Washington, D. C.
23. *Hearings* before the Subcommittee on Separation of Powers, p. 44.
24. U. S. Congress, Senate, Senator Fulbright speaking against ABM, S. 2546, 91st Cong., 1st sess., July 25, 1969, *Congressional Record,* 115, No. 125, p. S 8609.

The Fulbright record is not only one of importance, but is one of unusual independence and prescience. He was one of the earliest advocates of rebuilding American conventional forces as a sane alternative to a reliance on nuclear massive retaliation. Long ago he explored the connection between American economic growth and our capacity to act effectively in both the domestic and foreign sectors. Fulbright has been unique in resisting some of the erratic turns in American policy in recent years. For his venturesome spirit, his willingness to expose himself to criticism because of his theories and philosophies, and his underlying political pragmatism, J. William Fulbright deserves special attention in any study of the complexities of modern history.

The clash between J. William Fulbright and Lyndon Johnson in the late 1960s over foreign policy perhaps stands as one of the most significant historical examples of such a struggle between a Senator and the President. Important as this issue is, however, it does not stand alone in American history. Fulbright's changing views have deep historical and constitutional roots. A disagreement between the executive and legislative branches on any issue is not unusual. In a dissenting opinion in 1926, Mr. Justice Brandeis wrote:

> The doctrine of the separation of powers was adopted by the convention of 1787, not to promote efficiency but to preclude the exercise of arbitrary power. The purpose was not to avoid friction, but, by means of the inevitable friction incident to the distribution of the governmental powers among three departments, to save the people from autocracy.[25]

The relationship between Congress and the President in the field of foreign policy today is the product of neither formal amendment nor judicial interpretation. It is the result of changing custom and the pressure of world events.[26] Historian Henry Steele

---

25. *Myers* v. *United States*, 272 U. S. 293 (1926).
26. Ernest S. Griffith, *Congress: Its Contemporary Role* (New York: New York University Press, 1967), p. 4.

Commager has concluded that the period of Senator Fulbright's Chairmanship of the Senate Foreign Relations Committee has seen new ingredients added to the familiar problem of reconciling the various pressures related to the separation of powers in this field.[27] The Constitution vests the executive authority in the President, and it also makes him Commander in Chief of the Army and Navy. To Congress, however, is given the power to declare war and the responsibility of supporting the armed forces. The Senate has the special function of ratifying treaties and approving the appointments of ambassadors and other officials; the framers apparently thought that the Senate would function as an executive council to the President.[28]

The war power was a subject of discussion at the Constitutional Convention and by the nation's early leaders. The founders were impressed with the power of the British King to declare war, and they feared giving the American executive any similar power.[29] The original proposal at the Convention was to give Congress the power to make war, but Madison and Gerry moved to substitute the word *declare* in order to enable the executive to repel sudden attacks.[30] There is evidence that the framers expected that troops would never be sent outside the country without Congressional approval, except in the case of such response to attacks.[31] Jefferson regarded the retention by Congress of the financing of military activity as a significant restraint on the President:

We have already given in example one effectual check to

27. Henry Steele Commager, "Can We Limit Presidential Power?," *New Republic* (April 6, 1968), p. 15.
28. Edward S. Corwin, *The President: Office and Powers 1787–1957* (New York: New York University Press, 1957), p. 210.
29. Ruhl J. Bartlett of the Fletcher School of Diplomacy in a statement before the Committee on Foreign Relations. U. S. Congress, Senate, Committee on Foreign Relations, U. S. *Commitments to Foreign Powers, Hearings,* before the Committee on Foreign Relations, Senate, on S. Res. 151, 90th Cong., 1st sess., 1967, p. 9.
30. Max Farrand, ed., *The Records of the Federal Convention of 1787* (New Haven: Yale University Press, 1966), 2: 318.
31. "Notes: Congress, the President, and the Power to Commit Forces to Combat," *Harvard Law Review* 81 (June 1968): 1776.

the Dog of war by transferring the power of letting him loose from the Executive to the Legislative body, from those who are to spend to those who are to pay.[32]

The military problems and operations of the eighteenth century were undoubtedly much more readily available and understandable to Congressmen and Senators of that day than are some aspects of war in later periods. It has been argued that this has lessened the relevance of the power of the purse.[33]

The Constitution certainly did not provide a full blueprint of the exact roles of the executive and the legislative bodies, nor did it define the boundaries of power. During the First Congress, Alexander White of Virginia offered this principle in the face of ambiguity:

It would be better for the President to extend his powers on some extraordinary occasions, even where he is not strictly justified by the Constitution, than the Legislature should grant an improper power to be exercised at all times.[34]

Perhaps the course that was followed was that the Constitution merely issues "an invitation to struggle for the privilege of directing American foreign policy."[35]

George Washington sought to start a tradition of strict compliance with the Constitution. This did not involve a surrender to the Congress of powers that he regarded as being properly those of the President, as he demonstrated in making the procla-

---

32. As quoted in U. S. Congress, Senate, Committee on Foreign Relations, *U. S. Commitments to Foreign Powers, Hearings* before the Committee on Foreign Relations, Senate, on S. Res. 151, 90th Cong., 1st sess., August, September, 1967, p. 11.

33. Edward A. Kolodziej, "Congressional Responsibility for the Common Defense: The Money Problem," *Western Political Quarterly* 16 (March 1963): 150, 151.

34. Quoted in U. S. Congress, Senate. Senator Fulbright speaking on The Administration's Middle East Proposal, S. J. Res. 19, 85th Cong., 1st sess., February 11, 1957, *Congressional Record*, 103, Part 2, p. 1857.

35. Edwin S. Corwin, *The President: Office and Powers 1787–1957* (New York: New York University Press, 1957), p. 171.

mation of neutrality in 1793 despite the contention of Madison that his act infringed on the powers of Congress.[36]

The concept of using the Senate as an executive council that could both "advise and consent" was tried by Washington in 1789. He called on the Senate about a treaty with the Southern Indians and offered seven points that could be voted on *yes* or *no* on the spot. The Senators did not wish to dispose of the matter so speedily, however, and Robert Morris of Pennsylvania moved that the papers Washington had presented be referred to a five-man study committee for further consideration. William Maclay, Pennsylvania's other Senator, and the writer of the *Journal* from which the account was drawn, said his comments in favor of Morris's motion were delivered in a low tone of voice from which "peevishness itself could not have taken offense. . . ." Nevertheless, Washington "started up in a violent fret," and stated, "this defeats every purpose of my coming here." Washington remarked that he had brought the Secretary of War along so that all needed information could be given to the Senate without requiring any delay. The President found the whole experience a distasteful one and since that time no President has ever gone to the Senate for personal consultation about the advisability of a proposed negotiation.[37] The need for such a study committee resulted in 1816 in the creation of the Committee on Foreign Relations.

By 1796 Washington refused to give the House of Representatives papers that dealt with the negotiations concerning the Jay Treaty. He said the nature of the papers did not make it appropriate to disclose them "at this time," and this precedent has since extended to such disclosures to the Senate.[38]

Both Alexander Hamilton and James Madison in their writings laid out lines of argument that have persisted since that time.

---

36. Daniel S. Cheever and H. Field Haviland, *American Foreign Policy and the Separation of Powers* (Cambridge: Harvard University Press, 1952), pp. 14, 15.
37. Corwin, pp. 210, 211. As will be mentioned below, Wilson and Truman paid visits to attempt to persuade the Senate.
38. Corwin, p. 182.

Washington's neutrality proclamation sparked one such exchange. Madison, assuming the name "Helvidius," argued that since foreign affairs can easily lead to war, power over them should be Congress's under the war-declaring clause of the Constitution.[39] Hamilton, using the name "Pacificus," claimed that the exercise of foreign policy is an inherent or implied part of the executive function.[40]

To a substantial degree Hamilton's views have prevailed more often than Madison's. Hamilton earlier conceded, however, that the power of the President, while comparable to that of the British King as Commander in Chief, was "in substance much inferior" to the King's, since Congress must raise armies.[41] He added in Number 75 of *The Federalist* that treaty-making "partakes more of the legislative than the executive character, although it does not seem strictly to fall within the definition of either of them." Hamilton also went on to observe that

the history of human condition does not warrant that exalted opinion of human virtue which would make it wise in a nation to commit interests of so delicate and momentous a kind, as those which concern its intercourse with the rest of the world, to the sole disposal of a magistrate created and circumstanced as would be a President of the United States.[42]

Although Madison's argument has not been the dominant one through most of American history, Madison's own Presidency happened to fall during one of the periods of strongest Congressional domination of foreign policy. The House, under Henry Clay, was especially powerful, and it was able to force Madison into war with Great Britain in 1812. In 1813 the Senate invited

39. James Madison, *The Writings of James Madison*, ed. Gaillard Hunt (New York: G. P. Putnam's Sons, 1906), Helvidius No. 1, 6: 138–51.
40. Alexander Hamilton, *The Papers of Alexander Hamilton*, ed. Harold C. Syrett (New York: Columbia University Press, 1969), Pacificus No. 1, 15: 33–43.
41. Alexander Hamilton, James Madison and John Jay, *Selections from The Federalist*, ed. Henry Steele Commager, (New York: Appleton-Century Crofts, 1949), No. 69, p. 94.
42. *Selections from The Federalist*, No. 75, pp. 110, 111.

Madison to come to its meetings to consult on foreign affairs in the manner that Washington had tried. Madison refused.[43]

Like Madison, Thomas Jefferson experienced events as President that ran counter to his earlier-espoused positions. Jefferson argued for strict construction, but this did not prevent his purchase of the Louisiana Territory without authorization, an act that he privately admitted was "beyond the Constitution." Nor did his act prevent later Senate ratification of the purchase treaties.[44] Apparently most of the Senators saw the merit of the transaction and were pleased to overlook what Jefferson characterized the "metaphysical subtleties" of its Constitutional aspects.[45]

Jefferson used similar initiative when he committed forces to combat. In 1801 under provocation from pirates led by the Bey of Tripoli, Jefferson sent a squadron of ships to protect American commerce. He informed Congress afterwards when the *Enterprise* captured a Tripolitan ship:

> Unauthorized by the Constitution, without the sanction of Congress, to go beyond the line of defense, the vessel being disabled from committing further hostilities, was liberated with its crew. The Legislature will doubtless consider whether, by authorizing measures of offense also, they will place our force on an equal footing with that of its adversaries. I communicate all material information on this subject, that in the exercise of this important function confided by the Constitution to the Legislature exclusively their judgment may form itself on a knowledge and consideration of every circumstance of weight.[46]

In 1806 Jefferson actually violated the appropriate laws in

---

43. Woodrow Wilson, *Congressional Government* (Boston: Houghton Mifflin Company, 1913), p. 234.
44. Cheever and Haviland, p. 73.
45. Cheever and Haviland, p. 73. $2 million had been placed at Jefferson's disposal to buy Southern territories and Tucker of Virginia regarded this as an adequate injection of Congressional initiative. Corwin, p. 89.
46. U. S. Congress, Joint Committee on Printing, *Compilation of Messages and Papers of the Presidents*, ed. James D. Richardson (New York: Bureau of National Literature, 1897), 1: 314.

response to a British attack on the American frigate *Chesapeake*. Jefferson then gave this explanation to Congress:

> To have awaited a previous and special sanction by law would have lost occasions which might not be retrieved. . . . I trust that the Legislature, feeling the same anxiety for the safety of our country, so materially advanced by this precaution, will approve, when done, what they would have seen so important to be done if then assembled.[47]

James Monroe's administration was marked by contrasts in Presidential-Congressional relations in foreign relations. Congress showed initiative in encouraging the recognition of new South American nations. Congress went as far as to appropriate $100,000 for the establishment of such missions as the President "may deem proper."[48] Congress did not question Monroe's right to extend diplomatic recognition, and the President apparently did not resent the frank expression of the views of Congress. Monroe made use of his powers as Commander in Chief when he ordered Andrew Jackson to go into Spanish Florida in 1818 in "hot pursuit" of hostile Indians.[49]

President Monroe's best-remembered act is his statement of the "Monroe Doctrine," and it should probably be regarded as a sweeping declaration of intended action by Presidential initiative. Monroe himself, however, regarded his doctrine only as a broad policy. When asked in 1824 by Colombia as to the sort of defense action against European states that the newly independent nation might expect, he replied that ". . . by the Constitution of the United States, the ultimate decision of this question belongs to the Legislative Department of the Government. . . ."[50]

The first half-century of the Republic saw both Presidential and Congressional initiative in foreign policy, but Washington's

47. Quoted in *Congressional Record*, 103, Part 2, p. 1858.
48. Corwin, p. 188.
49. "Notes," *Harvard Law Review*, p. 1789.
50. Quoted in Ruhl J. Bartlett, ed., *The Record of American Diplomacy* (New York: Alfred A. Knopf, 1954), p. 185.

humiliation before the Senate preempted a close working relationship, and despite the force of Congress in the War of 1812, the general success of presidential initiative emerged, even with dubious constitutional basis. Congress remained, however, a relevant restraining force.

In 1846 James K. Polk told Congress that Mexico had crossed the U. S. border, and that war existed, "not withstanding all our efforts to avoid it. . . ." He called for a declaration of war and for funds to prosecute it. Senator John C. Calhoun regarded the message as an attempt by the President to usurp Congress's prerogative to declare war. Senator Cass of Michigan argued that declaration of aggressive war was the sole function of Congress, but that "another country can commence a war against us without the cooperation of Congress."[51] Since most, if not all, wars can be interpreted as defensive, this narrowed the scope of Congress's influence. Abraham Lincoln, as a Congressman from Illinois, disagreed with the way in which Polk secured the U. S. commitment. His views did not influence events and at the time, significantly, they were recorded from a letter he wrote to William H. Herndon February 15, 1848:

Allow the President to invade a neighboring nation, whenever *he* shall deem it necessary to repel an invasion, and you allow him to do so, *whenever he may choose to say* he deems it necessary for such purpose—and you allow him to make war at pleasure. Study to see if you can fix *any limit* to his power in this respect, after you have given him so much as you propose.

The provision of the Constitution giving the warmaking power to Congress, was dictated, as I understand it, by the following reasons. Kings had always been involving and impoverishing their people in wars, pretending generally, if not always, that the good of the people was the object. This, our convention undertook to be the most oppressive of all Kingly oppressions; and they resolved to so frame the Constitution that *no one man* should hold the power of bringing this oppression upon us.[52]

---

51. Corwin, p. 200.
52. Abraham Lincoln, *The Collected Works of Abraham Lincoln,* ed. Roy P. Basler (New Brunswick: Rutgers University Press, 1953), 1: 451, 452.

Even though Polk stretched the limits of his powers, he did not set a precedent that was seized upon by all of his immediate successors. President James Buchanan in December 1859 said that "without the authority of Congress the President cannot fire a hostile gun in any case except to repel the attacks of an enemy."[53] Such a view was constitutionally accurate, although it represented the narrow extreme of the spectrum of interpretation of presidential power and it was not adopted by later presidents.

One scholar has characterized Ulysses S. Grant's views as nearly the opposite of those of Buchanan.[54] President Grant, exercising the initiative and independence that had served him well as General, sought to annex Santo Domingo, claiming the necessity to protect American "interests." His Senate critics drew a distinction between American "interests" and "rights" and concluded that annexation could be justified only by rights. The Senate, with the leadership of Chairman Charles Sumner of the Senate Foreign Relations Committee, rejected the treaty that would have put the annexation into effect.[55]

Presidents Harrison and Cleveland did not make innovative use of their powers in foreign relations. Harrison's administration was a Congress-dominated one.[56] Cleveland's views were similar to Buchanan's.[57] In 1896 he ignored a Joint Resolution that called for recognition that a state of belligerence existed in Cuba. When he took office, President William McKinley suggested American intervention. A resolution "authorizing and directing" the President to use the Army and Navy to expel Spain from Cuba was passed by the Senate. An earlier-proposed Senate Resolution that acknowledged the independence of the Republic

---

53. As quoted in *U. S. Commitments to Foreign Powers, Hearings*, p. 11.
54. Robert William Russell, *The United States, Congress and the Power to Use Military Force Abroad*, Ph.D. thesis, Fletcher School of Law and Diplomacy, 1967, pp. 242–243. Quoted in U. S. Congress, Senate, Committee on Foreign Relations, *National Commitments*, S. Rept. 91–129, 91st Cong., 1st sess., 1969, p. 11.
55. Goldbloom, pp. 62, 63. Corwin, p. 201.
56. Rowland Egger, *The President of the United States* (New York: McGraw-Hill, 1967), p. 137.
57. Russell, pp. 242, 243.

of Cuba was rejected by the Senate on constitutional grounds, since it infringed on the executive's recognition function.[58] However, the potential for decisive action when Congress and the President agreed was dramatically illustrated during the war. In 1897 the power of an intransigent Senate was also demonstrated. The Olney-Pauncefote Treaty was rejected, despite the backing of McKinley and many prominent Americans and newspapers. The treaty provided for a system of arbitration of international disputes.[59] This rejection of a treaty again demonstrated the negative power possessed by the Senate.

In June of 1900 McKinley used American troops to help relieve the legations in Peking, which were under siege by the Boxers. The event has been cited as offering a precedent for the exercise of military force abroad.[60] In addition the action has significance in that it was directed against a rebel group that was not recognized as a government.

The more active and colorful Presidents usually tested the limits of their power in the foreign-policy field, and Theodore Roosevelt did this to an extent at least equal to Polk and in ways that set precedents for later twentieth-century chief executives to follow. The most important of Roosevelt's acts that extended the power of the President to use force on his own initiative in exercising foreign policy occurred in 1903. A rebellion was under way in the Colombian state of Panama, and Roosevelt wished to encourage it in order to bring into existence an independent government that would be favorable to deal with on the canal question. Roosevelt sent the United States Navy to prevent the landing of Colombian troops, which had been sent to put down the rebellion. The President justified his actions under the Colombian-American treaty of 1846, an authorization with an intent that was "highly doubtful."[61] This act against a sovereign state

---

58. Corwin, pp. 188, 189.
59. Cheever and Haviland, pp. 52, 53.
60. Robert A. Taft, *A Foreign Policy for Americans* (Garden City, New York: Doubleday & Company, 1951), p. 29.
61. As quoted in *U. S. Commitments to Foreign Powers, Hearings*, pp. 11, 12. The treaty bound the United States to maintain the "perfect neutrality" of the Isthmus.

could have brought war, and it was undertaken without the authority of Congress. Other military excursions into Cuba and the Dominican Republic were also justified by Roosevelt under similar treaties. As Secretary of War, William Howard Taft defended the unilateral actions of the executive under the theory that such treaties were the supreme law of the land and actions under them needed no authorization from Congress.[62]

Senate debate was sparked by Roosevelt's 1906 negotiation of the Algeciras Convention through the President's personal agents, who had not been appointed with the advice and consent of the Senate. Some in the Senate held that the President had the prerogative to negotiate treaties as he saw fit, while others expressed the opposite viewpoint under the theory that the foreign-relations power has a legislative as well as an executive nature.[63]

As President, Taft also used troops in foreign military actions on his own authority. In an intervention in Cuba Taft's actions were justified by his Secretary of State as being in defense of American life and property. This contrasts with Taft's own earlier rationale for Roosevelt's action in the same place; that had been defended as being justified by treaty. In 1912 President Taft sent the armed forces to Nicaragua, and this act served as the occasion for the State Department to issue a well-documented study of nineteenth-century practice in the use of military force by the President. The Department distinguished between "intervention," which involved political interference in a foreign country, and "interposition," which sought only to protect persons or interests of the United States. It was argued that interposition was used more than intervention, and that interposition could be justified solely by international law and thus did not require an authorization from Congress.[64]

Taft was the last President to operate in a world in which American foreign-policy commitments were either solely hemispheric or restricted to a few localities, such as China or Tripoli.

---

62. *U. S. Commitments to Foreign Powers, Hearings*, p. 12.
63. Cheever and Haviland, p. 69.
64. "Notes," *Harvard Law Review*, p. 24.

Under President Wilson, these commitments became global, and after the interlude of the 1920s and 1930s they became not only more extensive than ever but, as concern with the containment of Communism developed, they also became ideological in nature.[65] This combination of factors was to introduce new elements into the continuing debate over Congressional influence in determining foreign policy.

Wilson's earliest probings of the power balance between the President and the Congress in foreign affairs involved circumstances that closely resembled those that had faced his recent predecessors. Wilson opposed President Huerta of Mexico in 1914, despite the fact that he had been installed in a coup that the American minister had aided.[66] After the crew of an American barge had been arrested and released at Tampico, Wilson occupied the port and customs house at Veracruz. This cut off both Huerta's cash and his numerous imports, and he soon fled the country. Wilson justified the reprisal as one to "enforce respect" for the United States government.[67] In 1916 the Mexican Pancho Villa raided Columbus, New Mexico, and killed sixteen people. Wilson ordered 6,000 Army and National Guard troops, under General John J. Pershing, to chase Villa into Mexico in spite of the strenuous protests of Carranza, Mexico's new President.[68] Pershing's troops were not successful in capturing Villa, despite a one-year campaign, and in 1917, with war in Europe becoming a probability, Wilson withdrew the American force. As with Monroe's sending General Andrew Jackson into Spanish Florida 98 years earlier, Wilson justified his act by the need to be in "hot pursuit" of the raiders. After Pershing was in Mexico, the Senate adopted a resolution supporting Wilson's action; the resolution was never voted out of the House Foreign Affairs Committee.[69]

---

65. Commager, p. 15.
66. Samuel Eliot Morison, *The Oxford History of the American People* (New York: Oxford University Press, 1965), p. 844.
67. *National Commitments*, p. 5.
68. Morison, p. 846. For his opposition to Wilson Carranza became one of Mexico's heroes.
69. *National Commitments*, p. 5.

Wilson also invoked reasons used by Roosevelt and Taft in other armed interventions. In the Dominican Republic he claimed that a treaty violation justified the use of troops, despite the fact that the treaty did not provide for American intervention. In Haiti he intervened because he felt it necessary to protect American lives and property.[70]

As events related to the war in Europe started to draw the United States into the conflict, President Wilson's foreign-policy initiatives began to extend outside the Western Hemisphere. Acts against American shipping play a prominent role in the involvement of the United States in the First World War, and the President took actions that were closely related to the power of Congress to declare war. To counter Germany's unrestricted submarine warfare in 1917, Wilson sought to arm American merchant ships. Although he informed the Congress that he doubtless had the power to do this on his own initiative, he sought their backing for the action. A bill was introduced that stated that the President was "authorized and empowered to employ such other instrumentalities" as he found necessary to defend American ships.[71] The House deleted some portions of the bill, but passed it. The Senate delayed passage until after the end of the session. Wilson criticized "a little group of willful men" in the Senate, and in March 1917, before a later special session took action, he armed the ships on his own authority.[72]

As events proceeded, the following month Congress declared war and the question of proper constitutional authority was temporarily resolved for President Wilson. During the war Congress delegated very broad powers to him on most matters related to conduct of the war.[73] After the war Wilson attempted to continue to exercise his leadership in foreign affairs, but his

---

70. Thomas A. Bailey, *A Diplomatic History of the American People* (New York: Appleton-Century Crofts, 1969), pp. 553, 554. Also see *U. S. Commitments to Foreign Powers, Hearings*, p. 14.

71. *U. S. Commitments to Foreign Powers, Hearings*, p. 11.

72. Corwin, p. 197. See also *U. S. Commitments to Foreign Powers, Hearings*, p. 14.

73. Corwin, p. 235. These powers were not, however, without qualification. See Corwin, p. 468.

fight for the Versailles Treaty and the League of Nations ended in disaster for him. In his 1908 book Wilson had argued that the President had the only national voice and that he was the only one who could act for the whole country at once.[74] Once the pressures of war were removed, however, the Senate exerted power in a historic clash that had no comparable precedent. On July 10, 1919, Wilson became the second President to appear personally before the Senate on behalf of a treaty, and the results were for him far more humiliating than had been those for President Washington.

Neither the disposition of Wilson's three successors nor the nature of events in the 1920s and early 1930s produced an occasion for another test of presidential power in the foreign-policy field. Events in Europe were building, however, that would not make this possible for President Franklin D. Roosevelt. Roosevelt's first frictions with Congress over foreign policy came in his first administration, when the Senate refused to pass a resolution on neutrality in the form that FDR had sought. Roosevelt wanted the authority to embargo arms shipments to belligerents at his discretion; the House approved this. The Senate Committee on Foreign Relations, however, amended the resolution to apply to all belligerents. Preferring no resolution to this one, Roosevelt let the bill die in the House.[75] Through the 1930s the various neutrality acts became occasions for disputes between Congress and the Executive, with Roosevelt failing to match the legislative successes he experienced in domestic matters during the same period.

In September 1940 President Roosevelt made the first of the decisions that marked his exercise of increasing executive power in foreign policy. This was the exchange of fifty over-age but reconditioned American destroyers for British bases in the Western Atlantic. This was accomplished by executive agreement, not by treaty. It has been stated that this violated the international

---

74. Woodrow Wilson, *The Political Thought of Woodrow Wilson*, ed. E. David Cronon (New York: Bobbs-Merrill Company, 1965), pp. 68, 69.
75. James A. Robinson, *Congress and Foreign Policy-Making* (Homewood, Ill.: The Dorsey Press, 1967), pp. 24, 25.

law of neutrality and gave Germany legal cause to declare war on the United States.[76]

In April 1941, through another executive agreement, with the Danish Minister to the United States, Roosevelt acquired the right to occupy Greenland, despite protests from the Nazi-controlled government in Copenhagen.[77] In July of the same year Roosevelt announced to Congress that he had secured permission from the government of Iceland to take over from Great Britain the defense of Iceland in an emergency. The next month, again without consulting either house of Congress, FDR discussed with Churchill both lend-lease and the postwar peace program.[78] In September of the same year the U. S. destroyer *Greer* was helping British planes track a German submarine, and the sub fired two torpedoes at the *Greer*. The President then announced that the American Navy would shoot on sight all German and Italian vessels found west of the 26th meridian. This undeclared naval war continued for the remaining months before Pearl Harbor.[79]

During World War II President Roosevelt had various "Big Three" Conferences with Prime Minister Winston Churchill and Soviet Premier Joseph Stalin at such places as Casablanca, Teheran, and Yalta. The Yalta Conference is the best known and most controversial. Most significant at Yalta was the agreement to cede Eastern Poland to the U.S.S.R., and to give Russia gains in the Far East at the expense of Japan.[80] The fact of these "secret agreements" that went beyond military-strategy decisions of the sort a Commander in Chief should make on remaking the map of the world shocked many Americans.[81] These sweeping

76. Senate Committee on Foreign Relations, "Pro: Should Resolution 187 Concerning the Power of the Executive in Foreign Relations Be Adopted?," *Congressional Digest* 47 (October 1968): 236.
77. Corwin, p. 202.
78. Corwin, p. 203.
79. *Congressional Digest,* p. 236.
80. John C. Campbell and the Research Staff of the Council on Foreign Relations, *The United States in World Affairs 1945-1947* (New York: Published for the Council on Foreign Relations by Harper & Brothers, 1947), p. 13.
81. Charles O. Lerche, *Foreign Policy of the American People* (Englewood Cliffs, N. J.: Prentice-Hall, 1967), p. 103.

agreements were made without Congressional participation. A delayed negative response by Congress took place, however, and Yalta was to serve as an impetus to the attempted passage of the Bricker Amendment a decade later.[82]

Roosevelt not only stretched the powers of the presidency during the approach to World War II, but in his prosecution of total war he assumed even more extensive powers than had Wilson. When Harry S. Truman succeeded to the position of Chief Executive in 1945, he inherited not only an existing network of power, but a group of new challenges as well.

In one of his earlier major acts Truman appeared personally before the Senate in 1945 to request approval of the UN Charter. In his files a photostatic copy of Wilson's 1919 address to the Senate was found attached to an early draft of the speech. Unlike his predecessors, however, Truman's visit to the Senate was successful.[83]

In 1949, in connection with the North Atlantic Treaty Organization, a question arose in the Senate Foreign Relations Committee about the obligations of the United States under the treaty in case of an attack on a signatory power. The committee contended that NATO did not give the president the automatic power to go to war in case of such an attack. Secretary of State Dean Acheson made this reply:

> This does not mean that the United States would automatically be at war if we or one of the other parties to the treaty were attacked. Under the Constitution, the Congress alone has the power to declare war. The United States would be obligated by the treaty to take promptly the action which it deemed necessary to restore and maintain the security of the North Atlantic area. That decision as to what action was necessary would naturally be taken in accordance with our constitutional processes.[84]

---

82. Lerche, p. 103.
83. Robinson, p. 95.
84. *A Decade of American Foreign Policy, Basic Documents 1941–1949*, 81st Cong., 1st sess., Doc. No. 123, prepared for Senate Foreign Relations Committee by committee staff and Department of State (Washington: U. S. Government Printing Office, 1950), p. 1337.

In 1950 in Korea President Truman committed the nation to war without approval by Congress. When the North Koreans invaded South Korea, he did not consult Congress about his proper response. When he did meet with congressional leaders, it was to inform them of decisions he had already made. Significantly, the press was informed of the content of these meetings while they were still going on.[85] Senator Taft and others objected to the President's unilateral action, and a State Department document offered these arguments in favor of U. S. intervention in Korea:

1. The existence of an emergency that required immediate action and the possibility that the Congress might not respond quickly to a Presidential request for authority.
2. The assertion that the invasion was an immediate threat to the ultimate security of the United States.
3. The belief that a recommendation of the Security Council of the United Nations made assistance to Korea legal under international law.
4. The statement in various forms that the President as commander in chief could use the armed forces as he wishes, and particularly American foreign policy.[86]

War powers in areas such as strategic materials and price controls were granted to President Truman to a lesser extent than had been true during the two World Wars. On one occasion Truman seized the steel mills in order to expedite the war effort in the face of an impending industry-wide strike. This action was deemed illegal by the United States Supreme Court in the case *Youngstown Sheet and Tube Co.* v. *Sawyer.*[87] Truman's act had exceeded his constitutional powers, and it invaded those of Congress. It is significant that only on this domestic question did the highest court take part in the constitutional issue raised by Truman's action in entering and directing the war. With respect to

85. *U. S. Commitments to Foreign Powers, Hearings,* p. 16. See also U. S. Congress, Senate, Senator Church speaking for National Commitments, S. Res. 85, 91st Cong., 1st sess., June 20, 1969, *Congressional Record,* 115, No. 102, p. S 6880; "Notes," *Harvard Law Review,* p. 1791.
86. *U. S. Commitments to Foreign Powers, Hearings,* p. 17. Also see Appendix A.
87. 343 U. S. 579 (1952).

the international aspects of a President's foreign-policy initiatives the courts have played only a minor part, and to the extent that they have had anything to say at all they have backed the President's authority to exercise his powers as he sees fit.[88] It has not been changing judicial interpretations that have changed the constitutional position of Congress, however. In a number of cases the Supreme Court has interpreted the Constitution to support strong Presidential power.[89]

At the time of President Truman's initial commitment of American troops to combat in Korea almost no congressional dissent was heard. Senator Watkins of Utah did say that he would have sent a message to Congress asking for authority if he had been President.[90] By early 1951 Senator Taft's influential voice entered the discussion; Taft held that Truman had "simply usurped authority, in violation of the laws of the Constitution, when he sent troops to Korea to carry out the resolution of the United Nations in an undeclared war."[91]

As the war in Korea got underway, President Truman on September 9, 1950, announced his intention to make "substantial increases" in the number of American troops stationed in Western Europe.[92] The reason was to bolster defense of that section of the Continent against possible Soviet action while American attention

---

88. See cases cited in Louis Henkin, "Viet-Nam in the Courts of the United States: Political Questions," *The American Journal of International Law* 63 (April 1969): 286. One leading case that has been regarded as giving the President a broad scope in the conduct of international relations without Congressional approval, *U. S.* v. *Curtiss-Wright Export Corporation,* 299 U. S. 304 (1936). Eee "Notes," *Harvard Law Review,* p. 1802.

89. Griffith, p. 4. Also see *United States* v. *Sweeney,* 157 U. S. 281 (1895); *Myers* v. *United States,* 272 U. S. 293 (1926); *United States* v. *Belmont,* 301 U. S. 324 (1937); *United States* v. *Pink,* 315 U. S. 203 (1942); *United States* v. *Curtiss-Wright Export Corp.,* 299 U. S. 304 (1936); *Mora* v. *McNamara,* 389 U. S. 934 (1967).

90. U. S. Congress, Senate, Senator Watkins speaking about Truman's action in Korea, 81st Cong., 2d sess., June 27, 1950, *Congressional Record,* 96, Part 7, pp. 9229–33.

91. U. S. Congress, Senate, Senator Taft speaking against Truman's action in Korea, 82nd Cong., 1st sess., January 5, 1951, *Congressional Record,* 97, Part 1, p. 37.

92. Richard P. Stebbins and the Research Staff of the Council on Foreign Relations, *The United States in World Affairs 1951* (New York: Published for the Council on Foreign Relations by Harper & Brothers, 1952), p. 50.

was focused on the Far East. In December 1950 former President Herbert Hoover made a speech questioning the merit and opposing the expense of their troop commitment.[93] This soon touched off what came to be known as the "Great Debate" of 1951. Robert A. Taft was the chief spokesman against the President's expansion of the European force. In general Taft expressed a distrust of even friendly governments and a belief that air and sea power could be counted on without major ground force.[94]

Secretary of State Acheson defended the administration's decision in this way:

> Not only has the President the authority to use the armed forces in carrying out the broad foreign policy of the United States and implementing treaties, but it is equally clear that this authority may not be interfered with by the Congress in the exercise of powers which it has under the Constitution.[95]

The dissatisfaction over "Truman's War" grew; and when Dwight D. Eisenhower assumed the presidency, he started his administration taking the position that a stricter observance of constitutional separation of powers in foreign policy would be observed. In a March 10, 1954, press conference President Eisenhower made this statement:

> There is going to be no involvement of America in war unless it is a result of the constitutional process that is placed upon Congress to declare it. Now let us have that clear.[96]

The following year Eisenhower asked Congress for authority to use American armed forces to protect Formosa and the Pescadores. The resolution passed, and it included the word *authorize*. In debate over the resolution Senator Wayne Morse objected that "under the Constitution of the United States no

---

93. Dean Acheson, *Present at the Creation* (New York: W. W. Norton and Company, 1969), pp. 488, 489.
94. Stebbins, p. 50.
95. *U. S. Commitments to Foreign Powers, Hearings,* p. 17.
96. *Public Papers of the Presidents of the United States: Eisenhower,* 1954 (Washington: U. S. Government Printing Office, 1960), p. 306.

President has the right to commit an act of war against a sovereign power."[97]

In 1957 a generally similar resolution on the Middle East dropped the authorization concept and substituted the view that the President, as Commander in Chief, could use the armed forces to defend the "vital interest" of the United States.[98] Morse further claimed the presence of the troops would "encourage the Lebanese government in defense of Lebanese sovereignty and integrity." He did not refer to the resolution Congress had passed the previous year; rather he claimed to be acting under his inherent constitutional power.[99]

The foreign policies of President Eisenhower were aided by strong support from Republicans in the Senate. This partisan support compared to a similar situation in which Truman's Senate backing came mainly from Democrats. Malcolm Jewell made a careful study of 179 roll-call votes from 1947 to 1960 on foreign aid, reciprocal trade, and collective security. He found that while over 80 percent of Democratic Senators supported Truman on 71 percent of the votes studied, only 37 percent of Republicans voted for his measures a majority of the time. Eisenhower, on the other hand, secured the votes of a majority of Democrats on 71 percent of the roll calls, and he got a Republican majority on 83 percent.[100]

Eisenhower's movement away from the strict dependence on congressional authority in the use of troops in conducting foreign relations was underscored by Secretary of State John Foster Dulles's famous January 1956 statement in *Life* magazine that

97. U. S. Congress, Senate, Senator Morse speaking against Presidential authority to use Armed Forces to protect Formosa and the Pescadores, 84th Cong., 1st sess., January 24, 1955, *Congressional Record*, 101, Part 1, p. 766. Also see Appendix A.

98. U. S. Congress, Senate, Committees on Foreign Relations and Armed Services, *To Promote Peace and Stability in the Middle East*, S. Rept. 70, 85th Cong., 1st sess., 1957, p. 9.

99. *National Commitments*, p. 21. See U. S. Congress, Senate, President Eisenhower quoted on Middle East situation, 85th Cong., 2d sess., July 15, 1958, *Congressional Record*, 104 Part 11, pp. 13903, 13904.

100. Malcolm E. Jewell, *Senatorial Politics and Foreign Policy*, (Lexington: University of Kentucky Press, 1962), pp. 35, 36.

we had been on the "verge of war" in Indochina in 1954 and the Formosa Straits in 1955. He added, "if you are scared to go to the brink, you are lost."[101] "Brinkmanship" became a rallying cry for those who opposed the Secretary and his policies. Despite his prose, however, Dulles had a better-than-average record in seeking congressional backing for his action. The important Senate Resolutions on the Formosa Straits in 1955 (H. J. Res. 159) and the Middle East in 1957 (H. J. Res. 117) are the main tangible results of his efforts to involve the Congress in foreign policy. In 1954 Dulles sought congressional advice on the possibility of American intervention in Indochina. Congressional opposition to such intervention undoubtedly played a role in the decision not to become militarily involved.[102]

An important feature of the 1950s was the presence and influence of Senator Joseph P. McCarthy of Wisconsin. McCarthy's efforts were commonly called "witch hunts," and at the very least they were a "spectacularly destructive interference."[103] The intemperate nature of McCarthy's investigations into the State and Defense Departments was such that he inspired little reasoned criticism of the executive; it is much more likely that he brought broad discredit to Congress as a useful voice in foreign affairs.

In 1954 a constitutional amendment was proposed by Senator John W. Bricker of Ohio that would have limited the authority of the President, as well as the Senate, in international relations. It specified that no provision of a treaty that conflicted with the Constitution would have any force or effect. No treaty would be effective as international law unless implemented by legislation that would be valid apart from the treaty. The Bricker amendment also stipulated that Congress regulate executive agreements and that these agreements require the same procedures and

---

101. Grundy, p. 386.
102. Norman A. Graebner, *The New Isolationism* (New York: The Ronald Press Company, 1956), pp. 164–66. Also John Robinson Bear, *John Foster Dulles* (New York: Harper & Brothers, 1957), pp. 207, 208.
103. Stanley Hoffman, *Gulliver's Troubles, or the Setting of American Foreign Policy* (New York: McGraw Hill Book Company, 1968), p. 257.

limitations as treaties.[104] Although the Bricker amendment was modified considerably before any roll call was taken on it, it was defeated.

Two events in the presidency of John F. Kennedy involve important tests of executive-legislative powers in foreign policy. First was American support of the ill-fated invasion in 1961 of the Bay of Pigs in Cuba. Newspaper accounts of the training of anti-Castro units in Florida before the event brought no open congressional reaction, nor did late press reports that these units were being moved to forward bases. The President briefed congressional leaders during the few days it took to crush the invasion, but again no published objections were raised.[105] In later weeks some publicity was given to those who said that more force should have been used. The general restraint of Congress in the incident has been explained by the need to maintain national unity in a time of national humiliation and by President Kennedy's forthright acceptance of responsibility for the incident.[106] The Bay of Pigs would have fitted into the pattern established by McKinley and Theodore Roosevelt, or at least into Wilson's dispatch of Pershing into Mexico, except for the fact that it failed.

The Cuban missile crisis of October 1962 involved not only a confrontation with the Soviet Union, but also nuclear weapons. It thus broke out of earlier patterns, and fitted more into the

---

104. U. S. Congress, Senate, Senator McCarran introducing the Bricker Amendment for debate, Senate Joint Resolution 1, 83rd Cong., 2d sess., January 20, 1954, *Congressional Record*, 100, Part 1, pp. 478–86.

105. Senator J. William Fulbright was given an airplane ride by President Kennedy to a common destination, and during the course of the trip the President informed him of the invasion plan. Senator Fulbright expressed misgivings over the advisability of such action. President Kennedy invited Fulbright to the meeting at which the final decision on the Cuban invasion was made. Fulbright denounced the invasion once again, but was unable to convince the majority of presidential advisers. J. William Fulbright, private interview with the author, January 26, 1970, Washington, D. C. Also see Arthur M. Schlesinger, Jr., *A Thousand Days: John F. Kennedy in the White House* (Boston: Houghton Mifflin Company, 1965), pp. 233–66. Also see Appendix A.

106. Holbert N. Carroll, "The Congress and National Security Policy," in *The Congress and America's Future*, ed. David B. Truman (Englewood Cliffs, New Jersey: Prentice-Hall, Inc., 1965), p. 159.

nuclear-age image of the President as the man with his finger on the button that can trigger instant war. Kennedy's action to "quarantine" Cuba to force out the Soviet missiles had been preceded one month by a Joint Resolution, which stated American determination to prevent various acts of the Cuban government.[107] Before the resolution was passed, however, Kennedy stated in a press conference that as Commander in Chief he had full authority to do what he thought was necessary to protect American security.[108] Two hours before his historic television message of October 22, 1962, Kennedy made his only contact with Congress during the crisis and briefed its leaders on the decision he had already made. Theodore Sorenson later reported that this meeting had been the "only sour note of the day."[109]

In 1964 the war in Vietnam was of moderate proportions, although American troops were beyond the point of acting primarily in an advisory role. On August 2 of that year the American destroyer *Maddox* was on patrol in international waters in the Gulf of Tonkin 25 miles off the coast. It was approached by three North Vietnamese torpedo boats that fired their torpedoes but missed. Shells fired from the *Maddox* then hit one boat, and the other two were damaged by fighter planes sent from the carrier *Ticonderoga*. Two nights later the *Maddox*, now accompanied by the *Turner Joy*, reported that unidentified vessels approached them and that they were under continuous attack. Two of the attacking craft were sunk, although no damage was done to the American ships.[110] A series of reprisal raids was conducted against North Vietnam. In addition the administra-

---

107. *U. S. Commitments to Foreign Powers, Hearings,* p. 19. An Organization of American States resolution was also cited by Kennedy as authorizing his action. See "Notes," *Harvard Law Review,* p. 1792. See also Robert F. Kennedy, *Thirteen Days: A Memoir of the Cuban Missile Crisis* (New York: W. W. Norton and Company, 1969), p. 51.
108. *U. S. Commitments to Foreign Powers, Hearings,* p. 19.
109. Theodore C. Sorensen, *Kennedy* (New York: Harper and Row, 1965), p. 702.
110. *U. S. Congress, Senate, Committee on Foreign Relations, The Gulf of Tonkin, the 1964 Incidents, Hearings,* before the Committee on Foreign Relations, Senate, 90th Cong., 2d sess., February 20, 1968. See also Merlo J. Pusey, *The Way We Go To War* (Boston: Houghton Mifflin Company, 1969), pp. 116–19.

tion asked for a joint resolution to help deal with the situation. With very little discussion, on August 7, 1964, Congress passed a resolution stating that:

> the Congress approves and supports all the determination of the President, as Commander in Chief, to take all necessary measures to repel any armed attack against the forces of the United States and to prevent further aggression.
> . . . The United States is, therefore, prepared, as the President determines, to take all necessary steps, including the use of armed force, to assist any member or protocol state of the Southeast Asia Collective Defense Treaty requesting assistance in defense of its freedom.[111]

The resolution passed the House unanimously, and there were only two negative notes in the Senate. Under Secretary of State Nicholas deB. Katzenbach later characterized the resolution as the "functional equivalent" of a declaration of war, and it was so employed later.[112] There is no reason to assume that earlier resolutions might not have been subject to similar interpretation had the administrations chosen to do so.[113]

In the campaign of 1964 President Lyndon Johnson did not advocate a widening war effort in Southeast Asia. On October 21, 1964, he said this in a speech in Akron, Ohio: "We are not about to send American boys 9,000 or 10,000 miles away from home to do what Asian boys ought to be doing for themselves."[114] It is significant to note that President Johnson in 1967 stated that he did regard the Gulf of Tonkin resolution as sufficient notice to Congress that it would be asked to "stay the whole route" in Vietnam.[115] In 1966 the State Department legal adviser had al-

---

111. U. S. Congress, Senate, Committee on Foreign Relations, *Background Information Relating to Southeast Asia and Vietnam,* Committee Print, 91st Cong., 1st sess., March, 1969, p. 154.
112. *U. S. Commitments to Foreign Powers, Hearings,* p. 81.
113. See Appendix A.
114. Quoted in *National Commitments,* p. 23.
115. *New York Times,* August 19, 1967, p. 10.

ready written that the President also had full authority for the Vietnam action from Article II of the Constitution.[116]

Other than Vietnam the most significant foreign-policy event of the Johnson Administration was the landing of Marines in the Dominican Republic in 1965. This action was justified initially as necessary to protect the safety of American citizens. Later Johnson also said it was an exercise of the power to protect the security of the hemisphere in accordance with the principles of the treaty establishing the Organization of American States.[117] Critics of the episode have stated that U. S. Ambassador W. Tapley Bennett proposed the invasion to help a military junta, headed by General Wessin y Wessin, stay in power. The junta's opponents were thought to include Communists, although evidence is highly debatable.[118]

Events of the first year of the Nixon Administration centered around the de-escalation of the Vietnam War. The President did not embark on new acts that appeared to tend to conflict with the powers of Congress in foreign affairs. During this period objections raised by members of the Congress, and most especially by Senators, were indicative of the greater congressional unrest.

One demonstration of this restlessness was the passage by the Senate of the National Commitments Resolution. Senator Fulbright led in the effort to pass this resolution, which was essentially a reaction to the acts of President Johnson. The text of the relevant part of Senate Resolution 85 reads:

Resolved, That it is the sense of the Senate that a national commitment by the United States to a foreign power neces-

---

116. Leonard C. Meeker, "The Legality of United States Participation in the Defense of Viet Nam," *Department of State Bulletin* 54 (March 28, 1966): 484.

117. *New York Times,* May 2, 1965, p. 10 .

118. Theodore Draper, "The Dominican Crisis: A Case Study in American Policy," *Commentary* 40 (December 1965): 33–68. See Eugene J. McCarthy, *The Limits of Power* (New York: Holt, Rinehart and Winston, 1967), pp. 126–34. Also Seyom Brown, *The Faces of Power: Constancy and Change in United States Foreign Policy from Truman to Johnson* (New York: Columbia University Press, 1968), pp. 349–63.

sarily and exclusively results from affirmative action taken by the executive and legislative branches of the United States Government through means of a treaty convention, or other legislative instrumentality specifically intended to give effect to such a commitment.[119]

The resolution passed the Senate on June 25, 1969. (The names of the seventy Senators for and the sixteen against the National Commitments Resolution are shown in Appendix B.)

Congressional prerogatives in foreign policy were also asserted when Senator Frank Church proposed an amendment to the Defense Appropriation bill that specified that none of the funds appropriated by the Act could be used to finance the introduction of American ground-combat troops into Laos or Thailand.[120] President Nixon had endorsed this prohibition as consistent with Administration policy in Southeast Asia.[121] The amendment was passed 73 to 17. Their oversight in not including Cambodia under these restrictions later proved to be regrettable.

In late 1969 Senator Charles McC. Mathias of Maryland proposed the repeal of the Gulf of Tonkin and other resolutions that Presidents had relied on since the Korean War to defend their use of troops abroad. On March 14, 1970, the Associated Press reported that the State Department, in a letter to Senator Fulbright, said, "We neither advocate nor oppose Congressional action" on the Mathias proposal.[122] The balance of executive and congressional power can thus turn on formal constitutional questions, on events that give one side or another a position of strength at various points in time, on trends, such as technology, that can change the logic of authority, and on issues of institutional and even individual prerogative.

119. U. S. Congress, Senate, Debate on National Commitments, S. Res. 85, 91st Cong., 1st sess., June 20, 1969, *Congressional Record*, 115, No. 102, p. S 6878. Also see Appendix A.
120. U. S. Congress, Senate, Church Amendment to the Defense Appropriations Bill, 1970, H. R. 15090, 91st Cong., 1st sess., December 15, 1969, *Congressional Record*, 115 No. 208, S 16764.
121. *New York Times,* December 17, 1969, p. 1.
122. *Kansas City Times,* March 14, 1970, p. 18.

The Fulbright Premise

1

THE SENATOR
FROM ARKANSAS

In the 1830s Alexis de Tocqueville, the perceptive observer of American life and politics often quoted by many writers, including Senator J. William Fulbright, made this statement:

> that it is most especially in the conduct of foreign relations that democratic governments appear . . . to be decidedly inferior to governments carried on upon different principles. . . . Foreign politics demand scarcely any of those qualities which a democracy possesses; and they require, on the contrary, the perfect use of almost all those faculties in which it is deficient.[1]

Despite the handicap of a democracy in the conduct of foreign affairs, the United States in the past century has experienced geographic expansion, weathered wars, and become a seasoned international power. Even with this change, however, the question of the proper determination of American foreign policy is far from settled, and the nation has yet to develop fully those faculties in which Tocqueville found it wanting in its formative years.

The emergence of the United States into its status as a world power came with relative speed. We are reminded that "no other people have had to grow old so fast."[2] In the course of this

---

1. Alexis de Tocqueville, *Democracy in America* (New York: Alfred A. Knopf, 1945), 1: 234.
2. Robert Endicott Osgood, *Ideals and Self-Interest in America's Foreign Policy* (Chicago: The University of Chicago Press, 1953), p. 452.

growth the nation has gone through various crises. Political scientist Richard Neustadt observed in 1960 that "we may have priced ourselves out of the market for 'productive' crises. . . ."[3] By "productive" is meant those crises that can strengthen the President's chance for support *"within* the system."[4] The nature of the future environment in which American foreign policy will function can be characterized only as uncertain.[5] Amid the uncertainty and change at least two points stand out. One is the inevitability of United States involvement in world affairs. One author concludes that:

A style of Presidential politics which tended to leave the details of the international environment to others until the Commander-in-Chief's function was required would probably find this function required more often than a President who cultivated a facility with the rich arsenal of international inducements and sanctions at this nation's disposal, and would directly oversee their application in pursuit of our multiple interests across the globe. The White House, the entire nation, was fully implicated in this interdependent world. There was no escape from responsibility.[6]

The other certainty is that foreign policy will continue to be inextricably interwoven with domestic political considerations.[7]

In the 1950s and 1960s an important voice and force in American foreign policy was furnished by Senator J. William Fulbright, Democrat from Arkansas. In the Senate since 1944 and Chairman of the Senate Committee on Foreign Relations since 1959, Fulbright has played a role of increasing magnitude in the continuing discussion of American foreign policy. A topic of special

3. Richard E. Neustadt, *Presidential Power: The Politics of Leadership* (New York: John Wiley & Sons, 1962), p. 186.
4. *Ibid.,* p. 186.
5. Edgar E. Robinson and others, "Presidential Power in the Nuclear Age," *Powers of the President in Foreign Affairs, 1945–1965* (San Francisco: A Research Study Commissioned by the Commonwealth Club of California, 1966), p. 245.
6. Seyom Brown, *The Faces of Power* (New York: Columbia University Press, 1968), p. 372.
7. Francis H. Heller, *The Presidency: A Modern Perspective* (New York: Random House, 1960), p. 68.

importance that runs through Senator Fulbright's thought is the proper position of the President in the determination of foreign policy. Fulbright's views on the proper extent of presidential authority in foreign policy by no means follow a consistent theme; rather they vary widely at different times and under different circumstances.

One author points out that Fulbright's political discourse has influenced the public's views.[8] As he has gained public notice and even aroused controversy, the Senator's statements have served as the focal point for debate. These statements have special importance because in the Congress it is generally conceded that the chairmen of substantive committees are usually the most influential members.[9] This especially applies to their statements on matters related to the jurisdiction of their committees.

Senator Fulbright has emerged as more than an articulate voice. His Senate experience has spanned the post-World War II period during which the concept of the presidency has undergone important change.[10] It has been stated that if American foreign policy is to be changed from something other than the President's foreign policy, the President must therefore be crossed successfully by Congress, and especially the Senate.[11] By the late 1960s Senator Fulbright was crossing the President with great frequency.

In the 1970s and beyond, it appears likely that Senator Fulbright's efforts to restrict the independence and initiative of the President in the conduct of foreign policy will be remembered as his most important utterances on this subject. Despite this fact, these arguments will not remain as his only position on the subject, because Fulbright has always displayed an amazing flexibility in his thinking. In a "Meet the Press" interview on June 7,

8. Bruce M. Sapin, *The Making of United States Foreign Policy* (Washington, D. C.: Published for The Brookings Institution by Frederick A. Praeger, 1966), p. 53.

9. David N. Farnsworth, *The Senate Committee on Foreign Relations* (Urbana: The University of Illinois Press, 1961), p. 4.

10. Edgar E. Robinson, "Precedents: Powerful Presidents 1789–1945," *Powers of the President in Foreign Policy*, p. 3.

11. *Ibid.,* "Presidential Power in the Nuclear Age," p. 245.

1959, Fulbright made some telling remarks as part of a more
extended statement on the same theme:

> Our strong Presidents always have, if they are successful in
> this field, to counteract the parochial interests of our Congress.
> . . . It is a very complicated, difficult system, and I think when
> you are dealing with foreign relations, you must have a very
> strong, assertive President who uses all the powers of his
> office to get his way in the international field.[12]

In 1961 Fulbright again said that the President needs a free
hand in foreign policy.

> More specifically, I wonder whether the time has not ar-
> rived, or indeed already passed, when we must give the Execu-
> tive a measure of power in the conduct of our foreign affairs
> that we have hitherto jealously withheld.[13]

At other times, however, Senator Fulbright asserted the need
to restrain what he saw as excessive presidential commitments in
foreign policy, and by the late 1960s this side of the issue was
the only one stressed in Fulbright's public statements. An ex-
ceptionally forceful statement by Senator Fulbright, offered for
consumption by the general public, was published in *Look*
magazine in its December 2, 1969, issue. The article began with
this statement:

> We are overextended in our foreign commitments, especially
> our military commitments, and in the process of becoming
> overextended, we have allowed our national executive to ac-
> quire almost dictatorial powers in the field of foreign policy.[14]

---

12. J. William Fulbright, interview on "Meet the Press," N.B.C. telecast, June 7, 1959. Fulbright files, Washington, D. C.
13. *Ibid.,* "American Foreign Policy in the 20th Century Under an 18th-
Century Constitution," *Cornell Law Quarterly* 47 (Fall 1961): 2. This
statement was not lost on Senator Gale McGee, who quoted it to refute
Fulbright's later utterances, which took an opposite stand. See Gale W.
McGee, *The Responsibilities of World Power,* (Washington, D. C.: The
National Press Inc., 1968), p. 209.
14. *Ibid.,* "The Wars in Your Future," *Look* (December 2, 1969), p. 82.

More than the passage of time has led to these differences in viewpoint. These differences do not represent a simple change of mind caused by the passage of events or the effect of personalities. They do represent the drawing of lines of debate that will probably influence the whole position of Congress in foreign policy. The importance of this view has been summarized by political scientist James A. Robinson as a situation in which

history awaits Congress' response in the drama that will decide whether the world's most eminent legislature has an influential and constructive role to perform in an era marked by Earth's universal preoccupation with foreign policies among its own continents—and with other planets.[15]

Senator Fulbright's views on the proper role of the President in the determination of American foreign policy do not exist by themselves. His views on foreign-policy formulation are closely tied to his views on such matters as the role of public opinion in a democracy, the position of the United States among world powers, Communism, right-wing extremism, foreign aid, alliances, and the military.

Fulbright's views, in their totality, reflect his own background, his personality, and the events of his career. Especially important is the role he has played as Chairman of the Senate's Committee on Foreign Relations. This role has, in turn, been affected by the historic functions of this Committee and the nature of Senator Fulbright's predecessors in the chairmanship who influenced its traditions.

By 1970 one half of Fulbright's life had been spent as a member of Congress, and for all but the first two years of this period he has been a Senator. Even with this long tenure Fulbright is most often thought of, by supporters and critics alike, as a Rhodes Scholar and educator.

James William Fulbright was born on April 9, 1905, in Sumner,

---

15. James A. Robinson, *Congress and Foreign Policy—Making* (Homewood, Ill.: The Dorsey Press, 1967), p. 213.

Missouri, the son of Jay and Roberta (Waugh) Fulbright. His father, a farmer, moved his family to Fayetteville, Arkansas, in 1906, and there became highly successful. When he died, he left his widow and six children interests in a lumber business, farm properties, banks, real estate, a newspaper, a soft-drink bottling plant, and other prosperous enterprises. Fulbright's mother, who had attended the University of Missouri as a young woman, assumed the direction of these projects and published the *North-west Arkansas Times* of Fayetteville.

Several features of his youthful days in Fayetteville became important factors in the formulation of his later views. One was the location there of the University of Arkansas, which contributed to an intellectual environment that was greatly to influence his later public life.[16] Another was that Arkansas, less than most if not all other Southern states, did not have a tradition of war glory from the 1861–1865 period. The Civil War was not a popular one in Arkansas, and it brought the state few advantages of any kind to balance the extensive suffering and destruction.[17]

At the university young Fulbright gained recognition as a football star and student-body president, and his scholastic ability was recognized by an English professor who encouraged him to take the examination to qualify for a Rhodes scholarship to Oxford University in order to study economics and history. His studies at Oxford were fruitful, and he earned the bachelor's degree with honors there in 1928 followed by the master's degree with honors in 1931. He was also captain of the Pembroke College soccer team. He returned to the United States and went to Washington, where he earned a law degree with distinction at George Washington University. For a time he worked as a Justice Department lawyer.[18]

In 1936 Fulbright moved back to Fayetteville as a teacher

---

16. Tristram Coffin, *Senator Fulbright: Portrait of a Public Philosopher* (New York: E. P. Dutton & Co., 1966), p. 40.
17. *Ibid.*, pp. 41, 42. Arkansas is said to be the only Southern state without the statue of a Civil War General in the statehouse.
18. He was one of the lawyers who argued before the Supreme Court in the case *Schechter Poultry Corporation* v. *United States,* in which the NRA was declared unconstitutional, 295 U. S. 495, 1935.

in the university law school and directed several of his family's businesses. Three years later the president of the University was killed in an automobile accident and Fulbright was appointed President of the University of Arkansas at the age of thirty-four. In one of his first speeches as President, Fulbright reviewed some of his thoughts on the state of the nation, science, manufacturing, agriculture, and government:

> If it is granted as a premise that the functioning of our government has been and is our weakest point as a nation and society, then it seems to me that our universities should direct their efforts toward the improvement of this weakness.[19]

In 1941 Fulbright, despite his popularity with students, was dismissed as University President, at least in part because of the outspoken criticism of the Governor that his mother had made in the family-owned newspaper.[20]

In 1942 the Congressman from Fulbright's district gave up his seat, and Fulbright entered his first political campaign. On November 3 he was elected from the Third District of Arkansas. When he took office, Fulbright asked Speaker Sam Rayburn to appoint him to the Foreign Affairs Committee, and the request was granted. In his single term in the House, Fulbright took initiative unusual for a freshman legislator. However, his arguments for trying conditions related to peace-keeping to lend-lease were not accepted. Fulbright introduced a resolution in 1943 that called for an international peace-keeping organization. With support from President Roosevelt, the Fulbright Resolution passed 360 to 29 on September 21, 1943.[21] On November 5 the Senate passed

---

19. J. William Fulbright, "The Social Function of the University," speech at the University of Arkansas, December 10, 1939, printed in Haynes Johnson and Bernard M. Gwertzman, *Fulbright: The Dissenter* (New York: Doubleday and Company, 1968), pp. 269–70.

20. Coffin, pp. 50, 51.

21. U. S. Congress, House, Vote on Fulbright Resolution, Concurrent Resolution 25, 78th Cong., 1st sess., September 21, 1943, *Congressional Record,* 89, Part 6, pp. 7728, 7729. The resolution stated: "Resolved: that the House of Representatives hereby expresses itself as favoring the creation of appropriate international machinery with power adequate to prevent future aggression and to maintain lasting peace, and as favoring participation by the United States therein."

the Connally Resolution, named for Democratic Senator Tom Connally of Texas. Similar to the Fulbright declaration, it passed by a vote of 85 to 5.

As a delegate to an international conference on education held in London in 1944, Fulbright proposed a four-point program visualizing the reconstruction of essential educational facilities. The conference adopted his proposals and recommended the establishment of an organization to work for their realization. Its report was the basis for what later became the U. N. Economic and Social Council.

In 1944 Fulbright decided to run for the Senate. The decisive election was the Democratic primary and among his several opponents was Homer Adkins, the Governor who had ousted Fulbright as University President. Fulbright and Adkins were the frontrunners in the primary and, in a runoff election, Fulbright was the winner.

Fulbright exhibited primary interest in foreign policy from the start, but it was five years before he was appointed to the Committee on Foreign Relations. In one of his earliest speeches in the Senate, he not only stressed foreign affairs, but started these 1945 remarks with a sentence that foreshadowed his later work: "Mr. President, myths are one of the greatest obstacles in the formulation of national policy."[22] After the United Nations charter was drafted in 1945, Fulbright expressed disappointment with several features in its structure. One was the concept of national sovereignty. Another was the veto power. Generally, however, he supported the U. N.

During his first term as Senator, Fulbright was assigned to the Committees on Banking and Currency, Education and Labor, Public Buildings and Grounds, and Immigration. During the first session of the Seventy-ninth Congress, he voted for an extension of the Trade Agreements Act, the United Nations Charter, and the U. N. participation bill. He voted against an appropriation

---

22. U. S. Congress, Senate, Senator Fulbright, speech "American Foreign Policy-International Organization for World Security," 79th Cong., 1st sess., March 28, 1945. *Congressional Record*, 91, Part 3, p. 2896.

for the Fair Employment Practice Committee and a reduction in the excess profits tax.

In December 1945 an act providing that credits acquired by the United States through the sale of surplus property abroad be used for the exchange of students and professors to promote international understanding was introduced by Fulbright. The bill, known as the Fulbright Act, was signed by President Harry S. Truman on August 1, 1946. It granted travel expenses, tuition, and maintenance to American scholars for graduate study and research. It also provided traveling expenses for foreign students at American colleges and universities.

In 1946 Fulbright voted affirmatively in the second session of the Seventy-ninth Congress on the British loan, the Case strike control bill, and a constitutional amendment granting equality of rights under the law without regard to sex. He opposed cloture for an F.E.P.C. filibuster and state title to offshore oil lands. In 1947 he voted for the Greek-Turkish aid bill and to override the Presidential veto of the Taft-Hartley bill. He opposed the two-term limit for the presidency, the use of private injunctions in jurisdictional strikes, limiting foreign relief to $200,000,000, and granting exemption from antitrust suits to railroads.

In 1948 Fulbright voted for the tax reduction bill, for the Federal aid to education bill, to increase the soil conservation fund, and to admit 200,000 (as against 100,000) displaced persons. He opposed cutting the European Recovery Program appropriation.

In January 1949 Fulbright became a member of the Senate Foreign Relations Committee. During the 1949 session he favored a coalition revision of the Taft-Hartley law, the North Atlantic Security Pact, the foreign military aid bill, and the indefinite extension of ninety percent farm price supports. He voted against the prohibition of segregation in public housing, and a fifty percent reduction in European arms aid. The next year he supported an appropriation of $45,000,000 for the Truman Point IV Program and a loan of $100,000,000 to Spain.

When Fulbright ran for a second term in 1950, he was unopposed. In February 1951, after an investigation by a subcommittee (of the Senate Banking and Currency Committee), which Fulbright headed, he issued a report charging that political pressure and personal favoritism influenced the granting of Reconstruction Finance Corporation loans. Fulbright's conduct of public hearings was praised. He proved to be an adroit questioner. With his disarming smile and soft voice, he could reduce a complicated situation to a few simple and devastating questions. On the Senate floor he moralized: "Democracy is more likely to be destroyed by the perversion of, or abandonment of, its true moral principles than by armed attack from Russia."[23]

In 1951 during the first session of the Eighty-second Congress, he voted for the draft extension and universal military training bill, a bill to reduce Government civilian payrolls by ten percent, and a tax increase of $5,500,000,000. He opposed bills prohibiting the sending of additional troops to Europe without congressional consent, authorizing rent increases up to thirty-seven percent, and placing an absolute ban on Allied trade with the Soviet bloc.

During the second session in 1952, he approved the granting of power to the President to seize steel plants, use of the Taft-Hartley law in the steel strike, and overriding of the President's veto of the McCarran-Walter immigration bill. On the following measures he voted negatively: a bill to abolish the RFC, and a bill to end wage and price controls on June 30, 1952.

The following year (1953) Fulbright voted to confirm Charles E. Bohlen as envoy to the U.S.S.R., to return Senator Wayne Morse of Oregon to his former committee posts, and to admit 209,000 Iron Curtain refugees. He voted against the off-shore oil bill and a penalty against nations trading with the Communist bloc.

In the second session of the Eighty-third Congress in 1954, he voted to liberalize Congressional pensions, to build 140,000 public housing units, to revise the Atomic Energy Act, and to make membership in the Communist party a crime. He voted against

23. *Time*, April 9, 1951.

the St. Lawrence seaway bill, the Bricker treaty amendment, and statehood for Hawaii and Alaska. The preceding paragraphs give some indication of the independent stance that Fulbright took on different questions.

Early in his Senate career he had his first controversial brush with a President of the United States. After Election Day, November 5, 1946, the Republicans had taken control of the United States Congress for the first time in sixteen years. This resounding Republican victory in both houses of Congress led to a proposal that remains unique in political history. Carried on the front pages of the nation's newspapers for several days, this proposal "brought astonishment, shock and laughter to the political community."[24] Senator J. William Fulbright of Arkansas, a member of President Truman's own Democratic party, had suggested that the president should resign and let a Republican successor take over.[25]

Characterized by one author as "an immature first-termer," he nevertheless was "sober and scholarly."[26] Having studied at Oxford, he admired the British parliamentary system and thought that President Truman should resign in favor of a Republican, just as the British Prime Minister resigns when he loses a majority in the House of Commons.[27]

The journalistic furor that accompanied this suggestion originated with a conversation between Senator Fulbright and a female reporter for a press association in the Senate cafeteria prior to the election. When she predicted a Democratic defeat, Fulbright observed that this would lead to a stalemate and that under such conditions the president should resign because otherwise the nation would be "drifting for two years almost without a government, and the times are too critical for that."[28] Later,

---

24. Coffin, p. 96.
25. Cabell Phillips, *The Truman Presidency* (New York: Macmillan, 1966), p. 128.
26. *Ibid.*, pp. 128, 407.
27. Michael V. DiSalle, *Second Choice* (New York: Hawthorn Books, 1966), p. 189.
28. Coffin, p. 95.

she telephoned him and asked permission for a direct quotation. The text of Fulbright's statement to the press on November 10, 1946, contained the following:

> Under these conditions, neither party will have complete responsibility for or the authority to govern, and each party will place the blame for the inevitable stalemate on the other party. These times are too perilous for this nation to bicker and to drift for two years without a responsible government.[29]

Specifically, Fulbright suggested that Truman should consult with Republican members of Congress, then appoint a Republican Secretary of State, and resign. Contending that this procedure would be entirely legal, Fulbright quoted Article II, Section I of the United States Constitution and cited a March 1792, law that made provision for a method of resigning. Answering a question regarding the President's right to appoint his successor, the Senator stated that if the President accepted the recommendation of men chosen by a clear majority of the people in recent, hotly contested campaigns, this would be more representative of the will of the people than were delegates to national party conventions. In this connection he cited the Constitutional Convention of 1787, referring to debates favoring the selection of the President by the Congress. The alternative to a presidential resignation, he said, would be continual haggling. Other countries would lose faith in the United States, bipartisan foreign policy would be strained, and this would contribute to causes for another war.[30]

Fulbright thus argued that this course of action would promote the welfare of the nation because it would result in "a govern-

---

29. Karl E. Meyer, *Fulbright of Arkansas* (Washington: Luce, 1963), pp. 53–55. See also *New York Times,* November 10, 1946, p. 7. Meyer points out that on July 18, 1954, Fulbright "with bipartisan scrupulousness" suggested that Eisenhower resign if the Democrats won. See p. 53.

30. Meyer, *Fulbright of Arkansas,* pp. 53–55. See also *New York Times,* November 7, 1946, pp. 1 and 3, and November 8, 1946, p. 19. Fulbright named Senator Arthur Vandenberg of Michigan, Republican leader in foreign affairs, as the most logical choice, "because of his position in international affairs."

ment capable of functioning in a definite, positive manner." He argued that it would also promote the welfare of the Democratic party, because it would be wise political strategy to accede to the wishes of the people, who had indicated in the election that the administration was unacceptable, and then conduct a thorough review of party policies and a close examination of party organization.[31] Fulbright predicted "a disastrous defeat" in 1948 if the Democrats tried to hold power in the face of public disapproval. He advocated using the next two years to revitalize the party in order to more effectively challenge the rising tide of Republicans. A presidential resignation would give the Republicans an opportunity to develop a constructive, statesmanlike program, he said; and if they failed, the people would know where to place the blame in future elections.[32]

Senator Fulbright insisted that his suggestion was no reflection on the character or capacity of President Truman, saying that this circumstance was evidence of a serious defect in the electoral system, not of malfeasance on the part of the president. He later stated, "There was nothing personal about it. Why, I liked the President and I still do."[33] It is true, however, that Fulbright had called on President Truman during autumn, 1945, to express disagreement with certain presidential policies, and had afterward been quoted by one author as saying, "I didn't make a bit of an impression on the President. He didn't know what I was talking about." In November 1945 Fulbright had made a radio speech opposing administration policy on the United Nations and the atomic bomb.[34] Fulbright's proposal was privately and publicly discussed by members of the Truman Administration for some weeks after. Such discussions led President Truman there-

---

31. Meyer, *Fulbright of Arkansas,* pp. 53–55.
32. *New York Times,* November 8, 1946, p. 19, and November 10, 1946, p. 7.
33. Meyer, *Fulbright of Arkansas,* pp. 53–55, xix.
34. Alfred Steinberg, *The Man From Missouri* (New York: Putnam, 1962), p. 263, and Coffin, *Senator Fulbright,* pp. 80–83. (Quotation from Steinberg.) Coffin places the time of the visit as "a few weeks after Truman moved into the White House." See p. 76.

after to nearly always make reference to "Senator Halfbright."[35]
In 1946 Fulbright also pointed out that he had changed his mind
on a basic issue:

> Last summer, or even six months ago, I had little difficulty
> in discussing what I thought should be our foreign policy. The
> United States was the machinery by use of which well inten-
> tioned and forthright people could discuss and compare their
> difference. . . . Today I could confess that I am troubled and
> I find it exceedingly difficult to arrive at any convictions
> about the future of international relations.[36]

A major issue of the Truman Administration in which Senator
Fulbright became involved was the President's proposal in late
1950 to make major increases in American troops strength in
Europe. This set off the "great debate" of late 1950 and early
1951. Senator Fulbright supported Truman's decision and he
made this statement in a Senate speech:

> One important issue has been clearly defined. That issue is
> whether the President should seek the advice of Congress on
> the question of sending troops to Europe now, or whether his
> discretion should be subject to the consent of Congress. Ap-
> parently the President is agreeable to the idea that it is proper
> for Congress to give him its advice about this question, leaving
> him the full responsibility for making the final decision. He
> is not willing, however, to accept the principle that the consent
> of the Congress is necessary to validate his decision. In other
> words, he does not agree that his decision in this matter must
> be subject to the approval of Congress. Personally, I agree with
> the position of the President.[37]

One of Fulbright's most important encounters in his early

35. Phillips, *Truman Presidency,* p. 128.
36. J. William Fulbright, "Our Foreign Policy," speech before a joint
meeting of the American Academy of Arts and Letters and the National
Institute of Arts, New York City, May 17, 1946. Fulbright files, Washington, D. C.
37. U. S. Congress, Senate, Senator Fulbright speaking on the question of
sending troops to Europe, 82d Cong., 1st sess., January 22, 1951. *Congressional Record,* 97, Part 1, p. 520.

years on the Foreign Relations Committee took place in April of 1951 when he questioned General Douglas MacArthur when the latter appeared before the Committee following his being relieved of command in Korea. Fulbright and MacArthur clashed over the merit of the General's idea of how to conduct a war: "I believe that when you enter into a war, you should use sufficient force to impose your will upon the enemy."[38] Fulbright saw the issue as a decision between "a moment of imperial glory" and the "difficult, democratic process of persuasion and compromise."[39]

From 1953 through 1956 Fulbright generally supported the Eisenhower administration on foreign policy, although he did oppose Secretary Dulles's doctrine of "massive retaliation."[40] One of the issues of this period was the Bricker amendment to limit the treaty-making power of the President, and Fulbright opposed it. Fulbright was one of the most vigorous opponents of the destructive Senator Joseph R. McCarthy during the years of the Wisconsin Republican's peak activity. At one point Fulbright was the only one in the Senate who voted against giving McCarthy funds to continue his work.[41] In a 1954 speech Fulbright warned that "McCarthyism" was leading to the "tyranny of the majority."[42]

The Formosa Straits Resolution in 1955 was a significant specific issue. (See Appendix A.) The Resolution was still in effect in 1970, and an effort to repeal it at that time was mounted. Senator Fulbright voted for the 1955 Resolution to back the

---

38. U. S. Congress, Senate, Committee on Armed Services and the Committee on Foreign Relations, *Military Situation in the Far East, Hearings* before the Committee on Armed Services and the Committee on Foreign Relations, Senate 82d Cong., 1st sess., May, 1951, p. 146. For an analysis of MacArthur's value structure and motivational makeup, see Joseph H. deRivera, *The Psychological Dimension of Foreign Policy* (Columbus, Ohio: Charles E. Merrill Publishing Company, 1968), pp. 247–52.

39. Quoted in Coffin, p. 108.

40. Grundy, p. 384.

41. Alex Campbell, "Fulbright on Camera," *New Republic* (May 2, 1966), p. 21.

42. Andrew Kopkind, "The Speechmaker: Senator Fulbright as the Arkansas de Tocqueville," *New Republic* (October 2, 1965), p. 15.

President in his efforts to protect Formosa and the Pescadores with military force.[43]

The Suez crisis of 1956 brought Senator Fulbright into a major dispute with the Eisenhower administration. On "Martha Rountree's Press Conference" on ABC television on December 30 of that year, Fulbright characterized American Middle East Policy as a "failure" and as a "very serious matter" that the country needed to know about, but about the facts of which the Senate had not been informed.[44] Eisenhower asked for a joint resolution that would give him, among other things, authority to use U. S. troops in the Middle East "as he deems necessary. . . ." Fulbright offered a substitute resolution that actually gave the President no powers he did not already possess.[45] The Senator opposed Secretary Dulles vigorously, but he stressed that this was not a partisan matter.[46]

In January of 1959 the Chairman of the Senate Committee on Foreign Relations, Senator Green of Rhode Island, resigned from his chairmanship at the age of 91. Fulbright was next in line, and he assumed the post. A major clash with John Foster Dulles was foreseen by some, but this never occurred, since the Secretary died a few months later. Serving as Chairman of this important committee has been instrumental in the development of Fulbright's career. The committee itself is a prestigious one. Membership on it is sought after; many Senators seek a place on it, and few try to leave it. Foreign policy measures that ordinarily receive united support in the committee usually find approval in the Senate.[47]

---

43. See Appendix A. Also *Congressional Quarterly Almanac* 11: 115.
44. J. William Fulbright, interview on "Martha Rountree's Press Conference," ABC telecast, December 30, 1956. Fulbright files, Washington, D. C.
45. *Congressional Record,* 103, Part 2, 1855–1858.
46. "Martha Rountree's Press Conference."
47. Donald R. Mathews, *U. S. Senators & Their World* (Chapel Hill: University of North Carolina Press, 1960), pp. 149, 150. Mathews analyzed the change of Senators from one committee to another during a ten-year period and found that the Foreign Relations Committee was the most popular, having net gains from nearly all others and net losses to none. The recent extensive press coverage of the voluntary transfer of Senator Eugene McCarthy from the Foreign Relations Committee would demonstrate the rarity of such a move.

THE SENATOR FROM ARKANSAS

As Chairman and chief spokesman for the Committee, Fulbright has achieved major prominence. When he assumed the post in 1959, Walter Lippmann predicted that "the windows of the Senate will be open to the fresh air of a new time."[48] Fulbright himself planned from the beginning to play an active role in foreign affairs. He acknowledged, however, that while the objectives and ideals sought for foreign policy were easy to enunciate, "we have only the foggiest notions of how even to approach our prescription for an ideal world."[49] The Senator and his committee set about to clear that fog.

The Committee that Senator Fulbright has led since 1959 is one of those established in 1816 when the first standing committees were established in the Senate. Foreign Relations stood first on this original list.[50] The original committee had five members and this grew to 23 by the time the Legislative Reorganization Act of 1946 was passed and cut it back to 13. Since then it has been raised to 15, 17, and 19 members in 1953, 1959, and 1965 respectively. The increases that have taken place reflect both the committee's workload and its successful efforts to make the majority party have representation on the committee proportional to that which it possesses in the Senate as a whole.[51] The House Foreign Affairs Committee is the counterpart of the Foreign Relations Committee, and such men as Fulbright and former Secretary of State Christian Herter have served on the House group. Despite such men and despite the House's appropriations power, the Foreign Affairs Committee has not had influence or prestige at the level of that enjoyed by the Foreign Relations Committee, although the House Committee has gained in importance in recent years.[52]

The primary jurisdiction of the Senate Foreign Relations

---

48. Grundy, p. 1.
49. J. William Fulbright, "Our Responsibilities in World Affairs," Gabriel Silver Lecture on International Understanding, Columbia University, May 7, 1959. Fulbright files, Washington, D. C.
50. U. S. Congress, Senate, *Background Information on the Committee on Foreign Relations United States Senate,* Committee Print, 90th Cong., 2d sess., February, 1968, p. 3.
51. *Background Information,* p. 4.
52. Farnsworth, p. 8.

Committee is stated as follows in the Legislative Reorganization Act of 1946:

1. Relations of the United States with foreign nations generally.
2. Treaties.
3. Establishment of boundary lines between the United States and foreign nations.
4. Protection of American citizens abroad and expatriation.
5. Neutrality.
6. International conferences and congresses.
7. The American National Red Cross.
8. Intervention abroad and declarations of war.
9. Measures relating to the diplomatic service.
10. Acquisition of land and buildings for embassies and legations in foreign countries.
11. Measures to foster commercial intercourse with foreign nations and to safeguard American business interests abroad.
12. United Nations Organization and international financial and monetary organizations.
13. Foreign Loans.[53]

The functioning of the Committee in modern times has often tended to reflect the influence of its chairman. In December 1924 Senator William Borah, Republican of Idaho, took over the Chairmanship following the death of the powerful Henry Cabot Lodge, who had led the successful fight against the League of Nations. Borah's tenure as Chairman (1924–1933) has been exceeded in length since his years in office only by Fulbright. Borah was a colorful figure whose ample mane of hair made him a favorite of cartoonists. Borah's record is that of an accomplished negativist. He had been against the League and against the Court, against the Pacific Pact and against the Wilson-Hughes Russian policy, against the Caribbean policy, against the Isle of Pines Treaty, against the exclusion of Count Karolyi and Mr. Saklatvala, against the Alien Property Administration, against

---

53. *Background Information*, p. 5.

the Child Labor Amendment, against Coolidge Republicanism, and against LaFollette insurgency.[54] Once President Coolidge saw Borah riding horseback. The President commented to his companions: "Well, there is Senator Borah on a horse, and they are both going the same way!"[55] Borah conceived of his function as Chairman as the prevention of action in the foreign relations field.[56] Senator Borah spoke extensively in support of his ideas, and took pride in his ability as a speaker.[57]

Borah was succeeded as chairman in 1933 by Senator Key Pittman of Nevada when the Democrats took control of the Senate. Senate debate on foreign policy in this period was often led by Robert A. Taft, who was never even a member of the Committee until the last year of his life (1953). Later Chairmen prior to Fulbright generally did not gain a stature comparable to that of Borah. Walter F. George was Chairman for a brief period in 1941 and then again from 1955 to 1957. Tom Connally saw the Committee through both World War II and the Korean War, and Arthur Vandenberg of Michigan stressed bipartisanship during his Chairmanship in the Republican 80th Congress. Alexander Wiley of Wisconsin held the seat during 1953–1955 and he sought to support President Eisenhower when his junior colleague from Wisconsin engaged in destructive criticism. Senator Green became Chairman after he was so old that he had difficulty staying awake during hearings.[58] The men who held the Chairmanship, along with such other Senators as William Knowland and Lyndon Johnson, were also often consulted by the administration on foreign policy during the period when they were not serving as Chairman.[59]

54. Walter Lippmann, *Men of Destiny* (New York: The Macmillan Company, 1928), pp. 143, 144.
55. Robert H. Ferrell, *Peace in Their Time* (New Haven: Yale University Press, 1952), p. 33.
56. Claudius O. Johnson, *Borah of Idaho* (New York: Longmans, Green and Co., 1936), pp. 3, 4.
57. Claudius O. Johnson, pp. 320–22.
58. Sidney Hyman, "Fulbright: The Wedding of Arkansas and the World," *New Republic* (May 14, 1962), pp. 19, 20. Also see Goldbloom, p. 64.
59. Jewell, pp. 80, 81.

In periods when leadership of the Committee was not especially strong and when the issues before it were not highly pressing, participation by Committee members was sometimes poor. At least one treaty hearing attracted only three or four members out of 23.[60] In more recent years, however, the Committee has been as powerful as any in the Senate.[61] This power seems to grow when an administration's foreign policies are not successful or when public support for them decreases.[62]

Senator Fulbright's first decade in the Senate did not mark him as a maverick.[63] At the same time such things as the international scholarship program that bears his name showed that he was innovative. It is as Chairman, however, that he has made his real influence felt. Fulbright served early notice that he would insist on full debate, since he does not believe "it is possible for a democratic government to have a viable, effective policy unless it is founded on the widest possible public discussion." He does not believe that our allies fear this debate. "Their great fears arise over precipitate announcements of foreign policy which neither Congress nor the President has properly considered."[64] Another early declaration of Fulbright's as Chairman was his intention, delivered in a May 7, 1959, speech at Columbia University, to work closely with the academic community:

> I am making a systematic endeavor, in my position as Chairman of the Committee on Foreign Relations, to promote a better two-way communications channel between government and universities especially at the policy level. The Committee on Foreign Relations has contracts with 20 educational institutions (including the Russian Institute here at Columbia) in connection with an over-all foreign policy review which we expect to have completed by early next year. This is an attempt

---

60. Robert A. Dahl, *Congress and Foreign Policy* (New York: W. W Norton, 1964), p. 132.

61. Malcolm E. Jewell, *Senatorial Politics & Foreign Policy* (Lexington: University of Kentucky Press, 1962).

62. Maurice Goldbloom, "The Fulbright Revolt," *Commentary*, (September 1966), p. 63.

63. Grundy, p. 383.

64. E. W. Kenworthy, "The Fulbright Idea of Foreign Policy," *New York Times Magazine*, May 10, 1959, p. 74.

to spur the rate at which ideas can flow directly from the universities to the practicing politician.[65]

In 1953 Lyndon Johnson began to subordinate seniority to other factors in making committee assignments.[66] In the following years such men as Hubert H. Humphrey, Mike Mansfield, and John F. Kennedy joined the Committee on Foreign Relations. This meant that Fulbright had to share his responsibilities with highly articulate and ambitious colleagues, but it also meant that the Committee would be very unlikely to take a passive or indifferent role.

Fulbright's own position within the Senate has been commented on by several writers. Some rate him as in the "middle group," neither an "insider" nor an "outsider."[67] Another considers him as part of a "small band of liberals" that "still dares to argue in terms of moral issues."[68] In 1962 Fulbright was characterized in this way: "He has been an independent, somewhat aloof figure in the Senate, not particularly amenable to Lyndon Johnson's influence and not a part of the 'inner circle' of party leadership."[69] An unnamed Committee member is quoted as describing Senator Fulbright as follows:

He will never be reconciled fully to human nonsense. But he is more understanding and more forgiving of human crotchets than ever before. In most matters, he could now lead the Committee wherever he wanted to go—which is saying something, considering that its membership represents the greatest collection of prima donnas this side of the Metropolitan Opera House.[70]

Still another scholar says Fulbright is the "archetypal loner, the

65. Gabriel Silver Lecture. Copies of the reports from these university studies may be obtained from the Government Printing Office, Washington, D. C.
66. Jewell, pp. 138, 139.
67. Lawrence K. Pettit and Edward Keynes, eds., *The Legislative Process in the U. S. Senate* (Chicago: Rand McNally & Company, 1969), p. 243.
68. Friedman, p. 184.
69. Jewell, p. 133.
70. Hyman, p. 21.

most anti-club of all the Senators."[71] Fulbright is also described
in these terms:

> Fulbright is not one of the Senate's 'inner club' members.
> How could he be? His intellectualism sets him somewhat apart;
> he does not always show proper respect for the Senate's solemn
> plausibilities; he cannot resist irony—a form of humor legis-
> lators distrust—and he at times gives irritation rein. (Once
> when a colleague asked if he thought the Senate lacked power
> to pass a law he thought absurd, Fulbright snapped: 'We have
> the power to do any damn fool thing we want, and we always
> seem to do it.')[72]

In his personal life, Fulbright's tastes tend toward the simple
things.[73] Many observers also discuss what has seemed a tragic
personal burden for him. Like many Southern politicians, Fulbright seems trapped by the civil rights question. It has been the
source of the most serious doubts cast upon Fulbright's principles,
and has diminished his stature nationally.

The race issue, once virtually the sole political issue in the
South, unquestionably has lost much of its former appeal. White
southern attitudes toward the Negro may have changed little if
at all, but the ability of the South to "keep the Negro in his
place"—at the bottom of the social order—has sharply declined.
All three branches of the federal government are now committed
to the goal of full racial equality. Time and again, Washington
has successfully intervened in behalf of Negro rights in the South.

Perhaps the most effective weapon for disfranchising southern
Negroes was the "white primary," which finally was declared
unconstitutional in 1944. Southerners defended the white primary on the ground that the Democratic party was a private
organization and hence not subject to the limitations of the
Fourteenth and Fifteenth Amendments. Because victory in a
southern Democratic primary was usually tantamount to election,

71. Kopkind, p. 17.
72. Kenworthy, p. 78.
73. Coffin reports that he drives a ten-year-old Mercedes, always flies
tourist class, and enjoys watching *Bonanza*. Coffin, p. 112.

the small numbers of registered Negroes were as effectively stripped of political rights as the vast unregistered majority. Arkansas was no exception in this Southern pattern.

The changing political complexion of the South has become strikingly evident in Congress. As long as the region remained solidly Democratic, and the Democrats controlled Congress, the South was able to exert disproportionate power in both House and Senate. The reason was that southern members, once elected, tended to win reelection repeatedly. Under the seniority system, they would rise to positions of power on congressional committees, positions that enabled them to kill or emasculate legislation of which they disapproved. Moreover, the southern bloc in both houses was the most cohesive regional bloc in Congress, and its members were in general masters of parliamentary maneuver.

Now the ability of southern members to work their will in Congress is clearly on the wane. The change is especially evident in the field of civil rights legislation. For years it was hardly worth the trouble to introduce a civil rights bill in Congress; it was certain, if not killed in committee, to be filibustered to death on the Senate floor. The 1957 and 1960 acts survived Senate filibuster, but not before they had been largely modified to southern specifications. A bill to outlaw literacy tests, introduced in 1962, was killed outright.

Southern power and parliamentary skill were unable to prevent passage of the Civil Rights Act of 1964 or the Voting Rights Act of 1965. In the case of the former, southern strategists in the Senate made the grave strategic error of refusing any sort of compromise; they were determined to bury the bill in its entirety. In embarking on this all-or-nothing course, the southern bloc misread the temper of the country. The filibuster on the bill lasted 75 days, but on June 10, 1964, the Senate voted to invoke cloture—the first time it had ever done so in connection with a civil rights measure. All subsequent southern efforts to water down the bill were unavailing.

Senator Fulbright's record throughout these important civil rights battles has marked him in the eyes of some observers as a tragic figure. He has never voted for a civil rights act. He caused great dismay among his most ardent admirers when he signed the "Southern Manifesto" in 1956, an angry pledge to resist integration. He voted against the Truman proposal for a permanent Fair Employment Practices Commission in 1946, and many years later he voted for the deletion of the fair employment section of the Civil Rights Act of 1964. He voted against the Voting Rights Act of 1965 as well as the Open Housing Bill of 1968.

The tragic quality in all this is that Fulbright is no bigot or racist. He is simply a captive of the political practicalities of his state and region. Through the years he has been given a more or less free hand in his foreign policy pronouncements by the voters of Arkansas. However, this privilege did not come about without the cost of his nearly unbroken opposition to civil rights. Many observers are certain that the "Fulbright problem" has kept him from a national stature that he so much deserves otherwise. Unhappily for him, they are certainly correct in these assessments.

In the area of foreign policy, however, Fulbright has seen his role as chairman as one of conducting public discussion on general principles. He consults more privately with the President and the State Department. Several Presidents have listened to his words carefully. Consultative subcommittees of the Committee on Foreign Relations deal with specific regions of the world and work with the appropriate State Department officials. Fulbright has been quite skillful in his handling of extensive public and private hearings.[74]

By 1965 the Senator extended his actions to public speeches highly critical of the Democratic Administration. He offered these thoughts in explanation of this action:

> First, I believe that the Chairman of the Committee on Foreign Relations has a special obligation to offer the best advice he can on matters of foreign policy; it is an obligation, I believe, which is inherent in the chairmanship, which takes precedence over party loyalty, and which has nothing to do

---

74. Goldbloom, p. 65.

with whether the Chairman's views are solicited or desired by people in the executive branch.[75]

Much of Fulbright's effectiveness as Chairman over the years can be measured from this deep-rooted sense of obligation, and the country has benefited from it in many ways.

Books, 1966), pp. 62, 63.
75. J. William Fulbright, *The Arrogance of Power* (New York: Vintage

2

CHAIRMAN FULBRIGHT

In 1970 Senator Mike Mansfield of Montana compared Senator Fulbright with other Foreign Relations Committee chairmen under whom he had served. Mansfield related that "Senator Fulbright is more aggressive, more knowledgeable, more interested and more concerned." He also added:

> I think Senator Fulbright has done an outstanding job as Chairman of the Committee because he has taken his concern to the Committee and through the Committee to the American people. In my opinion he has performed a most valuable service.[1]

Senator Albert Gore of Tennessee characterized Fulbright's leadership in this way:

> He is the ablest of all chairmen on whose committees I have served. He is unusually considerate with respect to the rights and abilities of individual members. There is really nothing autocratic in his Chairmanship. With respect to interrogation of witnesses, he is bright and persistent and contemptuous of phoniness. He is a man of great intellect, good sense of humor, and above all, enormous courage. He has made a major con-

---

1. Mike Mansfield, interview with author Lynn, January 27, 1970, Washington, D. C. Besides Fulbright, Mansfield has served on the Committee on Foreign Relations under the chairmanship of Alexander F. Wiley, Walter F. George, and Theodore F. Green.

tribution to the reemergence of the Senate as a factor in foreign policy.[2]

Fulbright is not like any of his immediate predecessors as Chairman. Senator Tom Connally of Texas was an imperious man with no real comprehension of post-World War II problems. Republican Senator Arthur Vandenberg, Connally's successor of 1947-1949, had a reputation for sagaciousness that he enjoyed after his conversion to internationalism. Senator Alexander Wiley, Chairman from 1953-1955, was caught in the cross-fire between McCarthyism and Eisenhower diplomacy and therefore his role was largely ceremonial. In 1955 the Chairmanship passed to Democrat Walter George of Georgia who was not particularly effective. His successor was Senator Theodore Green, who was more than eighty years old when he became Chairman. To succeed Green, Fulbright had to resign as Chairman of the Senate Banking and Currency Committee.

It is quite easy to conclude that almost by default the Senate has in Senator Fulbright a spokesman and a leader who will rank among the upper house's influential members in its modern history. Senator Fulbright's views on selected policy issues are related to views of the proper role of the President in the determination of foreign policy. In 1945 Fulbright offered the thought that the American system of government "doesn't permit a change when the people want it."[3] He proposed that British-type general elections be held when there was a stalemate between Congress and the President.[4] Eighteen years later Fulbright still realized the need to consider public opinion, but he distinguished, in the case of foreign policy, between "transitory

---

2. Albert Gore, interview with the author Lynn, January 27, 1970, Washington, D. C. With respect to the interrogation of Dean Rusk, Gale McGee would not agree with Gore's estimation of Fulbright's treatment of witnesses. Gale W. McGee, *The Responsibilities of World Power* (Washington, D. C.: The National Press, Inc, 1968), pp. 206, 207.
3. Editorial, *Washington Post*, March 26, 1945, editorial page as copied from Fulbright files, Washington, D. C.
4. *Washington Post*, March 26, 1945. Also *New York Times*, November 8, 1946, p. 19.

popular emotions" that should be resisted, even at a "political price," and broad "popular support" which, if lost, could cause the failure of foreign policy.[5] He concluded that democratic leaders must both lead and follow public opinion. As they follow it, he points out, quoting Hans Morgenthau, it may occasionally be necessary to sacrifice the "merely desirable" in order to achieve the essential. Fulbright went on to express the view that the present (1963) policy processes rely too heavily on the more transitory aspects of public opinion.[6]

One of Fulbright's most colorful statements against excessive reliance on public opinion was made in 1958 in a speech on the Senate floor:

It is part of our litany in public life to say that the people speak with the voice of God. I do not question that. Much less do I question the institutions and practices of democracy that draw their vitality from that principle. But I would feel myself a toadying sycophant if I didn't speak one plain truth. It is that the people, for some years now, have spoken with the voice of a false God . . . and it is a voice which has impressed itself on what government itself has been doing during this period. If things have gone wrong, the people are not without blame in the matter.

The last thing that can be said about our foreign policy in the last few years is that it wasn't what the people wanted. Of course they wanted it! And what they got was exactly what they wanted . . . a foreign policy on the cheap, featuring a pact here, and a shipment of a few guns there.[7]

These statements do not necessarily reflect a mistrust of public opinion. Instead it is a recognition that policy action may have majority support and still be harmful to the nation and do considerable injustice to individuals. Democracy must respond not

5. J. William Fulbright, "Public Opinion and Foreign Policy," speech at Bowling Green State University, Bowling Green, Ohio, March 9, 1963. Fulbright files, Washington, D. C.
6. "Public Opinion and Foreign Policy."
7. U. S. Congress, Senate, Senator Fulbright, speech "The Character of Present-Day American Life," 85th Cong., 2d sess., August 21, 1958, *Congressional Record*, 104, Part 15, p. 18903.

only to the broad consensus in public opinion, but also to the great heterogeneity inherent in the public. Senator Fulbright makes this point in the following way:

It is I believe, an understanding of human diversity and of the inability of any one man or nation to determine what is best for all others, that forms the core of the democratic idea.[8]

Fulbright avoids making nationalistic statements and any conventional Fourth of July type oratory that might be classified as in the "my country right or wrong" tradition. Through many speeches spanning a long period of time he has developed the analogy between nations and individuals. In a 1966 Senate speech he quoted Dr. Jerome D. Frank, the psychiatrist, in support of this analogy:

Frightened, hostile individuals tend to behave in ways which aggravate their difficulties instead of resolving them, and frightened hostile nations seem to behave similarly.[9]

Fulbright said that the nation went through an irrational period with McCarthy in the 1950s, and had suffered a "nervous breakdown" with the Civil War.[10] In 1961 Fulbright said that the United States should act like a mature nation, and this meant acting like a mature person. We should accept responsibilities, but we should not entertain the adolescent illusion that we can solve all problems and do it immediately. "Above all, maturity requires a final accommodation between our aspirations and

8. U. S. Congress, Senate, Senator Fulbright speech, "The Basic Issue in Foreign Affairs," 88th Cong., 2d sess., September 8, 1964, *Congressional Record,* 110, Part 16, p. 21676.
9. Letter from Dr. Frank to Senator Fulbright, September 20, 1960, quoted by Fulbright in U. S. Congress, Senate, Senator Fulbright, speech "The United States and China," 89th Cong., 2d sess., March 7, 1966, *Congressional Record,* 112, Part 4, p. 5145.
10. "The United States and China." Fulbright pointed out that Southerners have a sensitivity other Americans may not have in this matter. He went on to contend that China is acting now in a hostile manner as a reaction to its humiliation by the West in the past.

our limitations."[11] Instead of this, however, the nation is aimless domestically and frustrated abroad.[12]

It might seem that a nation should strive to build its virtue, but Fulbright denies that this will solve the problem. He is fond of this quotation from Thackeray:

The wicked are wicked, no doubt, and they go astray and they fall, and they come by their deserts; but who can tell the mischief which the very virtuous do?[13]

From religious wars, to Robespierre, to Stalin, self-appointed "emissaries of God" have done great harm, being capable, as Djilas wrote of Stalin, "of destroying nine-tenths of the human race to 'make happy' the one tenth."[14] The United States has not been immune from the urge to impose its virtue on others, according to Fulbright. He cites "hotheads" on both sides as causing the Civil War, and President McKinley's annexation of the Philippines only after consulting the Supreme Being.[15] Franklin Roosevelt's crusading spirit allowed him to violate our traditional commitment to freedom of the seas and our obligations under the London Naval Treaty of 1930 by sinking Japanese merchant ships without first placing civilians in a place of safety; 105,000 civilians were killed.[16]

Fulbright has offered many suggestions with respect to our proper national posture. He warns that a rich nation may be

---

11. Quoted in an interview with E. W. Kenworthy in "Fulbright Becomes a National Issue," *New York Times Magazine,* October 1, 1961, p. 92.

12. J. W. Fulbright, "Some Aspects of American Foreign Policy," speech before the American Bar Association, Washington, D. C., September 1, 1960. Fulbright files, Washington, D. C.

13. William Makepeace Thackeray in *The Newcomes,* quoted by J. William Fulbright in "Ideology and Foreign Policy," the George Huntington Williams Memorial Lecture, Johns Hopkins University, Baltimore, March 12, 1965. Fulbright files, Washington, D. C.

14. "Ideology and Foreign Policy." The quotation from Milovan Djilas is from *Conversations with Stalin* (New York: Harcourt, Brace and World, 1962), p. 190.

15. Fulbright also quotes Mark Twain: ". . . shall we go on conferring our Civilization upon the peoples that sit in darkness, or shall we give those poor things a rest?" "Ideology and Foreign Policy."

16. "Ideology and Foreign Policy."

respected, but it is rarely loved. He points out that a democratic government in a middle-class society does not necessarily represent the ideal for everyone in the world.[17] He often advises that the United States can learn much from smaller nations.[18] In particular, the Senator advises his nation to give up what he calls the "victory and retreat obsession," which he regards as "sterile."[19] Thus in a February 1970 article Fulbright said that when President Johnson remarked that he did not want to be the first American President to lose a war, and when President Nixon warned on November 3, 1969, against "this first defeat in American history," they were projecting their own views about their standings in history into the position of being the national ego.[20] To Senator Fulbright it is necessary to admit it when you are wrong as a nation.[21]

People can become the victims of their own expectations, and so can nations, in Senator Fulbright's judgment. Aggressive feelings build up in people and countries, and for individuals various sorts of "safety valves" exist, but for nations there is "no moral equivalent of war." In recent times one crisis has led to another, and now, according to Fulbright, "the reshaping of the fatal expectancy of war is the foremost requirement of statesmanship in the twentieth century."[22]

National power occupies a conspicuous place in Fulbright's thought. Citing the case of Japan's remarkable postwar recovery,

17. J. William Fulbright, untitled speech before the American Society of Newspaper Editors, Washington, D. C., April 18, 1959. Fulbright files, Washington, D. C.

18. J. William Fulbright, "Education for a New Kind of International Relations," speech for the Annual meeting of the Swedish Institute for Cultural Relations, Stockholm, Sweden, December 5, 1966. Fulbright files, Washington, D. C. Also speech before the American Society of Newspaper Editors.

19. "Ideology and Foreign Policy."

20. J. William Fulbright, "Vietnam: The Crucial Issue," *The Progressive* 34 (February 1970): 17.

21. U. S. Congress, Senate, Senator Fulbright speaking on "Events Relating to the Summit Conference," S. Rept. No. 1761, 86th Cong., 2d sess., June 28, 1960, *Congressional Record*, 106, Part 11, p. 14734.

22. J. William Fulbright, "Human Needs and World Politics," speech at the commencement exercises of California State College at Long Beach, June 12, 1964. Fulbright files, Washington, D. C.

he states that power "is a dubious blessing and the absence or loss of it can have surprising rewards."[23] In a 1964 speech at California State College, Fulbright quoted the seventeenth-century Frenchman Jean de la Bruyère to make a similar point:

> How does it serve the people and add to their happiness if their rule extend his empire by annexing the provinces of his enemies; . . . how does it help me or my countrymen that my sovereign be successful and covered with glory, that my country be powerful and dreaded, if, sad and worried, I live in oppression and poverty.[24]

In 1966 Fulbright made his famous speech at Johns Hopkins University on "The Arrogance of Power." This arrogance on the part of nations is an outgrowth of a "power drive" that they have, which makes them want to show the superiority over others of their religions, their forms of government, and their people. Such motivations, according to Fulbright are very real, although they are not easy to explain:

> For lack of a clear and precise understanding of exactly what these motives are, I refer to them as the "arrogance of power"—as a psychological need that nations seem to have in order to prove that they are bigger, better, or stronger than other nations. Implicit in this drive is the assumption, even on the part of normally peaceful nations, that force is the ultimate proof of superiority—that when a nation shows that it has the stronger army, it is also proving that it has better people, better institutions, better principles, and, in general, a better civilization.[25]

The Senator goes on to show how he believes that many wars have been caused by the arrogance of power.

To a troubled nation and world Fulbright suggests a little less zeal and a little more tranquility. The Senator quotes with approval these words of George Bernard Shaw:

23. "Education for a New Kind of International Relations."
24. "Human Needs and World Politics."
25. *The Arrogance of Power*, p. 5.

All this struggling and striving to make the world better is a great mistake, not because it isn't a good thing to improve the world if you know how to do it, but because striving and struggling is the worst way you could set about doing anything.[26]

The Senator thus uses the human analogy frequently, particularly in his statements on the position of the nations. Critics disagree with each other, but one expresses the point that the attempt to apply individual psychology to nations is fallacious. Such psychological points might apply in individual cases but not to groups, except to a limited extent that would have to be verified statistically before it would be usable.[27]

Dealings with Communist governments have furnished the most sensitive area of American foreign policy for over two decades, and thus Senator Fulbright's views on Communist governments have special importance. The Senator has spoken at length in favor of a revision of American approaches in dealing with Communist states.

Fulbright viewed the postwar breakdown of the alliance with the Soviet Union with discouragement. In May of 1946 he made this statement: "Today I confess that I am troubled and I find it exceedingly difficult to arrive at any convictions about the future of our international relations."[28] The passage of years provided convictions. At the same time Fulbright continued to recognize that the existence of a Communist system that claimed 40 percent of the earth's population by 1960 posed a great problem, and one that Western policies did little to solve:

This should be enough to cause any thinking person to suspect that all is not well within the Western World and yet

---

26. George Bernard Shaw in *Cashel Byron's Profession* (1886), chapter 6, quoted in J. William Fulbright, "Prospects for Peace with Freedom," speech at the Rhodes Scholar Reunion, Swarthmore College, Swarthmore, Pennsylvania, June 19, 1965. Fulbright files, Washington, D. C.
27. Morton A. Kaplan, "Old Realities and New Myths," *World Politics* 17 (January 1965):357.
28. J. William Fulbright, "Our Foreign Policy, speech before a joint meeting of the American Academy of Arts and Letters and the National Institute of Arts, New York City, May 17, 1946. Fulbright files, Washington, D. C.

any significant change in our traditional methods of doing business is grudgingly considered and reluctantly accepted, if it is not rejected outright.[29]

Despite the signs of disunity within the Communist bloc, in 1960 the Senator pointed out that it was actually holding together much better than the remains of the Western Colonial empire were staying intact.[30] The Communists were certainly not going to bring about their demise through the exercise of a "suicidal mania" such as Hitler's Germany exhibited, according to Fulbright, and this actually makes the Soviet Union a more "formidable antagonist" than was Nazi Germany.[31]

Senator Fulbright sees ideology as a major barrier to American success in dealing with Communist governments. In particular there is a tendency to attribute to the "nature of Communism" anything about the Soviet Union that is being considered, whether this is its stubbornness about Germany, its inscrutable attitude on Vietnam, or its refusal to pay its United Nations dues.[32] Fulbright regards such a tendency as self-delusion. A person has a nature, but "Communism" is an abstract collection of ideas and premises that can have no "nature" of its own.[33]

Nikita Khrushchev receives special credit from Fulbright for "humanizing" the Communist system and its early rigidities. Khrushchev tolerated a degree of individual freedom and nationalism in Communist nations; even the bloodless manner in which the Premier was removed from power illustrates the change that took place.[34]

29. "Some Aspects of American Foreign Policy."
30. Ibid.
31. J. William Fulbright, "Russia and the West," William L. Clayton Lectures, The Fletcher School of Law and Diplomacy, Tufts University, April 29, 1963. Fulbright files, Washington, D. C.
32. "Ideology and Foreign Policy."
33. Ibid.
34. J. William Fulbright, "Lighting the Lamps of Europe," speech before the Austrian Foreign Policy Association on the 600th Anniversary of the University of Vienna, Vienna, Austria, May 11, 1965. Fulbright files, Washington, D. C. Morton Kaplan accuses Fulbright of creating a new myth by arguing that "Stalin's policy was one of utter and implacable hostility to the non-Soviet world or that Khrushchev's policy was one of wholehearted accommodation." Kaplan, p. 330.

The fullest expression of his views on Communist governments came in Fulbright's famous "Old Myths and New Realities" speech in the Senate on March 25, 1964. After refuting the
"master myth" that the Communist bloc is a "monolith" made
up of "organized conspiracies" rather than real governments,
Fulbright offered this thought:

It is time that we resolved this contradiction and separated
myth from reality. The myth is that every Communist state
is an unmitigated evil and a relentless enemy of the free world;
the reality is that some Communist regimes pose a threat to the
free world while others pose little or none, and that if we will
recognize these distinctions, we ourselves will be able to influence events in the Communist bloc, in a way favorable to the
security of the free world.[35]

The first essential, according to Fulbright, is "to learn to live
in an imperfect world."[36] To do this we will have to give up some
dreams of "a new era of world peace under world law" and curb
"our crusading tendency," which is so "noble in purpose" but
"so destructive in its consequence."[37] It seems clear that for
Fulbright himself the giving up of dreams of world peace under
world law was painful, but in giving up this cherished hope he
found it necessary to go beyond it to solutions that would be
practical under other circumstances. Part of living in the imperfect world is living with the Soviet Union. Fulbright suggests
that Khrushchev's well-remembered statement "we will bury
you" should be interpreted as a call to peaceful economic competition rather than as the manifestation of warlike interest.[38]
It also means that we must learn to live with mainland China,
and to do this we must find ways to use foreign policy as a means

---

35. U. S. Congress, Senate, Senator Fulbright, speech "Foreign Policy—
Old Myths and New Realities," 88th Cong., 2d sess., March 25, 1964, *Congressional Record*, 110, Part 5, p. 6228.
36. J. William Fulbright, "Bridges East and West," speech at the All-
University Convocation, Southern Methodist University, Dallas, Texas,
December 8, 1964. Fulbright files, Washington, D. C.
37. *Ibid.*
38. "Lighting the Lamps of Europe."

of survival.[39] We must learn to live with Cuba, a nation with respect to which our policy has been a failure.[40]

Fulbright concluded the "old Myths" speech by recognizing that he was asking that we dare to think "unthinkable thoughts," and various critics found them so. Even supportive editorials reprinted soon afterwards in the *Congressional Record* point out that charges of "soft on communism" and "appeasement" were being heard.[41] One prominent critic before and after the "old Myths" speech was Senator Barry Goldwater, the 1964 Republican candidate for President. Fulbright responded with vigor and humor to Goldwater's 1963 arguments against "coexistence." Fulbright quoted Goldwater's advocacy of "boldness and courage and determination," and suggested that this really meant a " 'bold,' 'courageous,' and 'determined' policy of 'coannihilation.' "[42] During the 1964 campaign Fulbright added partisan touches to his dialogues with the Arizona Senator:

> The Goldwater Republicans propose a radical new policy of relentless ideological conflict aimed at the elimination of communism and the imposition of American concepts of freedom on the entire world. The Democrats under President Johnson propose a conservative policy of opposing and preventing Communist expansion while working for limited agreements that will reduce the danger of nuclear war. The Republicans build their policy on ideologies that divide the world; the Democrats look beyond their ideology to the common hopes, the common interests, and the common dangers that unite the human race.[43]

39. Untitled speech before the American Society of Newspaper Editors, Washington, D. C., April 18, 1959. Fulbright files, Washington, D. C.

40. In the "old Myths" speech Fulbright argued that our trade sanctions against Cuba—the main continuing policy—have not inhibited economic expansion under Castro. *Congressional Record,* 110, Part 5, p. 6230.

41. U. S. Congress, Senate, Newspaper editorial comments on Senator Fulbright's "Old Myths and New Realities" speech, 88th Cong., 2d sess., April 20, 1964, *Congressional Record,* 110, Part 6, pp. 8466, 8467.

42. U. S. Congress, Senate, Senator Fulbright speech "Liberalism and Coexistence," 88th Cong., 1st sess., August 2, 1963, *Congressional Record,* 109, No. 118, p. 13173.

43. "The Basic Issue in Foreign Affairs."

Fulbright goes on from giving his advice on new attitudes toward Communist governments to offering proposals for a few new policies in dealing with these powers. With respect to the Soviet Union we must avoid provoking any "act of desperation." To do this we should learn the lesson of Britain during the *Pax Britannica* of the nineteenth century; this lesson is that it is not the possession of great power that counts, but rather the restraint with which that power is exercised that brings peace.[44] Fulbright points out that "our sympathy for those who cry out against poverty and social injustice . . . dissolves into hostility when reform becomes revolution; and when Communism is involved, as it often is, our hostility takes the form of unseemly panic."[45] We should also try to avoid the sort of mistake we made with regard to Cuba, especially in the 1965 invasion of the Dominican Republic:

> Rather than use our considerable resources to compete with the Communists for influence with the democratic forces who actively solicited our support, we intervened militarily on the side of a corrupt and reactionary oligarchy.[46]

And we should also use care in our use of rhetoric. Fulbright recounts a conversation he had with an East European diplomat in which the weekly celebration of the number of "Communists" killed in Southeast Asia by American forces was seen as an act and an expression of hostility against all peoples in all Communist nations.[47] We need, according to Fulbright, more of the spirit of Pope John when he said to Khrushchev's son-in-law:

---

44. "Russia and the West."
45. Quoted in John T. Campbell and the Research Staff of the Council on Foreign Relations, *The United States in World Affairs 1945–1947* (New York: Published for the Council on Foreign Relations by Harper & Brothers, 1947), p. 21.
46. *Ibid.*
47. J. William Fulbright, "The Vietnam Fallout," speech before the Bureau of Advertising of the American Newspaper Publishers Association, Hotel Waldorf Astoria, New York City, April 28, 1966. Fulbright files, Washington, D. C.

"They tell me you are an atheist, but you will not refuse an old man's blessing for your children."[48]

It is not surprising that the groups that Senator Fulbright terms the "radical right" have responded stridently to some of his views. Fulbright has long been an advocate of the pragmatic political proposition: "The first thing obviously that every legislator has to do is get himself elected to office."[49] Since Arkansas is by no means devoid of right-wing political strength, getting reelected there has meant a head-on clash with extremists.[50] Fulbright's stance on racial matters is a good indication of his political pragmatism in those clashes.

As he prepared to run for office in Arkansas in 1961, Senator Fulbright stressed to the state Chamber of Commerce the disproportionate amount of strength the state's congressional delegation had because of seniority. The two Senators and six Congressmen held four major chairmanships, while New York, Pennsylvania, Ohio, and California had none.

To counter the views of the radical right, Fulbright made these points:

> With regard to Communism, I *could* say that we have been betrayed by our national leaders, that we are misled here at home by disloyal Protestant clergymen, by Communist teachers in our schools, by members of the press who are Communist sympathizers, and by subversives in the Department of State. This thesis would tend to relieve all the rest of us from any responsibility, and would provide us with convenient scapegoats to blame for our troubles.
>
> This kind of approach was used by Hitler to enable *him* to liquidate all opposition to his regime. Both Stalin and Khrushchev have used it, in Russia, to destroy their opponents; and the Chinese leaders liquidate their opposition by calling them "subversives and agents" of the American capitalists.[51]

48. "Lighting the Lamps of Europe."
49. Kenworthy 1961, p. 21.
50. *Ibid.*
51. J. William Fulbright, untitled speech before the Arkansas Chamber of Commerce, November 8, 1961. Fulbright files, Washington, D. C. It might be observed that Fulbright did not use this occasion for his strongest expression of the contribution of Premier Khrushchev.

Fulbright went on to say that there was no validity in either the views of those on the right, who said that Communism had penetrated our society, or the statements of those on the left, that they would "rather be red than dead."[52]

For most of his Senate career, Senator Fulbright has supported foreign aid. This was not a policy that built great support in Arkansas.[53]

The argument is increasingly heard that the very nature of economic development requires the casting of foreign aid in new molds. Not only must economic aid to developing nations be put on a long-term basis to insure wise national planning; it should also be disbursed through international organizations capable of entering into institutional, rather than political, relationships with the recipients. The American penchant for bilateral disbursement is said to have involved the United States too deeply in the politics of too many countries, and to have reaped ill will instead of gratitude.

Fulbright is among those who believe that direct American assistance to undeveloped countries frequently gives rise to serious psychological problems. "It is a problem of pride and self-respect, which has everything to do with a country's will and capacity to foster its own development," he has written.

There is an inescapable element of charity in bilateral aid, and charity, over a long period of time, has a debilitating effect on both the recipient and the donor. It fosters attitudes of cranky dependency or simple anger on the part of the recipient and of self-righteous frustration on the part of the donor—attitudes which, once formed, feed destructively upon each other.[54]

---

52. Untitled speech before the Arkansas Chamber of Commerce, November 8, 1961, Fulbright files, Washington, D. C.

53. J. William Fulbright, interview on "Issues and Answers," ABC telecast, August 19, 1962. Fulbright files, Washington, D. C. Fulbright said in the interview that his support for foreign aid "was probably the greatest obstacle" in his very difficult struggle in the 1962 Democratic primary.

54. J. W. Fulbright, "Foreign Aid? Yes, But With a New Approach," *The New York Times Magazine*, March 21, 1965, p. 102.

Fulbright and others favor a new approach under which the United States would place most of its economic assistance funds at the disposal of international agencies—the United Nations, the World Bank, and the bank's soft-loan affiliate, the International Development Association.

United Nations technical assistance and development projects, dependent on voluntary contributions by member nations, have been on a relatively small scale. Most of the American development loans in Africa and Asia are committed under international arrangements. Aid to Latin America already goes through international channels of the Alliance for Progress. Fulbright contends that these arrangements consist largely of procedures for consultation and coordination, while final decisions about kinds and amounts of aid and the execution of programs remain bilateral. The multilateralists advocate a kind of arrangement that would vest in the international lending agency full authority to determine, according to objective economic criteria, who would receive development aid, and the amounts, kinds, and conditions of that aid.

On those occasions when he expressed reservations about some aspect of foreign-aid spending, as he did in 1962 when he proposed that prosperous Western European nations assume a greater share of the economic assistance programs, Fulbright stressed these views in his home state.[55]

Opponents of foreign aid ranged far beyond Arkansas, and Fulbright made many vigorous defenses of foreign aid on the Senate floor. In a 1959 Senate speech, Fulbright answered the argument that aid won us few friends:

I would remind anyone who feels this way that we are not running a popularity contest. Basically, we are trying to provide alternatives to Communism and to want, which on the record usually go together. The record also shows that people

---

55. Bruce Perry, *Senator J. William Fulbright on European and Atlantic Unity*, Ph.D. dissertation, University of Pennsylvania, 1968, pp. 86–88.

do not necessarily have to be pro-American in order to be profoundly anticommunist.[56]

In 1963 the Senator, conceding that foreign aid was not the single factor that brought world affairs to their current state, nevertheless made this point to his colleagues:

What I am saying is that the outlook for our nation and for the free world is at least as bright as any of us a decade ago had a right to expect it might be. In addition, it is quite apparent that we might have been in a radically different situation if Presidents Eisenhower and Kennedy had not been given the foreign policy tools to work with through congressional action on the program now before us.[57]

He has characterized foreign aid as an "indispensable instrument of American foreign policy."[58]

Fulbright made eloquent defenses of the aid program against critics who charged that spending was being wasteful. In 1960 he said that supporters of foreign aid felt they had to go through the "ritualistic ceremony" of deploring the element of truth in "an acknowledged small amount of waste," despite the fact that no human enterprise is perfect and that few enterprises undergo any more close and constant scrutiny than foreign aid.[59] In 1961 he cautioned against a "descent into black pessimism over the

---

56. U. S. Congress, Senate, Senator Fulbright speaking on the Mutual Security Act of 1959, S. 1451, 86th Cong., 1st sess., June 30, 1959, *Congressional Record*, 105, Part 9, p. 12276.

57. U. S. Congress, Senator Fulbright speaking on the Foreign Assistance Act of 1963, H. R. 7885, 88th Cong., 1st sess., October 28, 1963, *Congressional Record*, 109, Part 15, pp. 20337, 20338.

58. U. S. Congress, Senator Fulbright speaking on the Foreign Assistance Act of 1965, S. 1367, 89th Cong., 1st sess., March 4, 1965, *Congressional Record*, 111, Part 3, p. 4190. He has also called it a "normal instrument" and a "necessary instrument" of policy. U. S. Congress, Senate, Senator Fulbright speaking on the Foreign Assistant Act of 1964, H. R. 11380, 88th Cong., 2d sess., August 1, 1964, *Congressional Record*, 110, Part 3, p. 17718.

59. *Congressional Record*, 105, Part 9, p. 12274.

whole foreign aid program" because of a few instances of failure.[60] In 1964 he stated that it was an "impenetrable mystery" to him why the Senate authorized a $3.6 billion aid bill only after three weeks of "rancorous" debate, while the $5 billion space budget got only "perfunctory" debate and the $50 billion military budget received only "a few judicious queries."[61] Fulbright's support of foreign aid extended to South Vietnam, as late as 1964,

As a veteran of drawn-out debate over foreign aid, Fulbright deplored the introduction of "extraneous matters" into the hearings. At one point the Senator compared the amount of detail in this debate to the reply that the little girl gave to her aunt when she was asked if she learned anything about penguins from a book on the subject that the aunt had given her: "Indeed yes, much more than I care to know."[62] However, it may be noted that Fulbright did not refrain from excursions into peripheral issues when he questioned Dean Rusk during the Vietnam Hearings:

> If our national objectives were clear and generally agreed upon, it probably would not be too difficult to iron out differences about the costs and administration of the aid program. Unfortunately, we are not at present in agreement about our national objectives; there are, in fact, significant disagreements among us about the purposes of the aid program and the overall aims of American foreign policy. Imprecise statements about the defense of freedom and the national interest tend to disguise but not eliminate these disagreements. As long as they persist, they are bound to complicate our discussions of aid and other public programs, and we obviously cannot reach satisfactory decisions about amounts and kinds of foreign aid when we are in disagreement as to the purposes it is meant to serve.[63]

---

60. J. William Fulbright, speech on the Foreign Assistance Act of 1961. Fulbright files, Washington, D. C.
61. *Congressional Record,* 110, Part 3, p. 17719.
62. U. S. Congress, Senate, Senator Fulbright and others discussing the Foreign Assistance Act of 1965, H. R. 7750, 89th Cong., 1st sess., June 4, 1965, *Congressional Record,* 111, Part 9, 12609.

The question of long-range funding of foreign aid has occupied the Senator's attention at various times. In 1965 he pointed out that the very nature of economic development makes a one-year program too short.[64] He has argued that better administration could result, if there were more continuity.[65] He also pointed out that congressional time would be saved if the six-to-eight months spent per year in debate on the issue could be made to last for two years.[66] In 1966 Senator Fulbright changed his mind on the long-term financing question. He argued at this time in favor of the one-year limit. Senator Fulbright explained his change of position in terms of its misuse in Vietnam and also on "the tendency of the executive branch of Government to escalate the extent of our aid commitments."[67]

Even before he became an outspoken critic of the war in Vietnam, Fulbright advocated the separation of economic and military aid. Military aid was claimed by its supporters as part of the defense of the United States. If this is true, the Senator argued that it should be part of the Defense Department budget.[68] A major reason for this is the "billion dollar burden" that the military placed on the total foreign aid budget.[69] As time passed, however, it was the relationship between foreign aid and later American military commitments that led Fulbright not only to wish to separate military aid from the other aid, but to call for close congressional review of military aid.[70]

---

63. The Senator justified this tactic in U. S. Congress, Senate, Committee on Foreign Relations, *Foreign Assistance Act of 1968, Part 1—Vietnam, Hearings* before the Committee on Foreign Relations, Senate, on S. 3091, 90th Cong., 2d sess., March 11, 1968.

64. *Congressional Record*, 111, Part 9, p. 12609.

65. Undated Press Release. Fulbright files, Washington, D. C.

66. *Congressional Record*, 111, Part 9, p. 4189.

67. U. S. Congress, Senate, Senator Fulbright speaking about the Foreign Assistance Act of 1966, S. 3584, 89th Cong., 2d sess., July 18, 1966, *Congressional Record*, 112, Part 12, p. 16021.

68. *Congressional Record*, 111, Part 3, pp. 4190, 4191.

69. *Congressional Record*, 109, Part 15, p. 20338.

70. Untitled Press Release. Fulbright files, Washington, D. C.

Most American foreign policy aid has been bilateral, and Senator Fulbright argued that it should be multilateral. One of his best expressions of the reasoning behind this view was made in June of 1965:

> The fundamental difference between bilateralism and multi-lateralism in foreign aid is psychological. Bilateral aid carries a connotation of charity, which in the long run has a debilitating effect on both recipient and donor, fostering attitudes of cranky dependency or anger on the part of the recipient and of self-righteous frustration on the part of the donor, attitudes which, once formed, feed destructively upon each other. Multi-lateral aid, on the other hand, has the more dignified connota-tion of a community organized to meet its common and right-ful responsibilities toward its less fortunate members. The one is appropriate to a world of nation states with unlimited sov-ereignty, the other to a world that is at least groping toward a broader community.[71]

The Senator has gone so far as to express this thought in his proposal that aid be administered multilaterally through such agencies as the World Bank:

> I will offer this amendment because I have become con-vinced that bilateral development lending programs are hurt-ing us more than they are helping us.[72]

Fulbright's primary objections to bilateral aid are undoubtedly tied to his views on the Vietnam War:

> Foreign aid is not in a literal sense the cause or the reason for American military involvement in Vietnam. It was, how-ever, an important factor contributing to the state of mind of policy-makers who committed the United States to a major land war in Asia after having stated forcefully, repeatedly and, to many of us, quite convincingly, that that was exactly what they intended not to do. The relationship between American aid and the Vietnamese war is no less significant for being psy-

---

71. *Congressional Record,* 111, Part 9, p. 12609.
72. *Congressional Record,* 111, Part 3, p. 4189.

chological rather than juridical; indeed it is probably more significant.[73]

Senator Fulbright has long been counted in the front ranks of the supporters of American participation in its Atlantic alliance and in the United Nations. He has become a leading critic of our participation in alliances in Southeast Asia that involve military action. Fulbright's initial enthusiasm for the United Nations as an organ to solve a broad spectrum of international problems soon faded in 1946.[74] He continued, however, to back the UN through its various problems, such as the dispute over the Soviet refusal to pay its assessment for the Congo peacekeeping force.[75] He also advised that we use the opportunity to "play a constructive role" in the development of the many new nations that entered the UN.[76]

The Atlantic Alliance has received strong support from Fulbright:

In the last twenty years America has committed itself to partnership with the free nations of Europe and we have not faltered in that commitment. We have come at last to understand what we should have understood long ago, that, as Woodrow Wilson put it, "There can be no question of our ceasing to be a world power. The only question is whether we can refuse the moral leadership that is offered us, whether we shall accept or reject the confidence of the world."[77]

When in 1965 the alliance showed various signs of strain, the

---

73. *Congressional Record,* 112, Part 13, p. 17066.
74. "Our Foreign Policy."
75. J. William Fulbright, "Approaches to International Community," speech at Pennsylvania State University, University Park, Pennsylvania, March 6, 1965. Fulbright files, Washington, D. C. Fulbright said that although the American legal position on the financial crisis was strong, the fact remained that "in insisting on the enforcement of Article 19, the United States took a position lacking in political realism, and historical perspective."
76. "Some Aspects of American Foreign Policy."
77. J. William Fulbright, "Atlantic Partnership," speech before the Association for the Study of Foreign Affairs, Munich, Federal Republic of Germany, November 19, 1964. Fulbright files, Washington, D. C.

Senator, in a speech in Strasbourg, France, urged greater mutual understanding. He conceded that the United States had pursued the multilateral force with too much enthusiasm, only to react with "excessive despair" when things went wrong. He also urged the "new Europe" to accept "its responsibilities commensurate with its wealth and power."[78] He has encouraged the withdrawal of American troops from Europe.

Criticism of the military forms a consistent theme throughout Senator Fulbright's speeches and writings. He is often skeptical of the utility of military spending. He frequently expresses suspicion that the best-thought-out plans of the military establishment may be wrong.

In conversation he often refers to Alcibiades, the leader of the Peloponnesian War whose attack on Syracuse brought on wars that ended the great age of Greek culture.[79] In the Senate hearings in 1951 Fulbright had his famous exchange with General MacArthur. From the whole tone of his critical cross-examination of MacArthur it is clear that Fulbright had little confidence in the ability of this highly experienced military man to make objective judgments on military matters.[80]

The United States has generally overemphasized military matters in Fulbright's view. The Senator made this statement on a 1956 television interview about our policy with respect to Russia:

> I think this administration has given entirely too much emphasis to military treaties and military movements, and affairs, rather than an effort to restrain them in the political-diplomatic field.[81]

---

78. J. William Fulbright, "Atlantic Relations," speech before the Consultative Assembly of the Council of Europe, Strasbourg, France, May 4, 1965. Fulbright files, Washington, D. C.
79. Coffin, p. 68.
80. For example see Fulbright's comments on fighting China, U. S. Congress, Senate, Committee on Foreign Relations and Armed Services, *Military Situation in the Far East, Hearings* before the Committee on Foreign Relations and the Committee on Armed Services, Senate, 82nd Cong., 1st sess., May, 1951, p. 136.
81. "Martha Rountree's Press Conference."

The propensity of some military leaders to advocate what he refers to as "extremist" positions disturbs the Senator. In 1961 Fulbright objected to the Defense Department about this practice in a memorandum. He cited, among other things, an Air Force Officer who addressed a civic group in his official capacity and stated that "there is no question" that both American schools and churches have been infiltrated by Communists.[82] He also spoke on the Senate floor about eleven instances in which rightist "propaganda" was used by military people in official training sessions.[83]

If military overemphasis has handicapped our foreign policy, it has also severely inhibited domestic progress. In 1964 Fulbright said that programs in education, public health, and urban renewal had been sacrificed in order to build military forces. Fulbright deplored this:

> I sometimes suspect that in its zeal for armaments at the expense of education and welfare the Congress tends to over-represent those of our citizens who are extraordinarily agitated about national security and extraordinarily vigorous about making their agitation known.[84]

The Senator sees twin tendencies that are undesirable in the military emphasis of the modern United States. First is the thought that the expensive armaments really will not work as promised. In 1958 he compared the SAC bomber to the Maginot Line;[85] in a somewhat similar vein he opposed the ABM in 1969.[86] The second tendency is the more important one that the

82. Memorandum submitted by J. William Fulbright to the Department of Defense, 1961. Fulbright files, Washington, D. C.
83. U. S. Congress, Senate, Senator Fulbright discussing propaganda activities of military personnel, 87th Cong., 1st sess., August 2, 1961, *Congressional Record*, 107, Part 11, pp. 14433–39.
84. J. William Fulbright, "The Cold War in American Life," speech at the University of North Carolina 1965 Symposium "Arms and the Man: National Security and the Aims of a Free Society," April 5, 1964. Fulbright files, Washington, D. C.
85. *Congressional Record*, 104, Part 15, pp. 18903, 18904.
86. J. William Fulbright, "Militarism and American Democracy," Owens-Corning Lecture, Denison University, Granville, Ohio, April 18, 1969. Fulbright files, Washington, D. C. Also J. William Fulbright, "Foreign Policy Implications of the ABM Debate," *Bulletin of the Atomic Scientists* 25 (June 1969); 20–23.

arms race is likely to lead to war. In the "Old Myths and New Realities" speech Fulbright pointed out that past arms races have often done this. In a 1964 speech he quoted the social psychologist Gordon Allport:

> The crux of the matter lies in the fact that while most people deplore war, they nonetheless *expect* it to continue. And what people expect determines their behavior . . . the indispensable condition of war is that people must *expect* war and must prepare for war, before, under war-minded leadership, they make war. It is in this sense that "wars begin in the minds of men."[87]

The following year the Senator stated that the ultimate futility of war is that "the issues that cause great wars are often consumed in battle."[88] The avoidance of war is one of Fulbright's major objectives:

> It follows, I think, that one of the guiding principles of our foreign policy must be the accommodation of conflicting interests in the world by means other than military conflict.[89]

In Fulbright's judgment it is the right foreign policy, and not military power that will preserve peace.

Senator Fulbright has felt very free, as Chairman of the Committee on Foreign Relations, to conduct pointed inquiries into the qualifications of nominees for ambassadorial posts. In his early work as Chairman he expressed the thought that career foreign-service people tended to make better appointees than noncareer nominees:

> There is a presumption that career foreign service officers nominated for ambassadorial posts have some qualifications. There is, however, I believe, no such presumption, especially in diplomatic circles, that non-career nominees are qualified to serve the nation in ambassadorial posts.[90]

87. "Human Needs and World Politics."
88. "Lighting the Lamps of Europe."
89. "Bridges East and West."
90. J. William Fulbright, statement of May 12, 1959. Fulbright files, Washington, D. C.

Some noncareer people might be very well qualified, but the burden of proof is on them to show it. Fulbright cited Maxwell Gluck, former Ambassador to Ceylon, as "utterly unfitted" for his assignment.[91]

Senator Fulbright has assumed a role that has been played at some points in the past by powerful chairmen, such as Lodge and Borah. His immediate predecessors were not among the most activist occupants of the Chairman's post, but Fulbright has moved toward the more active pattern. The importance of this posture on the vital issue of presidential power in foreign policy will be treated in the next two chapters.

Fulbright's position on foreign aid and alliances, as well as his own often-mentioned Oxford background, have long planted him in the ranks of the internationally oriented public figures. On the other hand his skepticism about political doctrines, his lack of overriding concern about the alleged dangers posed for the United States by Communist government, and the suspicion with which he views military solutions and even the military itself, all add up to an opposition to many aspects of international action and extension of United States influence.

91. *Ibid.*

3

STRONG PRESIDENTS AND
AN ASSERTIVE SENATE

The heavy reliance on the President to initiate and carry out foreign policy is evidenced often in the speeches and writings of Senator J. William Fulbright. Fulbright has also considered in detail the reasons why the Congress can not and should not play a decisive role in foreign policy. These are major points in his thought, although the opposing side occupies a more voluminous and generally more recent place in his expressions. Several events during his first decade in the Senate served to underscore for Fulbright the actual and the potential detrimental influence that the Senate could exercise in foreign policy.

Senator Fulbright was an early and strong supporter of the United Nations. His own successful 1943 resolution had been one element building support for the principle of a postwar international organization to keep the peace when it came. As a student of history he had a clear knowledge of the Senate's role in keeping the United States out of the League of Nations after World War I.

In a November 23, 1945, speech on NBC radio Fulbright made an eloquent plea to the public to give support to the UN, and to work toward the extension of the rule of law to the international sphere. He conceded that the nation might give only lip service to the principle of international cooperation:

> The Senate formally disavowed isolationism in August and the President professes a faith in the United Nations, but his

actions and statements are not designed to give life or vitality to that organization.[1]

The formal disavowal of isolationism by the Senate could be a fragile thing in the face of insistence that he saw at that time on "the principle of absolute national sovereignty."[2] President Truman, through support of the Marshall Plan and other such measures, continued the generally active sort of international emphasis that characterized the administration of President Franklin D. Roosevelt. Toward the end of the Truman administration, however, two forces arose in the Senate to challenge the functioning of the presidency in foreign affairs. These were the Bricker Amendment to restrict the treaty-making power of the President, and the actions of Senator Joseph R. McCarthy in accusing various executive-department officials of participation in an international Communist conspiracy. The Bricker Amendment had little public support, although it was a major congressional issue; McCarthy became a cause of national embarrassment. The two events stood at the time as major examples of Congressional initiative in foreign policy, and both were opposed vigorously by Fulbright.

On February 2, 1954, Fulbright made a major Senate speech against the Bricker Amendment. After a detailed defense of the wisdom and reasoning of the Founding Fathers, Fulbright made this statement:

It is then no small thing to drastically alter the Constitution by an amendment that in effect throttles the President of the United States in his conduct of foreign relations. It is indeed bewildering to see the Constitution, which for so long has been the bulwark of our liberties and the primary source of our liberties and the primary source of our political strength, come under such violent attack as we have not witnessed since the 1850s. It is even more bewildering when one considers that, so far from being a "loophole" in our constitution as is now

1. J. William Fulbright, speech, NBC radio, November 23, 1945. Fulbright files, Washington, D. C.
2. NBC radio, November 23, 1945.

claimed, the treaty-making power was perhaps the most
urgent reason for calling the Constitutional Convention.[3]

Fulbright was not concerned about presidential abuse of executive agreements:

I believe that during the course of 165 years Presidents have
submitted the most important and serious political agreements
in the form of treaties.[4]

In a debate with Senator John Bricker of Ohio, the amendment's sponsor, Fulbright made this significant statement:

I do not see why we should throw the Constitution overboard
or amend the Constitution when it has served us well. . . .
But why the Senator should desire to change the basic law
when he cannot cite a single instance in which a treaty was
entered into which hurt the interest of the United States, I
cannot understand.[5]

Senator Fulbright has always been aware of the ability of
Congress, and especially the Senate, to "thwart" the President in
matters of foreign relations.[6] For a variety of reasons, however,

---

3. U. S. Congress, Senate, Senator Fulbright speaking against the
Bricker Amendment, S. J. Res. 1, 83rd Cong., 2d sess., February 2, 1954,
Congressional Record, 100, Part 1, p. 1105.
4. U. S. Congress, Senate, Senator Fulbright speaking against the Bricker
Amendment, S. J. Res. 1, 83rd Cong., 2d sess., February 25, 1954, *Congressional Record*, 100, Part 2, p. 2261.
5. U. S. Congress, Senate, Senator Fulbright speaking on the Bricker
Amendment, S. J. Res. 1, 83rd Cong., 2d sess., January 28, 1954, *Congressional Record*, 100, Part 1, p. 940. In an interview with author Lynn Senator
Fulbright made this reply, in answer to a question asking if he still agreed
with this statement:
No, of course not. Of course many of the treaties that we object to
now were made subsequent to that, I mean the SEATO treaty was after
that. The thing that has caused us so much harm were the series of
Dulles' treatment of treaties which were made subsequent and which I
think are being applied in a way directly contrary to what he represented them to be at the time, particularly SEATO.
6. J. William Fulbright, "Public Opinion and Foreign Policy," speech at
Bowling Green University, Bowling Green, Ohio, March 9, 1963, Fulbright
files, Washington, D. C.

ιe Senator has shown why the Congress has important limita-
ons that should prevent its being able to create and implement
foreign policy in the national interest:

> It seems clear to me that in foreign affairs, a Senate cannot
> initiate or force large events, or substitute its judgment of them
> for that of the President, without seriously jeopardizing the
> ability of the nation to act consistently, and also without con-
> fusing the image and purpose of this nation in the eyes of
> others.[7]

One important reason for the inability of Congress to play a
ading role in foreign-policy formulation, according to Senator
'ulbright, is the narrow view possessed by most members of the
Congress. In one Senate speech Fulbright referred to our "tra-
ition of States rights, the other aspect of which is a weak
'ederal Government."[8] He went on to make this statement:

> The members of the Congress, it has been said, regard them-
> selves as ambassadors of sovereign States whose first concern
> is the welfare and dignity of their own constituencies.[9]

n an important article in the Fall 1961 Cornell Law Quarterly
'ulbright summarized his views as to why the Congress was un-
ikely to be creative, or even adequate, in foreign policy:

> It is highly unlikely that we can successfully execute a long-
> range program for taming, or containing, of today's aggressive
> and revolutionary forces by continuing to leave vast and vital
> decision-making powers in the hands of a decentralized, inde-
> pendent-minded, and largely parochial-minded body of legis-
> lators. The Congress, as Woodrow Wilson put it, is a "dis-
> integrated ministry," a jealous center of power with a built-in
> antagonism for the Executive.[10]

---

7. Maurice Goldbloom, "The Fulbright Revolt," *Commentary* (September 1966), p. 65.
8. J. William Fulbright, remarks regarding Senate action on the Development Loan Fund, undated press release. Fulbright files, Washington, D. C.
9. *Ibid.*
10. J. William Fulbright, "American Foreign Policy in the 20th Century
Under an 18th-Century Constitution," *Cornell Law Quarterly* 47 (Fall
1961): 7.

The problem with the intrusions into foreign policy that Congress does make is that the actions taken have broader implications and consequences than those who made them can possibly realize. Little decisions, made in limited contexts, get linked to one another, with the result that large policies arise that no one has "*consciously* willed."[11] One author points out how Congressman Harold Cooley, a Chairman of the House Committee on Agriculture, developed a thorough knowledge of his specialty from a domestic standpoint, and also gained the power to decide from what nations, and in what amounts, the United States would buy sugar. As a by-product of his particular domestic concerns, he made foreign-policy decisions of great importance for countries that relied on their sugar for exports.[12] For such reasons as this Senator Fulbright said, "We need more international vision and less local politics in Congress."[13] If Congress was ever to enter effectively into foreign-policy formulation, a broader national perspective would have to be taken by more of its members.

An important point on which Senator Fulbright has never reversed himself is that Congress is not capable of handling the day-to-day management of foreign relations. While Congress can deliberate over broad aspects of policy, Fulbright maintains that it has neither the machinery nor the inclination to handle details.[14] As early as 1944 Fulbright pointed out that it was difficult to count on congressmen for action, and ". . . there is no known way to make a Senator do anything."[15]

Congress may play a part in offering some broad thoughts on policy, but these should not intrude very far into the functioning of the executive:

11. J. William Fulbright, Untitled speech before the American Society of Newspaper Editors, Washington, D. C., April 18, 1959, Fulbright files, Washington D. C. Emphasis in original.
12. Martin C. Needler, *Understanding Foreign Policy* (New York: Holt, Rinehart and Winston, Inc.), p. 41.
13. J. William Fulbright, "Our Responsibilities in World Affairs," Gabriel Silver Lecture on International Understanding, Columbia University, May 7, 1959, Fulbright files, Washington, D. C.
14. "Fulbright's Pilgrimage," *Economist* (June 4, 1966), p. 1081.
15. J. William Fulbright, Untitled speech before the Bond Club, New York City, December 11, 1944. Fulbright files, Washington, D. C.

A vital distinction must be made between offering broad policy directions, and interfering in the conduct of policy by the executive branch. Many of our difficulties in foreign policy arise . . . from a recurring tendency on the part of Congress to overstep its proper role.[16]

Congress has often played the role of an obstructionist in foreign relations, and Senator Fulbright in the 1950s opposed extensive Congressional participation in foreign-policy determination because of these obstructive tendencies.[17] In a 1963 speech Fulbright quoted Walter Lippmann with approval in showing how public opinion tended to impose a "massive negative":

The impact of mass opinion on vital issues of war and peace, in Lippmann's analysis, is to impose a "massive negative" at critical junctures when new courses of policy are needed. Lagging disastrously behind the movement of events, Lippmann contends, public opinion forced a vindictive peace in 1919, then refused to act against a resurgent Germany in the interwar years, and finally was aroused to paroxysms of hatred and unattainable hopes in a Second World War that need never have occurred. The impact of a public opinion, says Lippmann, has been nothing less than a "compulsion to make mistakes."[18]

He went on to show that the prudent politician in Congress reflects the negativism of his constituents and feels free to obstruct the conduct of foreign affairs. Fulbright concluded that the electorate and their representatives should influence foreign policy only in a very broad way, while "trained professionals" formulated and implemented most policies.[19]

The principal concern of Congress in foreign policy relates to the fiscal implications of foreign relations. In Senator Fulbright's view in 1961 this represented an important weakness:

---

16. Quoted in Goldbloom, p. 65.
17. Interview with Senator Fulbright.
18. "Public Opinion and Foreign Policy." The quotations from Walter Lippmann are from his *The Public Philosophy* (New York: The American Library of World Literature, 1956), p. 19.
19. "Public Opinion and Foreign Policy."

The appropriations process in Congress, moreover, is governed by a basically faulty attitude. The central consideration is invariably *money* rather than *policy*.[20]

The question was not what kind of foreign policy does the nation need, but how little money do we have to spend. This attitude represented an important manifestation of congressional obstructionism.

In the postwar period foreign aid became the focal point of Congress's negativism in foreign affairs. Fulbright was usually in the forefront of those who fought for foreign aid. Thus he felt the full brunt of the efforts of the economy-minded bloc who sought to curb foreign spending as useless "giveaways." In a 1959 speech regarding aid to Laos, he decried the misplaced emphasis of those who were far more concerned with some waste in the program than they were with the important results that aid could achieve in Laos.[21] After the 1963 foreign-aid debate in the Senate, when Senator Wayne Morse of Oregon almost single-handedly secured major cuts, one writer said that Senator Fulbright "appeared grateful to be alive."[22]

Presidents felt the impact of foreign aid foes too. In 1957 Representative Otto Passman of Louisiana was brought to the White House for tea in a presidential limousine in an attempt by President Eisenhower to lessen Passman's objection to the aid bill. The attempt was in vain, and the President was quoted as saying, "Remind me never to invite that fellow down here again."[23]

To lessen congressional obstruction for their foreign-policy programs the representatives of the President often consult with key Senators and Congressmen. Because of personality factors

---

20. *Cornell Law Quarterly*, p. 5.
21. *Congressional Record*, 105, Part 9, p. 12274.
22. Quoted from Mary McGrory, "Morse Tackles an 'Untidy World,' " *Washington Evening Star*, November 17, 1963, in Nelson W. Polsby, *Congress and the Presidency* (Englewood Cliffs, N. J.: Prentice-Hall, Inc., 1964), pp. 37, 38.
23. Rowland Evans, Jr., "Louisiana's Passman: The Scourge of Foreign Aid," *Harpers* 224 (January 1962): 80, 81.

this process can pose delicate problems. Dean Acheson cited the problems that he encountered when he worked with Senator Connally and Senator Arthur Vandenberg:

> Dealing with the two senior Foreign Relations Senators took a great deal of time. . . . The simple thing would have been to talk with them together; but simplicity would have been, if not disastrous, at least hazardous. Connally loved to heckle Vandenberg. Vandenberg when aroused could respond in a way calculated to move Connally another notch toward disagreement for its own sake. So the procedure was to see them separately, to get each so far committed that only the sheerest wilfulness could undo it. But which to see first? Here was a tricky decision. Both were fairly good about not leaking the "content" of our talk to the press. But each found it hard to resist leaking the fact of a private talk. Once this was done, the second to be seen knew that he was the second. With Connally, this was instant cause for offense.[24]

Former Vice-President Hubert Humphrey, in an interview with the author, discussed this problem of consulting with Senators:

> There are some personalities involved in this. I really believe that Senator Fulbright was of the opinion that if he had been consulted more often by President Johnson all of these things might not have happened. Now, you may have noticed that the Senate Foreign Relations Committee has pulled way back with Mr. Nixon and I think one of the reasons is that President Nixon has systematically and assiduously, carefully consulted with the leaders of the Congress all the time quietly on the side. In other words Bill Fulbright, Mike Mansfield, Albert Gore, Frank Church, many of the people that would ordinarily resist him have been brought in, given information etc.
> . . . and one thing I have learned about Senators is that they're all prima donnas. They all like to be individually consulted because if you have two Senators together, one has got seniority over the other of some kind and the minute you had one fellow who has to stand one-half step behind the other fellow, he never feels satisfied. There is only one way to meet

---

24. Dean Acheson, *Sketches from Life of Men I Have Known* (London: Hamish Hamilton, 1961), p. 138.

with a Senator and that's really [to] get him off in the kitchen or the men's room alone so that nobody else can get at you. And then he feels that he's got a *real* contact with the President.[25]

On various occasions members of Congress have either shown themselves responsive to what Senator Fulbright terms the "radical right" or they have not shown a willingness in sufficient numbers to oppose rightist positions on foreign policy. Because of Senator Fulbright's own attacks from rightist group and some self-styled "conservatives," this factor is a possible influence on his position opposing congressional determination of foreign policy.

In 1965 various groups, led by the Young Americans for Freedom, forced the Firestone Tire and Rubber Company to terminate plans to build a synthetic rubber plant in Rumania. The deal had State Department approval, but "conservative" opponents of it picketed Firestone and accused the company of selling strategic technical know-how to the Communists. Senator Fulbright, in a long Senate speech, criticized this successful effort to thwart national trade policy, and he deplored the lack of effective congressional and executive action to preserve the Firestone plans.[26]

Senator Barry Goldwater's 1964 campaign for the presidency as a "conservative" brought extensive criticism from Fulbright. One of Goldwater's points that received Fulbright's attention was this contention of the Arizona Senator:

I feel very strongly that the executive branch has taken too much power from the legislative branch.[27]

25. Interview with former Vice-President Hubert H. Humphrey, January 9, 1970, Manhattan, Kansas. Mr. Humphrey made this comment about his unique opportunity to observe the consultation process: "You know it's an interesting position to be Vice-President—all you can do is just shut your mouth, so to speak, and observe."

26. U. S. Congress, Senate, Senator Fulbright, speech "Public and Private Responsibility in the Conduct of Foreign Relations," 89th Cong., 1st sess., July 26, 1965, *Congressional Record,* 111, Part 13, p. 18226.

27. Quoted in *Congressional Record,* 110, Part 15, p. 19787. It is interesting to note that Barry Goldwater was one of only 16 Senators who voted against the National Commitments Resolution. See Appendix B.

Fulbright disagreed with Goldwater:

> In the field of executive-legislative relations the key idea seems to be that the President should turn over many of his powers to the Congress, which should then diligently refrain from exercising them.[28]

The thought of taking powers away from a progressive President to give to a conservative Congress has little appeal to Senator Fulbright.

Fulbright has always paid more than the usual lip service to the goal of avoiding war. He has seen "warlike tendencies" in Congress, and this accounts for many of his reservations about granting more foreign-policy power to Congress. In 1966 he made this statement on the Senate floor:

> What I said was that "Congress is more warlike than the President." . . . Although the Congress is more warlike than the President, it may well also be more warlike than the country. This remains to be seen.[29]

The Senator cited the efforts of Congressmen Passman and Sikes to give $54 million worth of war planes to Chiang Kai-shek, when this was not in the budget, as an instance of undesirable Congressional intervention. He also characterized Speaker John McCormack as "very warlike."[30]

It is very probably that the pervasiveness of the seniority system in Congress has been a factor influencing the Senator in his reservations about the role of Congress. What one author terms "accidents of seniority" distribute significant power.[31] Certainly Fulbright had an ample opportunity to observe the fact at first hand. The Committee on Foreign Relations was chaired by Senator Connally when Fulbright became a member; Connally left the Senate in 1952 at the age of seventy-five.

---

28. *Congressional Record,* 110, Part 15, p. 19787.
29. U. S. Congress, Senate, Senator Fulbright speaking on the political atmosphere in the United States, 89th Cong., 2d sess., August 22, 1966. *Congressional Record,* 112, Part 15, p. 20185.
30. Interview with J. William Fulbright.
31. Needler, p. 41.

Senator Wiley chaired the Committee at age seventy. When the Democrats got control of the Senate again after the 1954 election, Senator George became chairman at age seventy-seven. George was followed as chairman by Fulbright's predecessor, Senator Green, who finally retired at the record age of ninety-one.[32] Fulbright was a vigorous fifty-three when he assumed the chairmanship.

Regardless of the positive contribution made by these chairmen and others who rise through the Congressional seniority system, no perceptive observer could avoid the conclusion that regular reelection from a state with relatively little party competition plays a larger role than merit.[33]

Senator Fulbright has also made a strong case for giving a generally free hand to the President in the making of foreign policy. He could easily speak this way in retrospect, as he remembered in 1966 the coming to office in 1961 of a President he supported:

> The event was the coming to office in the United States of a creative new Administration, eager to strengthen the developing debate with the Russians, and eager as well to use a respite from international crisis to devise imaginative new programs for the betterment of American life.[34]

Fulbright's support for independent presidential leadership and initiative in foreign policy went far beyond support for a given President, however, and it also extended freely to Presidents of

---

32. Haynes Johnson and Bernard M. Gwertzman, *Fulbright: the Dissenter* (New York: Doubleday and Company, 1968), p. 157. Johnson and Gwertzman also describe how Senator Green was finally eased out as chairman, pp. 2–5.

33. Among the many books dealing with the problems of seniority are: Richard Bolling, *House out of Order* (New York: E. P. Dutton, 1965); Philip Conham and Robert J. Fahey, *Congress Needs Help* (New York: Random House, 1966); and Estes Kefauver and Jack Levin, *A Twentieth-Century Congress* (New York: Greenwood Press, 1959).

34. J. William Fulbright, "Higher Education and the Crisis in Asia," speech before the 21st National Conference of Higher Education, Chicago, Illinois, March 14, 1966.

both parties.[35] The Constitution, according to Fulbright, puts the President in this position in foreign relations:

It makes him the leading actor; not a spectator and leading witness. . . . It was never intended by the Founding Fathers that the President of the United States would be a ventriloquist dummy sitting on the lap of Congress.[36]

One of the main reasons that the Senator has given for his support of presidential initiative is the contention that foreign-policy action must inherently lie with the executive. Where Congress is not well equipped to handle day-to-day problems and to execute policy, the President is so equipped. It was in recognition of such realities that Fulbright on July 16, 1958, expressed support for the sending of troops to Lebanon, even though he regretted the necessity of the act and had vigorously opposed the "Eisenhower Doctrine." Stating that only the future could finally vindicate the wisdom of the act, he said, "We must therefore support it, if only because it has been done."[37] Action seemed inherent in the function of the Presidency.

In his 1961 *Cornell Law Quarterly* article Fulbright took his strongest position ever on giving the President a free hand in foreign policy. At that point he saw far more than a need to support a chief executive in actions that had already been taken; he advocated giving the President sweeping new powers that would authorize him to act even more. He was undoubtedly influenced by his confidence in President Kennedy and his general agreement with the administration's foreign-policy position. Several passages from this article demonstrate his argument:

My question, then, is whether we have any choice but to modify, and perhaps overhaul, the 18th-century procedures that govern the formulation and conduct of American foreign

---

35. Data to substantiate this point will be presented in chapter 4.
36. *Congressional Record*, 100, Part 1, p. 1106.
37. U. S. Congress, Senate, Senator Fulbright discussing the Middle East Situation, 85th Cong., 2d sess., June 16, 1958, *Congressional Record*, 104 Part 11, p. 13908.

policy. More specifically, I wonder whether the time has not
arrived, or indeed already passed, when we must give the
Executive a measure of power in the conduct of our foreign
affairs that we have hitherto jealously withheld. . . .
It is not within our powers to confer wisdom or perception
on the Presidential person. It is within our power to grant or
deny him authority. It is my contention that for the existing
requirements of American foreign policy we have hobbled the
Presidency by too niggardly a grant of power.[38]

Fulbright did not view his proposal to grant new powers to the
President with great satisfaction; he merely deemed the idea
essential:

> The President alone can act to mobilize our power and re-
> sources toward the realization of clearly defined objectives and
> to wean the American people and their representatives from
> the luxuries of parochialism and self-indulgence that they can
> no longer afford. The enhancement of Presidential power is, as
> I have said, a disagreeable and dangerous prospect. It is seen
> to be a compelling necessity, however, when set against the
> alternative of immobility, which can only lead to consequences
> immeasurably more disagreeable and dangerous.[39]

By the close of the 1960s Senator Fulbright had changed his
mind on the arguments stated above. Generally similar arguments, however, were presented by Hubert H. Humphrey in an
interview with the author:

> Ultimately though the President must be in charge. You
> cannot run foreign policy by committees. You can give advice,
> you can give counsel, but that doesn't mean you are going to

38. *Cornell Law Quarterly*, p. 2. In 1967 in referring to this speech Fulbright said that he had been concerned about events such as the paralysis
of the State Department due to the exploits of Cohn and Schine and the
tensions of the cold war of that period. He added, "We are all susceptible
to the human tendency to give undue weight to concerns of the moment."
Fulbright's critics might characterize this as an understatement. See U. S.
Congress, Foreign Relations, *U. S. Commitments to Foreign Powers, Hearings* before the Committee on Foreign Relations, Senate, on S. Res. 151,
90th Cong., 1st sess., August, September, 1967, p. 2.
39. *Cornell Law Quarterly*, pp. 12, 13.

satisfy the critics in Congress because ultimately the President must make the decision, and whatever goes wrong, even though he got advice from Congress, they will be able to say, "Well, I didn't mean it that way." "The buck stops here," said Mr. Truman, when he had that little sign on his desk. It is Mr. President that has the responsibility for really defining the interests of national security of this country. He is the man that is Commander-in-Chief. He is the man that must sift out the information and come to a value judgment as to what he recommends or what he can do. . . .

There is no way in the world that you can design a political system that is going to be responsive to the world, to the needs of your country or to the needs of security if you put it in a strait jacket. This system doesn't work so much by law as it does by tradition and as it does by trust. As I tell the critics of the present government and all "We have done pretty well."

I have not seen very many Presidents that are overly anxious to commit American forces. I have seen Presidents that have anguished over the commitment of American forces, but I would have hated to wait for the Congress of the United States to have given Andrew Jackson the authority at the time of the Tariff of Abominations. I'd have hated to wait for the Congress of the United States to have given Thomas Jefferson authority over the Barbary pirates. We have certain things that a President is supposed to do.[40]

Besides the underlying argument that decisive action is an inherent executive function, Fulbright has made two other important points. One, which ties in with former Vice-President Humphrey's remark about the Barbary pirates, is Fulbright's 1967 point that in an emergency speed is essential and consultation with Congress is impractical.[41] The second is that a need for secrecy, or at least confidentiality, exists in many segments of foreign relations, and it is the executive branch that is geared to attaining it. In a 1963 speech Senator Fulbright pointed out that "the public prefers a hero to a horse trader . . .," but it is

---

40. Interview with Hubert H. Humphrey.
41. U. S. Congress, Senate, Report of the Committee on the Judiciary made by its Subcommittee on Separation of Powers, *Separation of Powers*, S. Rept. 91–549, 90th Cong., 1st sess., 1967.

not heroism that strikes viable bargains.[42] A free people must know and consent to the content of this nation's agreements, but the actual bargaining process must be carried on "between professional negotiators."[43] Fulbright quoted with approval Harold Nicolson's paraphrase of President Wilson that we must have "open covenants, but not openly arrived at."[44]

On various occasions these thoughts led Fulbright to follow the general principle: when in doubt, back the President. In January 1955 he voted for the Formosa Resolution that the Administration had requested, despite some doubts on some of its provisions.[45] In the debate on the Eisenhower Doctrine, when President Eisenhower asked Congress for authority to provide armed support to any Middle Eastern nation wanting protection against "overt armed aggression from any nation controlled by international Communism," Fulbright spoke against such an extensive grant of power to the President.[46] He conceded at the time, however, that the President, as Commander in Chief, had the power to defend the nation's "vital interests," and the Senator contended that the resolution (S. J. Res. 19) would actually have the effect of limiting that power.[47] The same spirit can explain Fulbright's vote, in 1964, for the landmark Gulf of Tonkin resolution.[48] It also is reflected in the Senator's speech on June 15, 1965, offering guarded approval of the Vietnam War policy:

It cannot be denied that there have been mistakes over the

---

42. "Public Opinion and Foreign Policy."
43. *Ibid.*
44. Quoted in *Ibid.*
45. Kenneth W. Grundy, "The Apprenticeship of J. William Fulbright," *Virginia Quarterly Review* 43 (Summer 1967): 385.
46. *Congressional Record,* 103, Part 2, pp. 1855–70.
47. U. S. Congress, Senate, Committees on Foreign Relations and Armed Services, *The President's Proposal on the Middle East, Hearings* before the Committees on Foreign Relations and Armed Services, on S. J. Res. 19 and H. J. Res. 17, Senate, 85th Cong., 1st sess., January, to February, 1957, p. 28.
48. U. S. Congress, Senate, Committee on Foreign Relations, *National Commitments,* S. Rept. 91–129, 91st Cong., 1st sess., 1969, p. 23. See also U. S. Congress, Senate, Debate on Southeast Asia Resolution, S. J. Res. 189, 88th Cong., 2d sess., August 5, 6, 1964. *Congressional Record,* 110, part 14, August 5, p. 18403 and August 6, p. 18409.

years in our policy in Vietnam, not the least of which was the encouragement given in the mid-1950's to President Ngo Dinh Diem to violate certain provisions of the Geneva accords of 1954. Even when past mistakes are admitted, the fact remains that over the past 4½ years the United States has consistently sought to negotiate compromise settlements on southeast Asia. I believe that President Kennedy and President Johnson have been wise in their restraint and patience, that indeed this patience has quite possibly averted a conflict that could be disastrous for both the Communist countries and for the United States and its associates.[49]

The Presidency of Dwight D. Eisenhower shaped one of Senator Fulbright's basic concepts about the approach of the Senate to the issue of presidential power in foreign relations. This is the point that an inactive or passive President must be not only backed, but also positively encouraged. This point remains as an active one in Senator Fulbright's thought as late as 1970, and it can be applied to President Eisenhower with validity, despite the latter's occasional excursions into ventures, such as the Middle East activities, that Fulbright opposed.[50]

In 1970 the Senator looked beyond the events of the Johnson era to a time when an entirely different kind of President might call forth responses different from those of the 1960s:

Now, you get a very weak and retiring President following him and what are you going to do? You react to him. You certainly cease the same kind of reaction. There is no need for it. This politics in government is a day to day matter that goes on. The Constitution is a basic set of principles. Now after they are applied they vary according to the personalities in power and issues of a given time.[51]

President Eisenhower provided Senator Fulbright his only

---

49. U. S. Congress, Senate, Senator Fulbright speaking on "The War in Vietnam," 89th Cong., 1st sess., June 15, 1965. *Congressional Record,* Vól. 111, Part 10, p. 13657.
50. Interview with Senator J. William Fulbright. Senator Fulbright attributes the improper treatment of treaties during the Eisenhower years as the work of Secretary of State Dulles rather than President Eisenhower.
51. Interview with J. William Fulbright.

experience in public life with a chief executive who would qualify for the passive-inactive classification. Fulbright did not hesitate to criticize what he felt was a weakness in Eisenhower's leadership, before and after the General's term in office. In 1959 Fulbright said, "We need more concentrated energy instead of buckshot spray in the White House."[52] In 1961 Fulbright summarized Eisenhower's executive leadership in contrast to President Truman's in these words:

> President Eisenhower, on the other hand, was an exemplary head of state, a virtual personification of the American ideal, but his failure to exercise the *full* measure of his powers and duties as "Prime Minister" was the cause of basic failures and omissions in our foreign policy.[53]

Fulbright did not join the critics of President Eisenhower's "personal diplomacy." He said he did not regard personal diplomacy as "the next worse thing to Original Sin," and he welcomed signs that the President was returning to something approaching the "Ike" of pre-1952 days:

> The "Ike" of those days embodied in his person the whole spirit of what NATO was meant to be. He was the prophet of warning and encouragement, the negotiator of operating agreements where each member nation could see that its own national interest was best served in the context of a security arrangement that served simultaneously the national interest of every other member. His renown was vastly augmented by that fact. And if now he returns to the scene and source of the accomplishments which carried him into the White House, and if there sets in motion the material programs necessary to restore the integrity of his earlier accomplishments, the actions which will add luster to his name will also add strength to the Grand Alliance.[54]

Fulbright came also to appreciate and agree with Senate Majority

52. "Our Responsibilities in World Affairs."
53. *Cornell Law Quarterly*, pp. 7, 8.
54. Quoted in Sidney Hyman, "The Advice and Consent of J. William Fulbright," *Reporter* (September 17, 1959), p. 25.

Leader Lyndon B. Johnson's policy of supporting President Eisenhower. While such support

> may have been wrong with respect to particular issues and events, it was basically right as a proper long-term procedure because failure to support the President, particularly a weak one, and particularly at a time of divided government, easily could have led to political warfare between the parties over foreign policy.[55]

Contrary to his announced policy of speaking in public to Republican Presidents, Senator Fulbright had numerous private meetings with President Eisenhower, and his encouragement of the President to use his powers more fully must reflect this more personal acquaintance. With Fulbright, Eisenhower apparently achieved the sort of close personal consultation that former Vice-President Humphrey pointed out as being necessary. Fulbright served as a private critic of the Eisenhower administration's foreign policy. On various occasions Fulbright and a small group of Senators such as Johnson, Dirksen, and Knowland, and perhaps Speaker Sam Rayburn, would be invited to President Eisenhower's office for informal 5 P.M. drinks.[56] This apparently built mutual trust.

The need to support and encourage a relatively inactive President stands as a major point in Senator Fulbright's thought, especially in view of the fact that the alternative of foreign-policy determination by the Congress tends to approach unworkability. But Fulbright's view that Congress, especially the Senate, should reassert its influence in foreign-policy formulation reflects a gradual and genuine change in his thinking. This change has deep roots in the Senator's experiences, but it assumed its fullest form during the administration of President Lyndon B. Johnson. As early as 1945 in a letter to the Editor of the *Washington Post* Fulbright advocated change in the American system of government to permit the resolution of a stalemate when the executive

---

55. Quoted in Goldbloom, p. 64.
56. Johnson and Gwertzman, p. 157.

and legislative branches could not agree on a course of action.[57] This certainly suggests that he did not feel then that such conflicts should be resolved by having the executive's policies take precedence. The question of executive-legislative disagreements was to occupy a prominent place in the Senator's thought.

The most convincing demonstration that he has changed his views on the proper role of the President of the United States with regard to foreign policy is the frank admission of the fact by the Senator himself. The most forthright acknowledgment of this change for the public record was made by the Senator on June 19, 1969, on the Senate floor. Senator Gale McGee of Wyoming, who disagrees with many of Fulbright's later views, quoted with approval from Fulbright's 1961 *Cornell Law Quarterly* article discussed earlier. It will be recalled that he argued for fuller grants of foreign policy power to the executive. Senator Fulbright's reply to Senator McGee included this paragraph:

> However, I did state what the Senator has read, and under the circumstances of that time I felt that it was correct. We had then a President who was very reluctant to exercise Executive power and had been all during that period. He was almost the opposite in his approach to the exercise of power, as a President, from the one in the office when the present resolution was introduced. Of course, as the Senator knows, the circumstances under which we operate often, as of a given time, influence a judgment. However, in view of the experience of the relatively quiescent period of President Eisenhower and the very active period under President Johnson, there is no doubt that I have changed my mind as to which is the more dangerous to the welfare of the country. The restraining influence of Congress upon an overactive and overambitious President is the much safer course for the country.[58]

Senator Fulbright in his interview with the author reaffirmed this point. He is not ashamed to admit it when he changes his mind. He has often admitted that he made a mistake in voting

---

57. J. William Fulbright, letter to the Editor of the *Washington Post*, dated March 25, 1945. Fulbright files, Washington, D. C.
58. *Congressional Record*, 115, No. 101, p. S 6838.

for the Gulf of Tonkin Resolution.[59] In his 1970 interview with the author the Senator summed up his thoughts and actions in these words:

> I would like to put it this way, that I think the reaction along about the time of the end of the Eisenhower regime was simply a reflection of the feeling that the administration was entirely too passive and that a number of Congressmen with special interests were seeking to insert these into our foreign policy by way of the foreign aid bill. . . . Afterward when you come into the regime of President Kennedy and the Bay of Pigs and then Johnson and Vietnam, of course I was impressed with the need of restraint on the part of the Congress on an overactive President. I don't think it is a deep intellectual distinction there. I think it is simply that you are faced with a situation in which you have a President who is seeking to override the Congress and pays no attention to them.[60]

Several major events caused the Senator to revise the views that he expressed in such statements as his 1961 *Cornell Law Quarterly* article. Essentially, this was the change from advocating the need for more Presidential power in foreign affairs as a general rule to the recognition that giving such a free hand to the chief executive is actually a special case, appropriate only when the President is passive. The chief concept that Senator Fulbright learned, and which he passes on to political scientists and the public, is that the lessons taught by limited events must not be learned too well or held uncritically for too long, because newer events take place.

Fulbright's earliest major perception of excessive executive power came in the Eisenhower years in connection with the work of Secretary of State John Foster Dulles.[61] The 1954–1955 actions relative to the Formosa Straits aroused Fulbright's doubts about

---

59. J. William Fulbright, "Meet the Press., NBC telecast, January 22, 1967. Fulbright files, Washington, D. C.
60. Interview with J. William Fulbright.
61. Fulbright still adheres to the concept of the dichotomy between the passive President Eisenhower and the overactive Secretary of State Dulles. Interview with J. William Fulbright.

Dulles, but not his active questioning.[62] Later Dulles's pronouncements, such as his famous terms *massive retaliation*, and *the
brink of war* deepened Fulbright's doubts, as did Dulles's loose
talk, prior to the 1956 Hungarian uprising, of "liberating" Eastern
Europe.[63] Fulbright favored American support of the Aswan Dam
project in Egypt, and when Dulles withdrew support from this
economically feasible project and thus precipitated the Suez
crisis of 1956, Fulbright repeatedly expressed opposition to the
Secretary's action.[64]

In 1957 when Secretary of State Dulles testified before the
Foreign Relations Committee that the Soviet Union's foreign
policy was a failure and that the Russians were losing the Cold
War, Senator Fulbright answered Dulles in a speech delivered
in the Senate and reprinted in the *New York Times:*

> I want to draw the attention of this body to a matter that
> dwarfs all other things before it. To put it plainly, the matter
> is this:
> Will Secretary of State Dulles tell America the truth about
> our present peril or will he say one thing publicly and an
> opposite thing privately?
> . . . But I ask you: are these systems of government well
> served when a Secretary of State misleads public opinion, con-
> fuses it, feeds it pap, tells it that if it will suppress the proof
> of its own senses, it will see that Soviet triumphs are really
> defeats, and Western defeats are really triumphs?[65]

Dulles and Fulbright had numerous encounters in Foreign
Relations Committee hearings that served to identify the disagreements between the two men. One exchange between them
occurred in 1957 in connection with the "Eisenhower Doctrine."

62. Grundy, p. 385.
63. J. William Fulbright, "Bridges East and West," speech at Southern
Methodist University, Dallas, Texas, December 8, 1964, Fulbright files,
Washington, D. C.
64. U. S. Congress, Senate, Senator J. William Fulbright discussing his
recent trip to the Middle East, 86th Cong., 2d sess., June 15, 1960. *Congressional Record*, 106, Part 10, p. 12617. See Grundy, p. 393. For an interesting discussion of Dulles and the Aswan Dam decision see Herman Finer,
Dulles Over Suez (Chicago: Quadrangle Books, 1964).
65. *New York Times*, February 28, 1957, p. 4.

Fulbright denounced Dulles publicly and to the Secretary's face during the hearings:

> Mr. Secretary, I think that points up our difference perhaps better than anything I can say. I simply think you were completely wrong in your evaluation of events which were well-known to everybody. Why you misjudged it of course I don't know, but I did not, and I submit that events since then have not borne you out.[66]

In the end Dulles won the vote on the resolutions, but Fulbright formed views about the Secretary that have persisted to the current period. He also used rhetoric of a type that would be repeated a decade later:

> This, I think is also symptomatic of the fact that our policies have lost touch with the ideals and aspirations of the common man. People everywhere who aspire to the good life are unable to identify their desires with our policies. Unless our long-range policies can be adapted to the opinions of mankind, our foreign policies are doomed to continued failure.[67]

The ill-fated Bay of Pigs invasion of 1961 provided the principal point of disagreement between Senator Fulbright and President Kennedy. The casual way in which the Senator learned of the invasion plan while on an impromptu airplane ride with the President dismayed Fulbright. Nor was the Foreign Relations Committee briefed. Fulbright later sent a memo to the President that encouraged calling off any plan to remove Castro by force of arms. Fulbright said that the Communists seek to impose their system, by force if necessary, and "if we intervene unilaterally in Cuba, we prejudice our cause in the hemisphere. . . ."[68]

---

66. U. S. Congress, Senate, Committee on Foreign Relations and Armed Services, *The President's Proposal on the Middle East, Hearings,* before the Committee on Foreign Relations and the Committee on Armed Services, Senate, on S. J. Res. 19 and H. J. Res. 117, 85th Cong., 1st sess., January–February, 1957, p. 384.
67. *Congressional Record,* 104, Part 11, p. 13908.
68. Kenworthy, 1961, p. 96. Also see J. William Fulbright, tape-recorded interview with *Washington Post* Staff writer Chalmers M. Roberts, reprinted in U. S. Congress, Senate, 89th Cong., 1st sess., October 22, 1965, *Congressional Record,* 111, Part 21, p. 28390.

The manner of the President's briefing of Fulbright and other congressional leaders at the time of the Cuban Missile Crisis is also remembered by the Senator as an example of improper procedure.[69] About 5:00 P.M. the leaders started their "consultation." By 6:30, when it became known that Kennedy was going on nationwide television at 7:00, it was clear that no advice was being sought, nor had any been sought from Fulbright on this question earlier.[70] During the short briefing Fulbright suggested invading Cuba. He later said:

> Had I been able to formulate my views on the basis of facts rather than a guess as to the nature of the situation, I might have made a different recommendation. In any case, the recommendation I made represented my best judgment at that time, and I thought it my duty to offer it.[71]

Kennedy's effort in this case is almost universally regarded as highly successful as a matter of national policy. It was for Fulbright, however, an exercise of the sort of independent presidential initiative that he had earlier advocated but has since led him to question the wisdom of broad and continuing grants of power to the occupant of the White House.

While his disagreement with the Johnson Administration about the wisdom and propriety of escalating the war in Vietnam has been the major continuing issue that led Senator Fulbright in the late 1960s to accuse the President consistently of exceeding his authority in foreign policy, it was not the key issue that brought this side of the Senator's thinking to the forefront. In 1963 Juan Bosch, the constitutionally elected President of the Dominican Republic, was overthrown in a bloodless military coup, and a civilian junta, under the leadership of Donald Reid Cabral, took control of the nation. On April 24 military supporters of Bosch started a revolution, which led to the fall of the

---

69. Interview with J. William Fulbright.
70. *Ibid.*
71. As quoted in Tristram Coffin, *Senator Fulbright: Portrait of a Public Philosopher* (New York: E. P. Dutton and Company, 1966), p. 150.

Cabral government the following day. Fighting between the two factions, however, continued. On April 28 a group of congressional leaders, including Senator Fulbright, were called to an emergency meeting at the White House, where President Johnson told them that a force of 400 Marines would be landed in Santo Domingo for the purpose of protecting the lives of the 2,500 American citizens in the Dominican Republic.[72] In the following days more American troops were landed, and by May 2 14,000 were there. On that date President Johnson declared that the pro-Bosch forces had been taken over by "a band of Communist conspirators."[73] Johnson did not propose to allow another Communist state in the Western hemisphere, even if it meant giving armed support to a military dictatorship in violation of the nonintervention principle of the OAS treaty, if it was needed in order to prevent it.

Senator Fulbright proceeded to have the Committee on Foreign Relations make a detailed investigation of the intervention by the United States. On September 15, 1965, he made a major speech on the Senate floor disagreeing with the whole American action. He questioned the unexplained change in American attiture toward Bosch and his people that took place from 1963 to 1965. He criticized the fact that the saving of the lives of American citizens was initially used as a pretext for the interference in the affairs of an independent nation. The fact that Johnson subsequently justified the act as fighting Communism did not satisfy Fulbright:

The point I am making is not—emphatically not— that there was no Communist participation in the Dominican crisis, but simply that the administration acted on the premise that the revolution was controlled by Communists—a premise which it

72. J. William Fulbright, *The Arrogance of Power* (New York: Vintage Books, 1966), p. 49. Also see U. S. Congress, Senate, Committee on Foreign Relations, *Background Information Relating to the Dominican Republic,* Committee Print, 89th Cong., 1st sess., July, 1965.
73. *Ibid.,* p. 20.

failed to establish at the time and has not established since.[74]

If the action was excused as a fight against certain "Communists" whose presence or even existence was not proven, it was an act of the sort that would have been committed by the most irresponsible representative of the radical right. Fulbright contended that the Dominican invasion was an act that would certainly harm the reputation of the United States throughout Latin America.[75]

Senator Fulbright's September 15 speech brought extensive reactions, which caused him some surprise. President Johnson was quoted as saying that the speech would cause the United States embarrassment in its future relations with the Dominican Republic.[76] The President also dropped Fulbright from the White House social list for six months.[77] There was extensive press comment on the speech. In the October 22, 1965, *Congressional Record*, Senator Fulbright had reprinted 33 editorials supporting his position and 32 opposing him. What the Senator found most surprising was the fact that much of the comment about his views centered not on the proper policy in the Dominican Republic, but on Fulbright himself.[78] Later he described the matter in this way:

> When in the wake of the Dominican Hearings, I publicly stated my criticisms of American policy, there followed a debate not on the substance of my criticisms but on the appropriateness of my having made them.[79]

The speech was criticized as "irresponsible" and "unpatriotic," not to mention as damaging to the "consensus."[80]

---

74. U. S. Congress, Senate, Senator Fulbright commenting on the situation in the Dominican Republic, 89th Cong., 1st sess., October 22, 1965, *Congressional Record*, 111, Part 21, p. 28376.
75. *Arrogance of Power*, p. 96.
76. *Congressional Record*, 111, Part 21, p. 28390.
77. Alex Campbell, "Fulbright on Camera," *New Republic* (May 21, 1966), p. 19.
78. *Congressional Record*, 111, Part 21, pp. 28372, 28373, 28379–406.
79. U. S. Congress, Senate, Committee on the Judiciary, *Separation of Powers*, Part 1, *Hearings* before the Subcommittee on Separation of Powers of the Committee on the Judiciary, Senate, 90th Cong., 1st sess., 1967, p. 45.
80. *Hearings* before the Subcommittee on Separation of Powers, p. 45

The very special significance of this experience for Fulbright he sums up in these words:

> This was the first of many occasions on which no one questioned the right of dissent but many people had something to say about special circumstances making its use inappropriate.[81]

He had worked hard to investigate the situation, and he had found that in his opinion major mistakes had been made. When he spoke out against these mistakes he was told by some that he should not have done so. This was a revealing experience, one that would never again permit him to seek to preserve the executive immune from Senate influence in the formulation and exercise of foreign policy. In the specific case of President Johnson, it was to contribute to a loss of Fulbright's confidence and trust in connection with the far larger issue of the war in Southeast Asia.

At the same time that the events of 1965 in the Dominican Republic showed Fulbright that efforts to reveal executive misrepresentation would be unwelcome, the war in Southeast Asia was being escalated. In the presidential campaign of 1964 Fulbright had spoken at length in support of Johnson and against Goldwater. Fulbright's attacks on Goldwater focused on the latter's talk of pursuing a military "victory" in Vietnam, defoliating part of that country's terrain, and using small nuclear weapons against the Chinese.[82] When President Johnson sent more troops into an expanding conflict, Fulbright felt deceived.

On March 14, 1966, Senator Fulbright spoke of the contrast between the early and later parts of the President's term. He praised the fact that Johnson "embraced and expanded" the innovations begun by John F. Kennedy. He spoke of Johnson's ability "to utilize his own extraordinary political talents to make the first session of the 89th Congress the most productive in a generation."[83] After further praise of the "Great Society," Fulbright said:

---

81. *Ibid.*
82. *Congressional Record,* 110, Part 15, p. 19786.
83. "Higher Education and the Crisis in Asia."

Then came Vietnam. The war had been going on for many years but before 1965 it had been a small and distant war and, as our leaders repeatedly assured us, a war which would be won or lost by the Vietnamese themselves. Then about a year ago it became clear that the Saigon government was about to lose the war and we radically changed our policy. Intervening with a large army of our own, we changed our role from adviser to principal belligerent and expanded what was essentially a civil war into a contest between the United States and Asian communism.[84]

Senator Fulbright thus indicated the importance of the Vietnam War issue in the change in his thinking regarding not only President Johnson but the larger issue of presidential power in general. While Vietnam was important, however, it was not the only issue. On January 29, 1970, one of the present authors asked Senator Fulbright: "It it weren't for Vietnam would there be so much concern about presidential power?" The Senator made this response:

It is the symbol of the distortion of our relationships between the executive and the Congress. It could have been something else. We might have intervened in the Middle East or been dragged into the Congo. It could have been any one of those places. I think the President went pretty far this morning in a statement for which there is no Constitutional basis; that is there is no treaty. There is no commitment of that kind. If you take his words literally it almost gives a carte blanche to the Israelis—anything they want they get.[85]

In 1967 Fulbright made this statement, which indicated that his concern over presidential power went beyond Vietnam:

The cause of the constitutional imbalance is crisis. I do not believe that the Executive has willfully usurped the constitu-

---

84. *Ibid.*
85. Interview with J. William Fulbright. President Nixon had sent a message to the Conference of Presidents of major American Jewish Organizations, which was meeting in Washington. The message included the statement that "we will not hesitate to provide arms . . . as the need arises." See *New York Times*, January 26, 1970, p. 5.

tional authority of the Congress; nor do I believe that the Congress has knowingly given away its traditional authority, although some of its members—I among them, I regret to say —have sometimes shown excessive regard for Executive freedom of action.[86]

Despite the fact that Fulbright's stated concern over the presidential power issue went far beyond Vietnam, the war there has been an object of his major opposition, and it has highlighted his views as perhaps other issues could have, but did not. He opposed the war because of what he considered to be the useless loss of American lives and property, the loss of Asian lives and property, the loss of friends such as Sweden, the fact that federal power was becoming more centralized, and because of the undemocratic character of the South Vietnamese government.[87] In his doubts about the existence of political advantage for the United States in its emphasis on military matters in Southeast Asia and elsewhere, Fulbright was supported by Professor Hans J. Morgenthau of the University of Chicago, whom Fulbright often quotes in his speeches.[88] Fulbright himself advocated for South Vietnam *self-determination* and *neutralization*.[89]

In July 1966 President Johnson announced an "Asian Doctrine," which was aimed at defeating aggression on that continent and, according to Vice-President Humphrey, also aimed at "realizing the dream of the Great Society in the great area of Asia, not just here at home."[90] Fulbright opposed the doctrine in a Senate speech:

---

86. *Hearings* before the Subcommittee on Separation of Powers, p. 42.
87. The Senator has spoken extensively on his reasons for opposing the Vietnam War. Many of the best sources have already been cited. An excellent summary of his objection is contained in J. William Fulbright, "Vietnam: A Proposal for the Democratic Party in 1968," statement to the Platform Committee of the Democratic National Committee, August 20, 1968. Fulbright files, Washington, D. C.
88. U. S. Congress, Senate, Committee on Foreign Relations, *What is Wrong with Our Foreign Policy, Hearings* before the Committee on Foreign Relations, Senate, 86th Cong., 1st sess., April 15, 1959.
89. "Vietnam: A Proposal for the Democratic Party in 1968." Emphasis in original.
90. Quoted in *The Arrogance of Power*, p. 53.

The emerging Asian doctrine about which so much is currently being said and written represents a radical departure in American foreign policy in that it is virtually unlimited in what it purports to accomplish and unilateral in its execution. Without reference to the United Nations and with only perfunctory reference to the nonfunctioning SEATO treaty, the United States on its own has undertaken to win a victory for its protégés in the Vietnamese civil war and thereupon to build a "great society" in Asia, whatever that might turn out to mean. I think it is extremely important that the Senate, which used to be asked for its advice and consent on major foreign commitments, consider some of the sweeping implications of the Asian doctrine before it becomes an irrevocable national commitment without the consent or even the knowledge of the Senate.[91]

On April 2, 1970, Senator Fulbright made a major Senate speech updating his "old Myths and New Realities" theme. He said that the "master myth" was that Vietnam really mattered to American security. In fact, a friendly government there would be a convenience, but not a necessity. The importance of Indochina in United States policy arises from the "most indestructible myth of them all: the myth of the international Communist conspiracy." This myth, according to Fulbright, has persisted because of American leaders "whose education in Communism began—and ended—with Stalin." The Senator contended that we should accept the "new reality" that Indochina is North Vietnam's "sphere of influence," just as Eastern Europe is the Soviet Union's and Latin America is the United States."[92]

The escalation discussed above had its roots in the Gulf of Tonkin Resolution of August 7, 1964. This resolution followed two days after President Johnson's request for such a resolution in response to attacks by North Vietnamese torpedo boats on the destroyers *Maddox* and *C. Turner Joy*. Senator Fulbright served

---

91. U. S. Congress, Senate, Senator Fulbright speaking on "The Asian Doctrine," 89th Cong., 2d sess., July 22, 1966, *Congressional Record,* 112, Part 13, p. 16806.
92. U. S. Congress, Senate, Senator Fulbright speaking on "Old Myths and New Realities–I," U. S. Cong., 2d sess., April 2, 1970, *Congressional Record,* 116, No. 51, pp. S 4928, S 4929.

as Senate floor manager of the resolution, and he recommended its approval after only perfunctory hearings. The American vessels were said by Secretary of Defense Robert McNamara to have been carrying out routine patrol operations in international waters of the sort that are done at all times over the world.[93] The Senate vote on the resolutions, as has been said earlier, was 88 to 2.

Later hearings created doubts about whether or not the attack actually took place, although even Senator Morse, one of the two who voted against the resolution, conceded that a "minor engagement" occurred.[94] Senator Fulbright determined at the 1968 hearings, however, that no damage was done to the American ships. More important was the finding that the American destroyers were equipped with "electronic spy equipment"; this was in the form of a "black box" that was used to "stimulate the electronic instruments of North Vietnam, to frighten them, to create the jitters."[95] The ships got as close to North Vietnam as four miles.[96]

The facts of the patrol in question are subject to dispute, both with respect to what they really were and with respect to what they signified. The Johnson Administration later used the resolution as justification for the escalation of the war, and it was termed by Under-Secretary of State Katzenbach as "the functional equivalent" of a declaration of war.[97] Senator Fulbright came to regard the Resolution as a "mistake." He admitted later that his partisan support for Johnson had influenced his actions, since he thought Barry Goldwater's election would have been a

93. U. S. Congress, Senate, Committee on Foreign Relations, *The Gulf of Tonkin, The 1964 Incidents, Hearings* before the Committee on Foreign Relations, Senate, 90th Cong., 2d sess., February 20, 1968, pp. 9, 10.
94. U. S. Congress, Senate, Committee on Foreign Relations, *Foreign Assistance Act of 1968, Part 1—Vietnam, Hearings* before the Committee on Foreign Relations, Senate, on S. 3091, 90th Cong., 2d sess., March, 1968, p. 31.
95. *Foreign Assistance Act of 1968, Part 1, Vietnam, Hearings*, p. 31. See also *The Gulf of Tonkin, The 1964 Incidents, Hearings*, pp. 24–26.
96. *The Gulf of Tonkin, The 1964 Incidents, Hearings*, p. 27.
97. *U. S. Commitments to Foreign Powers, Hearings*, p. 82.

"disaster for the country."[98] In 1967 Fulbright summed up why he regarded the speedy passage of the Resolution as an error in procedure as well as a mistake on the particular matter:

> The error of those of us who piloted this resolution through the Senate with such undeliberate speed was in making a personal judgment when we should have made an institutional judgment. Figuratively speaking, we did not deal with the resolution in terms of what it said and in terms of the power it would vest in the Presidency; we dealt with it in terms of how we thought it would be used by the man who occupied the Presidency. Our judgment turned out to be wrong, but even if it had been right, even if the Administration had applied the resolution in the way we then thought it would, the abridgment of the legislative process and our consent to so sweeping a grant of power was not only a mistake but a failure of responsibility on the part of the Congress. Had we debated the matter for a few days or even for a week or two, the resolution most probably would have been adopted with as many or almost as many votes as it actually got, but there would have been a legislative history to which those of us who disagree with the use to which the resolution has been put could now repair. The fundamental mistake, however, was in the giving away of that which was not ours to give. The war power is vested by the Constitution in the Congress, and if it is to be transferred to the executive, the transfer can be legitimately effected only by constitutional amendment, not by inadvertency of Congress.[99]

In his 1970 interview with present author Lynn, Senator Fulbright gave additional insights into his later views on the resolution and the strength of his convictions on the subject:

> The Gulf of Tonkin Resolution was used by the President as a substitute for the declaration of war. The way he got it was entirely unorthodox and out of line. . . . I still think the only protection is to follow the Constitution in that respect. The reason for it is the assumption that 100 men in the Senate have some contribution to make. The basics are the very es-

---

98. *The Arrogance of Power*, p. 52.
99. *Congressional Record*, 113, Part 15, p. 20704.

sence of democracy. If you think the President is wiser in his sole judgment then you are saying that the Constitution is obsolete. In view of the terrible disaster that he got us into, I think there is still the possibility of a wiser decision if the Congress, or in these particular cases, the Senate itself were given an opportunity to consider the subject.

. . . When they brought the Gulf of Tonkin Resolution in, they brought it to the House, passed it unanimously, and they brought it to the Senate about 9 o'clock. The main thrust was that this is a psychological matter. The North Vietnamese have attacked us on the high seas with absolutely no provocation on our part. They attacked our ships and we must react immediately and by show of unity show we are behind the President. (Of course, we had responded and bombed the hell out of them.) Why, *they* were widening the war. The whole purpose of this resolution was to prevent the widening of the war, to prevent the spreading of the war, and to prevent North Vietnam from having any illusions about our purposes. This is the way to stop this from becoming a major conflict—that was the whole thrust of it. Now it is extremely important that it be done *now*—I mean *today*. Under the impact of being told that our ships, peaceful men are going along on these ships and these dreadful Communists came out and attacked them without any reason, everybody's emotions were aroused. You can't stand for this and so on. Everybody was unanimous in the House and in the Senate no one suspected this wasn't true.[100]

Supporters of the resolution, of course, continue to hold the opposing view. This view was forcefully developed by former Vice-President Humphrey in his interview with one of the authors (Lynn) on January 9, 1970:

It really isn't that important as to whether or not they got all the facts because you can always drag up another incident or fact. I think we got most of the facts. But what was important was the decision that was made. Here is what was said in the Gulf of Tonkin Resolution—they didn't recite all the little details or the little whereases. It was resolved that the President of the United States is hereby authorized to take

---

100. Interview with J. William Fulbright.

whatever steps are necessary, including the use of the Armed Forces of the United States to defend American Forces, to defend American manpower, ships etc., and to resist aggression in this area. Now, no Senator can come to Hubert Humphrey and say that he didn't know what he was voting on. I was the majority whip. I was there. I was in the debate. I heard the questions asked. Questions were asked of Senator Fulbright— Does this mean that the President of the United States is hereby authorized to send American forces into Vietnam? And the answer was, "It does and you need to know it." If you look in the *Congressional Record,* I said the same thing as majority whip. I said I don't think any Senator here should be under any misapprehension. . . . What the Resolution said was if we were fired on, if we ever got into trouble, Mr. President, you are authorized hereby to protect the American forces and if need be, to use the Armed Forces of the United States not only to protect our own people but also to resist aggression. Now the Congress can go around and pretend they didn't know what was in that Resolution but they did know.

. . . Now, if the Senate is going to say that because a couple of shots were fired at a destroyer we became so emotional that we had no more judgment—then they have disqualified themselves to give advice and consent.[101]

Despite such reasoning, Senator Fulbright continues to look back on the resolution that he backed in 1964 as a mistake and as the product of deception by President Johnson in his dealings with the Senate.

Senator Fulbright's attitude shifted from one of unquestioning support in 1964 to good-humored disagreement in 1965, when he was still able to make this statement: ". . . I emphasize that I speak as an individual Senator and not as a representative of President Johnson." He went on to point out that the American system of separation of powers has advantages:

It frees a Senator from responsibility for an Administration's policies and it frees the executive from responsibility for a

---

101. Interview with Hubert H. Humphrey.

Senator's speeches—an arrangement for which both at times are profoundly grateful.[102]

Before long, however, opposition reached the point where such soft touches as these were absent. The deep disagreement with the Administration over Vietnam has been cited above.

Aside from the major issues themselves, such as the Dominican Republic and the Gulf of Tonkin, a principal aggravating factor in the deterioration of Fulbright's support of Johnson was the nature of the briefings the Senator received from the President. To this could be added the lack of real substantive consultation that Johnson sought from Fulbright. In the Dominican Republic matter, Fulbright recalled in 1967, he and others had been "summoned to the White House" to be told that Marines would be landed to protect the lives of American citizens:

> Had I known that the real purpose of our intervention was the defeat of the Dominican Revolution, as subsequently became clear in the course of extensive hearings before the Senate Foreign Relations Committee, I would most certainly have objected to massive American military intervention.[103]

The method of consultation used by President Johnson came to be regarded by Senator Fulbright as basically defective. First is what Fulbright calls the "hastily arranged 'consultation'— really a briefing" at the White House, which puts Senators against a "psychological barrier."[104] This is because the White House is the President's home ground and it is difficult to "contradict kings in their palaces . . . with the freedom and facility with which one contradicts the King's Ministers in Parliament or the President's Cabinet members in Committee."[105] Second is

---

102. J. William Fulbright, "The Commonwealth and the United States in Eastern Asia," speech delivered at the Eleventh Parliamentary Conference, Wellington, New Zealand, December 8, 1965. Fulbright files, Washington, D. C.
103. *Hearings* before the Subcommittee on Separation of Powers, p. 45.
104. *Ibid.* p. 48.
105. *Ibid.*

the fact that such consultations do not involve *listening* on the part of the President.[106] Proper consultation should start with a preliminary consultation of "provisional views," with the Administration receptive to the views of the Senators present.[107] President Johnson did not use this approach.

The consultation technique President Johnson did employ was strongly criticized by Senator Fulbright in his interview with author Lynn:

> In the case of President Johnson, I think his spokesman deliberately, deliberately may not be the right word, *affirmatively, positively* misled the Senate at the time of the Bay of Tonkin and on many other occasions would not consult with the Senate at all.[108]

The Senator described Johnson in these words:

> Now in the case of President Johnson, you had a man who is extremely active, a very dynamic and aggressive man, who had been a leader of the Senate, who understood the Congress and who knew how to subvert it, who knew how to push it around to get his way. He had done favors for many Senators. He knew how to play the political game. He was able to dominate the Senate and even the Congress for quite a while from the White House. This was not only because of his personality, but his knowledge of it. He had grown up in it. He had been in the House and in the Senate. He had studied under Sam Rayburn, and so forth.[109]

Fulbright had this to say about Johnson in connection with the Gulf of Tonkin incident:

> The President himself at that time, right at the beginning, about the time of the Gulf of Tonkin was himself in public statements saying that he was opposed to a wider war. He was opposed to American boys doing the fighting that Asians

106. *Congressional Record*, 113, Part 15, p. 20705. Emphasis in original.
107. *Congressional Record*, 113, Part 15, p. 20705.
108. Interview with J. William Fulbright.
109. *Ibid.*

should do. This is the grossest kind of deception it seems to me. When he was saying that publicly, he was promoting this intrusion into North Vietnam and getting ready for a major expansion of the war. I don't know how you deal with this kind of deception. Our system is based upon an assumption of a sort of a minimum of good faith. Democracy is not going to work at all with this kind of dealings. I don't know whether it can work. It has never worked in a country as big as ours and with such a complex society. I hope it will and we will do what we can to make it work, but it certainly has difficulties.[110]

The exact consultation process with President Johnson worked like this:

You get a phenomenon like Lyndon Johnson and he was very aggressive in the Senate. He made the Senate perform, that is act, quite affirmatively. He was a good operator in that sense. Then he goes to the White House and combines his knowledge of the Senate plus the power in the White House and you get an imbalanced creativity inside the government. It destroys what we think of as a normal balance, checks and balances between the legislature and executive. And yet he had his ways, very difficult for people to understand. It is difficult to describe it. When he had a controversial matter coming up, particularly in foreign affairs, he would invite what he called the "leadership" down for a "consultation." He wouldn't just consult, he would have all his top people in—Joint Chiefs, Secretary of State, Secretary of Defense, and the head of the CIA. He would always start out "We are all unanimous," and he would brief you and *then* he would call upon you. There would be about 15 or 20 of us—Speaker and the majority leader, etc. He would call upon you—"What do you think?" In effect he was endeavoring to commit you before you had ever had a hearing of your own, relying solely upon what you had been told just by his people. After a while this got to be in complete distortion of the whole system. He would say, "What do you think?" He would call, he wouldn't wait for them to volunteer. Formerly, whenever you went there with Eisenhower or Kennedy they would usually brief you and then you would go home. Usually no one committed themselves. Occasionally someone would say, "Well, you know Mr. President,

110. *Ibid.*

you are our leader and we follow you right down to the last"—
this was the tendency on the part of some people, particularly
like the Speaker, he was very warlike anyway. But most people
didn't commit themselves this way. But President Johnson
would insist upon it, and I just got so I would use every possible device to keep from going.[111]

The effect on Fulbright of this method of "consultation" may
not have been fully understood at the time by some of the President's closest advisers.

As the Senate reasserts its power, according to Fulbright, it
will be taking back authority that actually has been usurped by
the executive. Senator Fulbright expressed the point in this way:

> The concept of the President being permitted to do anything
> he likes in the field of foreign relations is a concept that has
> grown up. It is a misguided concept, dating back to certain
> resolutions adopted by the Senate, one relating to Formosa,
> in the Eisenhower administration, and one more recently in
> the Johnson administration, with respect to the Gulf of Tonkin.
> This has led some Senators to believe that there is no restraint
> whatever on any President; that he can do as he pleases. It is
> true that he has the power, but that does not mean he has the
> legitimate, constitutional right to use it.[112]

Other Senators have agreed with Fulbright. Senator Church
pointed out that the situation has gone so far that for Congress
to reassert its role is regarded by some members as an attempt
to usurp the power of the Executive.[113] Senator Ervin said that

---

111. *Ibid.* One writer reports that Johnson quit inviting Fulbright to
briefings; even Senator Mansfield sometimes did not include Fulbright
in briefings related to foreign affairs. Undoubtedly this and the differences
in viewpoints publicly expressed by members of the Committee on Foreign
Relations diminished Fulbright's power as Chairman. See Randall B. Ripley,
Power in the Senate (New York: St. Martin's Press, 1969), p. 11.
112. *Congressional Record,* 111, Part 19, p. 25623. On June 25, 1969 Senator
Tydings used this sentence: "But as we have become a world power, the
Executive has usurped the role of the Congress." *Congressional Record,*
115, No. 105, p. S 7151.
113. U. S. Congress, Senate, Committee on Foreign Relations, *What Is
Wrong With Our Foreign Policy, Hearings* before the Committee on Foreign
Relations, Senate, 85th Cong., 1st sess., April 15, 1959, p. 17.

in foreign policy Congress has submitted an ". . . abdication of its constitutional responsibilities."[114] Fulbright himself has stated that the check-and-balance system has been lost in foreign policy matters, and it must be reestablished.[115]

The Foreign Relations Committee did not agree with Nicholas Katzenbach's contention that the limit of presidential authority should be set "by the instinct of the nation and its leaders for political responsibility."[116] Fulbright has stated that the convenience of the President has often been confused with the national interest, and this must not be allowed to happen.[117] Assertion of its constitutional role by the Senate may well inconvenience or delay the administration, but in the interest of their constituents, Senators must insist on sufficient time to pursue adequate hearings on issues.[118]

One presidential practice that has brought special criticism from Senator Fulbright is that of presenting the Senate with a *fait accompli*. Upon such presentations, one of which Fulbright asserted took place with the Thailand military buildup in 1966, Congress is "counted on to come to heel."[119] For such causes the Senator considers reassertion of Congressional power in foreign policy to be essential.

One attempt to regain the foreign-policy position of the Senate was the passage of the Resolution on National Commitments in 1969.[120] Senator Fulbright first introduced the resolution on July 31, 1967, but he was unable to gain the necessary support until 1969. President Nixon did not mount major opposition to the resolution at the time of its passage, although the executive

114. U. S. Congress, Senate, Senator Ervin speaking on National Commitments, S. Res. 85, 91st Cong., 1st sess., June 25, 1969, *Congressional Record*, 115, No. 104, p. S 7122.
115. "Vietnam: A Proposal for the Democratic Party in 1968." See *Congressional Record*, 112, Part 18, pp. 24777, 24778.
116. Quoted in *Congressional Record*, 115, No. 104, p. S 7080.
117. *The Arrogance of Power*, p. 54.
118. *Ibid.*, pp. 54, 55.
119. *Congressional Record*, 112, Part 18, p. 24777. Fulbright used the same point in opposing the *fait accompli* approach in the Formosa Straits issue in 1955 and the Middle East question in 1957. See Grundy, pp. 392, 294.
120. See Appendix A.

branch went on record as opposing it in a letter of March 10, 1969, from Assistant Secretary of State William B. Macomber, Jr., to Fulbright. The letter also included this point:

> The executive branch tends to doubt the usefulness of attempting to fix by resolution precise rules codifying the relationship between the executive and legislative branches in the broad area of national commitments.[121]

Senator Fulbright is frank to admit that the resolution could not have won support in the House of Representatives:

> The House has been much less inclined to criticize the Vietnam policy. The Speaker of the House and the leadership have been all-out in support of the President, so this is a practical matter. I think at that time at least it would have been foolish to try to pass it in the House. If you do undertake to pass it in the Senate and the House as a concurrent resolution and it fails, you get nowhere. But in the Senate we did pass it, and the Senate has a special role in foreign relations in any case. Under the Constitution the Senate is the one that advises and consents to treaties and approves ambassadors and so on. So there is reason for taking it to the Senate rather than the House. However the commitment resolution doesn't just say the Senate, it says Congress. It's a sense of the Senate so there is nothing wrong with our saying the Congress in that connection.[122]

One factor that helped sway the Senate vote was the finding by Fulbright of a secret assurance given to Franco of Spain a year earlier.[123] The passage of the resolution after lengthy discussion in which many Senators expressed approval of his work

---

121. *National Commitments*, p. 35.
122. Interview with J. William Fulbright.
123. *National Commitments*, pp. 28, 29. "Secret Agreements," *New Republic*, July 26, 1969, p. 5. The commitment to Spain concerned the protection of American bases there, but could easily be interpreted as a commitment to defend the Franco government against internal disruptions.

stands as a major example of the exercise of effective leadership by Fulbright.[124]

Historian Henry Steele Commager, while very sympathetic to Senator Fulbright's objective of controlling the power of the President in foreign affairs, doubts that this resolution will accomplish that objective. Commager writes that the National Commitments Resolution would not have changed the reaction at the Gulf of Tonkin, since the SEATO treaty could have been invoked; it would not have prevented Eisenhower's intervention in Lebanon or the Pescadores, since these had a degree of Senate approval; it would not have prevented the intervention in the Dominican Republic in 1965, since protection of American lives was an issue. In addition, the President could always "have invoked the amorphous concept of 'vital interest.' "[125]

Despite these shortcomings the resolution stands as a major interim step in Senator Fulbright's campaign to restore the Senate to what he regards as its proper place in foreign-policy formulation.

124. For a sample of these opinions, see U. S. Commitments to Foreign Powers, Hearings, pp. 190, 191 and 236, 237; *Congressional Record,* 113, Part 15, pp. 20706–19; *Congressional Record,* 115, No. 102, pp. S 6878–914; *Congressional Record,* 115, No. 104, pp. S 7122–25; *Congressional Record,* 115, No. 105, pp. S 7122–53.
125. Henry Steele Commager, "Can We Limit Presidential Power?," *New Republic* (April 6, 1968), p. 17.

4

THE CONTINUING STRUGGLE

Upon first reading the public pronouncements and writings of Senator J. William Fulbright concerning the question of the proper role of the President in foreign-policy formulation, the impression of some sort of conspicuous inconsistency is gained. Probably no other authority has articulated both sides of the issue in such full form as has Fulbright. This seeming contradiction poses no difficulty for the Senator. He acknowledges mistakes in judgment and finds it difficult to understand those whose pride does not permit this kind of self-criticism and thus self-correction. This particular quality has been noted by Daniel Ellsberg. He observed that of all the officials connected with the passage of the Gulf of Tonkin Resolution Fulbright was the only one he had heard admit responsibility and regret, and he praised Fulbright for having the courage to acknowledge these publicly.[1]

Because of his ability to acknowledge error, Fulbright finds it difficult to be tolerant of Presidents like Johnson and Nixon, who seem to him overly concerned with their position in history. He may not be fully cognizant of the extent to which a President feels locked in by a past policy which, if changed, could seriously damage his prestige and reputation.

In a 1965 interview with Chalmers M. Roberts of the *Wash-*

---

1. Daniel Ellsberg, *Papers On the War* (New York: Simon and Schuster, 1972), p. 230. For an excellent discussion of Fulbright's personality see Betty Glad, "The Significance of Personality For Role Performance. As Chairman of the Senate Foreign Relations Committee: A Comparison of Borah and Fulbright," Paper delivered at the Annual Meeting of the American Political Science Association, September 3, 1969.

ington Post Senator Fulbright said: "I think the great merit of our system is that it's adaptable."[2] He also pointed out that the relationship between the Congress and the President . . . is nearly altogether dependent on the strength of the President."[3] By 1970 when he spoke with the author, Fulbright contrasted his general support of the Eisenhower foreign policy, which he characterized as "entirely too passive," with the changed circumstances later when the country had "an overbearing President."[4] He went on to make this point: "If I was a professor trying to perfect the long-term philosophy, I suppose I would come down on one or the other side, but I don't see how you can with much realism."[5] He also pointed out that the basic system of government is established by the Constitution, but "these systems are not self-executing."[6] They must be executed by men adapting their actions to changing circumstances and personalities. The process, as scholar Hans Morgenthau has put it, is "a continuous struggle."[7] Fulbright agrees.

The adaptable approach is always opposed by those who regard themselves as the possessors of a great and ultimate truth. Sometimes these "truths" are based on historical analogy. Modern American foreign policy has been influenced by the desire not to repeat the errors of 1919, and they have been significantly shaped by a desire not to commit the sort of "appeasement" that is commonly supposed to have encouraged Hitler in the 1930s. In fighting in Vietnam, Fulbright thinks, we are excessively preoccupied with the desire to avoid another Munich.[8] A more

---

2. Reprinted in *Congressional Record*, 111, Part 21, p. 28390.
3. *Ibid.*
4. Interview with J. William Fulbright.
5. *Ibid.*
6. *Ibid.*
7. U. S. Congress, Senate, Committee on Foreign Relations, *What is Wrong With Our Foreign Policy, Hearings*, before the Committee on Foreign Relations, Senate, 86th Cong., 1st sess., April 15, 1959, p. 17.
8. J. William Fulbright, "Vietnam: A Proposal for the Democratic Party in 1968," statement to the Platform Committee of the Democratic National Committee, August 20, 1968, Fulbright files, Washington, D. C. Also see Henry F. Graff, "Thinking Aloud: Participatory Foreign Policy," *New Leader* (March 2, 1970), p. 11.

pragmatic approach, however, does not learn more from an event
than there is in it to learn. The pragmatist also is not concerned
with implementing doctrines. Such doctrines, Fulbright relates,
guided the abolitionists of the North and the "hotheads" of the
South in the Civil War. They guided the "puritan spirits" whose
slogans like "manifest destiny" led to our "unhappy adventure
in imperialism" in 1898.[9] It guides those who feel that national
honor can accept nothing less than victory in Vietnam.[10] Fulbright has quoted Robert Southey's 1798 poem "The Battle of
Blenheim" to illustrate the futility of the "total victory" goal:

> "And everybody praised the Duke,
> Who this great fight did win."
> "But what good came of it at last"
> Quoth little Peterkin.
> "Why, that I cannot tell," said he;
> "But 'twas a famous victory."[11]

Perhaps the most constant theme in Senator Fulbright's thought
is his propensity to quote Tocqueville to support his positions
in such diverse writings as the 1961 *Cornell Law Quarterly* article
and *The Arrogance of Power*.[12] Beyond this he is both adaptable
and flexible.

Fulbright's philosophy affects his approach to a number of
issues besides the basic one of Presidential power in foreign
policy. One such issue is foreign aid. Where he had once spoken
convincingly of the need for long-term foreign aid where there
were long-term developmental projects, in 1966, when he was

---

9. J. William Fulbright, "Ideology and Foreign Policy," The George
Huntington Williams Memorial Lecture, John Hopkins University, Baltimore, Maryland, March 12, 1965. Fulbright files, Washington, D. C.
10. Professor Henry F. Graff of Columbia University terms this the desire to "nail the coonskin to the wall." Graff, p. 11.
11. "Ideology and Foreign Policy." Fulbright also said, "The West has
won two 'total victories' in this century and it has barely survived them"
in the same speech.
12. J. William Fulbright, "American Foreign Policy in the 20th Century
Under an 18th-Century Constitution," *Cornell Law Quarterly* 47 (Fall
1961): 13 and J. William Fulbright, *The Arrogance of Power* (New York:
Vintage Books, 1966), p. 28.

trying to restrain the administration, he changed to advocacy of an annual review. His main reason for this was the fact that foreign aid to Vietnam had been given by Dean Rusk as a basis for the commitment of 3,000,000 troops there.[13] Where once he opposed those Senators who used the foreign-aid hearings as a vehicle for airing their foreign-policy opposition to the President, by 1968 Fulbright was doing so himself.[14]

His opposition to reliance on the military has been one of the most constant points in the Senator's thought, but he has been flexible in his reasons for this opposition. His principal reversal on a military matter, that over the Gulf of Tonkin Resolution, has already been discussed; political support for Johnson as against Goldwater was a major reason for this aberration.[15] Back in the 1950s he opposed military intervention in the Middle East as alienating the "ordinary people" of that region, and he opposed the military portion of foreign aid as shoring up despotic regimes when the money could better have been applied to other projects.[16] The dominant position of military factors in our foreign policy upset Fulbright later, as did the apparent lack of control in Congress over the "military-industrial complex."[17] The influence of the military in introducing into the intellectual community such concepts as "megadeaths" to describe what is really "hideous carnage" revolted the Senator.[18] When the anti-ballistic-missile debate of 1967 took place Fulbright was eager

13. *Congressional Record*, 112, Part 12, p. 16021.
14. *Ibid.* Fulbright quoted from a speech Dean Rusk made in Las Vegas on February 16, 1966, in which he gave as one reason for American commitment to Vietnam "the aid approved by bipartisan majorities in Congress over a period of twelve years."
15. U. S. Congress, Senate, Committee on Foreign Relations, *Foreign Assistance Act of 1968, Part 1, Vietnam, Hearings*, before the Committee on Foreign Relations, Senate, on S. 3091, 90th Cong., 2d sess., March, 1968, p. 57.
16. Alex Campbell, "Fulbright on Camera," *New Republic* (May 21, 1966), p. 19.
17. *Congressional Record*, 104, Part 11, p. 13908. Also see *Congressional Record*, 105, Part 9, p. 12274.
18. J. William Fulbright, "The Cold War in American Life," speech at the University of North Carolina 1965 Symposium "Arms and the Man: National Security and the Aims of a Free Society," April 5, 1964, Fulbright files, Washington, D. C.

to join it, not only because of what he regarded the ill-advised nature of the proposal, but because it became a "symbolic" issue. The ABM controversy was the first large-scale confrontation between the President and the Congress on a military spending matter and Senator Fulbright hoped it would become a turning point as Congress reasserted its constitutional prerogative to control military spending.[19]

In his interview with author Lynn in 1970 the Senator regarded the invasion of another country without Congressional approval as something he would oppose regardless of the passive or overactive nature of the President who did it:

> Well, I don't think troops should be sent abroad at any time, whether it's a weak or strong President, without the authorization of Congress. There is a difference now. We make the clear distinction between repelling an attack, nobody is contesting that; you have the right to defend yourself and brothers. But to go into a foreign country where we don't have any bases or interests there and attack someone else, is going pretty far. I wouldn't have much trouble defending that no matter what kind of President it is.[20]

With the Presidency of Richard M. Nixon Senator Fulbright has another presidential "style" and personality to deal with. Fulbright rates Nixon as another President of the overactive type. Fulbright deplored Nixon's pledge of military support to Israel. He also opposed the "secret war" that he believed Nixon was fighting at that time in Laos.[21] A few weeks later Fulbright expressed in the Senate his opposition to American participation in combat in Laos.[22] On March 11, 1970, Senator Fulbright intro-

19. J. William Fulbright, "We Must Not Fight Fire With Fire," *New York Times Magazine,* April 23, 1967, p. 122.
20. U. S. Congress, Senate, Committee on Foreign Relations, *Psychological Aspects of Foreign Policy, Hearings* before the Committee on Foreign Relations, Senate, 91st Cong., 1st sess., 1969. Also see U. S. Congress, Senate, Senator Fulbright speaking against ABM, S. 2546, 91st Cong., 1st sess., July 25, 1969, *Congressional Record,* 115, No. 125, pp. S 8601, S 8602.
21. Interview with J. William Fulbright.
22. *Ibid.*

duced Senate Resolution 368, which was referred to the Committee on Foreign Relations:

Whereas, the United States has not by treaty or other constitutional procedure undertaken to engage American military forces in combat in Laos; and

Whereas, United States Air Force and other American military personnel have nevertheless become increasingly involved in, and have suffered casualties as a result of, combat activities in Laos, distinct from the interdiction of military supplies or forces destined for South Vietnam; and

Whereas, the full nature and extent of U. S. military involvement in Laos has not been completely communicated to the American people: Now, therefore be it

Resolved, that it is the sense of the Senate that the Constitution of the United States requires that authority for the use of United States armed forces in combat in or over Laos must be predicated upon "affirmative action taken by the executive and legislative branches of the United States Government through means of a treaty, convention or other legislative instrumentality specifically intended to give effect" to the commitment of American forces in Laos as agreed to by the Senate in the so-called commitment resolution (S. Res. 85, 91st Congress, 1st session.)[23]

By the introduction of this additional resolution Senator Fulbright futilely attempted to force the administration to live up to the spirit and the letter of the National Commitments Resolution.

Essentially, Senator Fulbright remains skeptical of alleged "solemn commitments" and claimed "vital interests."[24] As he does so, however, he maintains a flexible posture which, on another day and under changed circumstances, could yet find him encouraging a chief executive to exercise more initiative in foreign policy and urging his colleagues not to block the President as he

23. U. S. Congress, Senate, Senator J. William Fulbright speech, "What is the National Interest of the United States in Laos?" 91st Cong., 2d sess., March 3, 1970, *Congressional Record*, 116, No. 31, pp. S 2818–20.

24. U. S. Congress, Senate, Senator Fulbright's submission of a resolution to express the sense of the Senate on armed forces in Laos, S. Res. 368, 91st Cong., 2d sess., March 11, 1970, *Congressional Record*, 116, No. 37, p. S 3507.

does so. The Senator does this with the avowed intent of holding to as few doctrines and dogmas as he can and meeting problems as they come without taking backward glances to make sure he is not contradicting an earlier assertion.

Another conclusion that could follow is that Senator Fulbright is concerned about presidential power only when the President takes action in foreign policy with which he disagrees. This, of course, is the privilege of an experienced politician.

The relationship between the President and the Congress has been described as the "Achilles' heel of United States foreign policy."[25] One author has stated that "the experience of the past three decades suggests that the question of the relationship between the two branches of government charged with control of American foreign policy will never be resolved satisfactorily."[26] It has become commonplace to say that there has been an increase in presidential power since World War II. This increase has been accepted by many members of Congress and many citizens as a by-product of the Cold War and the speed of decision needed in the atomic age. Despite his traditional lack of trust in the military, before 1965 Senator Fulbright generally supported giving the President a free hand in foreign policy. He held that the executive actions that in his view were mistakes (as in the Middle East in the 1950s) were probably less troublesome than would be the greater errors and the chaos of congressionally-led foreign policy. The war in Indochina, the invasion of the Dominican Republic in 1965, and his feeling that he was deceived by President Johnson in connection with the 1964 Gulf of Tonkin crisis increasingly led Senator Fulbright to change his mind and become a leading advocate of more congressional, and especially senatorial, power. He has conceded, however, that the reassertion of such Congressional power is not necessarily a permanent ad-

25. J. William Fulbright, "Political Semantics," speech before the American Society of Newspaper Editors, Washington, D. C., April 17, 1968. Fulbright files, Washington, D. C.
26. Daniel S. Cheever and H. Field Haviland, *American Foreign Policy and the Separation of Powers* (Cambridge: Harvard University Press, 1952), p. 172.

vantage; future events might call for a new era of more presidential supremacy in foreign policy.

The work of Senator Fulbright has thrust the executive-legislative relationship into renewed focus as an issue. Some of the implications of his thought for the development of a more satisfactory working relationship should certainly be considered. No one expects perfect harmony to take place, for this would be unattainable, and perhaps even undesirable. Hubert H. Humphrey stressed this important point in an interview:

> You must remember that there is a natural conflict, and rightly so, between the executive and the legislative. There is always arm's length suspicion. There always has been. This is part of the Constitutional process, checks and balances.[27]

The events of the Vietnam War, according to Senator Jacob Javits, have pointed ". . . the need to find a new 'check and balance' in the Congressional role in foreign policy. . . ."[28] This new relationship will need chiefly to be the product of the executive and legislative branches; the judicial branch will do little, if anything.[29] The statements of Senator Fulbright, and the statements of others in response to the Senator, suggest a number of approaches that may help to build a better working relationship between the President and Congress in the field of foreign-policy determination.

There is certainly room for improvements, and no careful review of the literature of this field can be made without the realization that an improved attitude of each group toward the other would be of help. Brooks Hays, who served with both the legislative and executive branches, has related a story that illustrates this point:

> When Mr. Hays was a US Representative from Arkansas, a

27. Melvin Small, "Democracy and Foreign Policy," *Journal of Conflict Resolution* 12 (June 1968): 252.
28. Interview with Hubert H. Humphrey.
29. Jacob K. Javits, "The Congressional Record in Foreign Relations," *Foreign Affairs* (January 1970), p. 226.

service station attendant once noticed the initials "MC" on the Congressman's license plate and speculated that they might stand for "mental case." Some years later, when Mr. Hays was Assistant Secretary of State for Congressional Relations, his grandson recalled the episode at the filling station. Pointing to the door of his grandfather's State Department office, the boy wondered of the initials "A.S.S." had an even more obvious and literal significance. "You know," observes Mr. Hays, "one of our real problems is to keep the people in the Executive Branch from thinking the folks up on the Hill are a bunch of mental cases, and to keep members of Congress from thinking those in the Executive are a bunch of asses."[30]

While both the Congress and the President must play important roles in working out a more constructive relationship in foreign-policy matters, it is appropriate to begin with the executive. In a 1963 speech Senator Fulbright summed up the rigorous tasks that faced the President in shaping a new kind of foreign policy for the 1960s:

He must lead our people to the acceptance of partial rather than complete solutions, to the acceptance of continuing responsibility rather than a single national effort. He must lead the American people toward a new consensus about the world and their place in it: one of patience as well as boldness, wisdom as well as resourcefulness, quiet determination as well as righteous dedication and, most of all, one of moral as well as physical courage.[31]

This statement sets an unrealistically high goal for the President, and it is inevitable that no man will be able to achieve it. While Fulbright somewhat unfairly expected the President to work near-miracles in the foreign-policy field, the President must also succeed in the wearing of his other hats: he must handle domestic problems, must respond to a variety of interest and pressure groups, must lead his own party with its many factions, and must

30. "Notes: Congress, the President and the Power to Commit Forces to Combat," *Harvard Law Review* 81 (June 1968): 1794.
31. Quoted in Alton Frye, "Gobble 'uns and Foreign Policy: A Review," *Journal of Conflict Resolution* 8 (September 1964): 314.

contend with the need to win elections.

Despite the fact that the difficulties in carrying out the consultation process are very real, the need for better consultation is so great that the improvement of this process is of vast importance. Aside from the "assumption," as Senator Fulbright puts it, that "the 100 men in the Senate have some contribution to make," if Senators do intend to assert their prerogatives, the President should improve his consulting system purely as a matter of self-defense.[32]

As early as 1956 Senator Fulbright, on a television program, pointed out that while Senator George had been consulted on the Middle East problems, he had not been: "I was not consulted, but I haven't been consulted at any time by this Administration. All I know is what was in the paper."[33] As have others, the study that the Brookings Institution completed for the Senate Committee on Foreign Relations in 1960 assigned a high priority to better consultation:

> A greater effort should be made by the executive branch to consult, on a continuing and consistent basis, with Senators and Representatives, including those who are Members of the Senate Committee on Foreign Relations or the House Committee on Foreign Affairs. The Congress should give increased support to arrangements, such as the existing consultative subcommittees for the foreign policy committees, in order that full advantage may be taken of the opportunities for fruitful contacts between the executive and legislative branches.[34]

Casual consultations, such as the accidental one between Senator Fulbright and President Kennedy in 1961, would not fit this requirement, despite the value of some informal contacts.

Former Vice-President Humphrey has made a strong case for a systematic approach to presidential-congressional consultation:

32. J. William Fulbright, "Public Opinion and Foreign Policy," speech at Bowling Green University, Bowling Green, Ohio, March 9, 1963, Fulbright files, Washington, D. C.
33. Interview with J. William Fulbright.
34. "Martha Rountree's Press Conference," A.B.C. telecast, December 30, 1956, Fulbright files, Washington, D. C.

I think we are going to have to find a way and a mechanism by which the President can more closely collaborate with the Congress on foreign policy. I made a suggestion some years ago of establishing in Congress a Joint Committee on National Security that would be the counterpart of the President's National Security Council. This Joint Committee on National Security would consist of representatives of the House and Senate in the field of Foreign Affairs and Foreign Relations, of the Armed Services of the two Houses, of the Joint Committee on Atomic Energy and of the Appropriations Committee. These would be the top committees of the Congress that deal with matters of national security and foreign policy. You would have the Chairman and the ranking Republican member of each of these committees—House and Senate. You would also have the majority leader of the House and the majority leader of the Senate, the majority whip of the House and the minority whip of the Senate and the Speaker of the House. This would give you the top echelon leaders of the Congress that could meet regularly with the President and his cabinet leaders. . . . I believe this would be helpful. I think our real problem on foreign affairs with the Congress is a lack of steady, regular communications and the fact that Congress is broken up into committee jurisdictions organized in a way that makes it difficult for it to effectively participate either in the administration of foreign policy or even in consultation. It is very easy for the executive branch under the present arrangement to play off one group against another—the Armed Services Committee against the Foreign Relations. . . . You can't even go to the Joint Committee on Atomic Energy even when you have the best and the highest clearance for other committees. So you have a kind of separatism, a fragmentation of the whole concept of national security in the Congress. Now this plays right into the hands of an executive, of a President that really wants to ignore or bypass Congress. I don't think any President really wants to bypass Congress, but I think he finds it very difficult to know how to work with it because of the way they are organized. The President has to make *ad hoc* arrangements when the country is in crisis. When you have the Dominican crisis, the Laotion situation in 1961–1962; when you have the Vietnam crisis at the Gulf of Tonkin, the President hastily calls together leaders of both parties, leaders of committees, calls them over to the White House, has a talk with them, and

then we go back to the normal processes of Congress again with
whatever needs to be done.[35]

The argument is heard that the speed with which events occur
in the modern world precludes prior consultation in many cases.
In most modern cases, such as the movement of troops to Iceland,
the sending of troops to Lebanon, and the invasion of Cambodia,
prior approval of Congress could have been sought.[36] In the
highly unusual cases where time does not permit full consultation
and approval before action is taken, such a consultation effort
can still be made by the President simultaneously with his policy
action.[37] Senator Fulbright has stressed the right of Senators
to know what is happening before it happens:

> I think the President doesn't have to take anybody's advice,
> but the Congress and the Senate is [sic], I think, entitled, if
> we operate our system properly, to be aware of what is being
> done before it is finally done. I mean in most cases, even if it
> doesn't require prior action by the Senate. But I think this
> makes for good government if they are not kept in the dark.
> This is the least you can expect in a democratic system—that
> the Congress and the people be aware, to know what is going
> on. They shouldn't be asked to sacrifice their lives and their
> property without even knowing what is going on.[38]

The Executive should maintain a receptive attitude to the
thoughts of the members of Congress as he consults with them.
Consultation should involve the President's "listening" as well
as his talking, and moreover he should listen with an "open
mind."[39] The consultations with President Johnson where he

35. U. S. Congress, Senate, Committee on Foreign Relations. *The Formulation and Administration of United States Foreign Policy*, study prepared
at the request of the Committee on Foreign Relations, Senate, by the
Brookings Institution pursuant to S. Res. 336, 85th Cong., and S. Res. 31,
86th Cong., No. 9, Committee Print, 86th Cong., 2d sess., January 13, 1960.
36. Interview with Hubert H. Humphrey.
37. "Notes," *Harvard Law Review*, p. 1798.
38. *Ibid.*, p. 1797.
39. Interview with J. William Fulbright.

merely told Senator Fulbright and others that he was "gonna do so and so," did little for Senator Fulbright except to build opposition to the President's effort to secure a commitment before, or without, formal hearings.[40] The President cannot expect to build an effective long-term relationship with Senators when he attempts to use consultations as a means of securing agreement from men who have not had a reasonable opportunity to form an opposing viewpoint.[41]

Vice-President Hubert Humphrey supported Fulbright's position when he said:

> Having said all of this I don't believe that we will be able to continue in the foreseeable future with quite the same degree of autonomy of the President in exercising judgment on foreign policy decisions. He is going to have to find and we are going to have to design with the Congress ways to communicate; otherwise we are going to get into a log jam.[42]

In the opinion of responsible observers, among them Fulbright, the process of security classification has been used by the executive in order to control the nature of information that reaches Congress. For example, writing in *Foreign Affairs*, Senator Jacob K. Javits of New York expressed the conviction that "it becomes apparent" that information about the Anti-Ballistic Missile was given to Congress on "a highly selective basis by Administration witnesses."[43] He went on to say, "Diligent and imaginative probing often uncovers additional classified information which supports opposite conclusions."[44] Congressional scrutiny can often lead to declassification of formerly classified information that was classified "more for the sake of bureaucratic convenience than for legitimate national security reasons."[45] This argument is not a new one, and some writers stress the fact that classified

40. "Notes," *Harvard Law Review*, p. 1797.
41. Interview with J. William Fulbright.
42. *Ibid.* See also Andrew Kopkind, "The Speechmaker," *New Republic* (October 2, 1965), p. 16.
43. Interview with Hubert H. Humphrey.
44. Javits, p. 224.
45. *Ibid.*

material is often made available to committees when they meet in executive session.

Senator Fulbright has been among the members of the Congress who have objected to habitual executive claims of the need for secrecy. In October 1960 Fulbright asked Secretary of State Herter for a transcript of a conversation in Russia between Vice President Nixon and Premier Khrushchev. He was answered not by Herter, but by Assistant Secretary of State William B. Macomber, Jr. Macomber made this statement:

> the Department does not normally make public records of such conversations between high Government officials and it does not plan to do so in this instance.[46]

To treat the Chairman of the Senate Committee on Foreign Relations as merely part of the "public" does not seem to be good judgment, and to do so in a letter from an official an echelon lower than the one addressed is not likely to build Senatorial support.

In 1969 Senator Fulbright made this criticism of the security process as a means of preventing the Congress from learning relevant information:

> Congress, in trying to appraise executive branch policies on national security matters is, in effect, playing a game where the rules are revised at will by the opposing side. Conflict is inevitable under our system of separation of powers but when one coequal branch of the Government, under the guise of security, withholds any information it chooses, and releases that information piecemeal in an effort to make its case, the democratic process suffers.
>
> There are few real secrets in the operations of a democratic Government as anyone who reads the *New York Times*, the *Washington Post*, or *Aviation Week*, knows. Much of the information given the Committee on Foreign Relations on a classified basis either has already appeared in print, or appears in print shortly thereafter—through executive branch leaks.[47]

46. *Ibid.*
47. Correspondence between Senator J. William Fulbright and officials of the Department of State. Fulbright files, Washington, D. C.

If the executive seeks Senate support, he must be more open with information than has often been the case in the past. At the same time, if the Senate is brought in more closely, members may have to observe a somewhat higher standard of discretion and responsibility than they have in the past. Former Vice President Humphrey observed that

> one of the reasons for it is when you go before too many members of the Congress with anything that is highly sensitive you just as well put it right out in the *New York Times*. And that's a fact. Now, that's why you have to have some mechanism. When we have one, for example, no information ever gets out about the relationship of the executive branch to the Appropriations Committee on Central Intelligence, because the people, and they are consulted, just understand that this is something you don't talk about.[48]

Presidents have sometimes been inclined to make commitments to various powers on what appears to be a casual basis. President Nixon's action of this type expressing assurances of backing for Israel in a routine speech to a Jewish group has already been cited in an earlier chapter. This practice is objected to strongly by Senator Fulbright, and it should be used as little as possible by a President who wishes to build good relations with potentially critical members of Congress. In 1969 Fulbright spoke out vigorously against statements of sweeping commitments which have been made to various nations by Presidents and Secretaries of State. The question being discussed involved the Philippines, but the point the Senator made was a general one.[49]

The problem that occurs in this instance is that the executive uses speeches to various groups at home and abroad to build political support or friendly relations. If such statements are not taken seriously by the speaker or the listeners, no difficulty arises. Members of Congress may need to tolerate some verbal commitments that are made lightly to gain popularity, but the

---

48. *Congressional Record,* 115, No. 67, p. S 4884.
49. Interview with Hubert H. Humphrey.

executive must control this process so that a high price in "national honor" is not collected in return for a moment's applause.

There are a number of ways in which the Executive can establish a better relationship with Congress on foreign policy. Even if a President is not concerned about such action, however, the Congress itself has a wide range of available options to exercise a fuller voice in foreign policy within the present processes of government. Congress can give advice more insistently than the President might wish, and it can often couple the giving of advice with effective means of seeing to it that such advice is taken.[50] If advice is consistently rejected, Congress can take "revenge," as one author puts it.[51] This in time will give the Chief Executive a message he can not continue to ignore indefinitely. Morgenthau has termed the restoration of congressional initiative in foreign policy with the instruments at its disposal as both "a great opportunity" and "a solemn obligation."[52] Congress does have power; what Senator Fulbright has advocated is the concerted will to use it.

Perhaps the most available tool possessed by the Congress is insistence on the holding of hearings on foreign-policy issues before and after a decision is made. This can replace mere acquiescence to the policy and the preferences of the President. Senator Fulbright, as has been pointed out, has exercised this insistence on hearings, in addition to his vigorous advocacy of the practice. This use of hearings is suggested in the Brookings Institution report of the proper functions of Congress in foreign policy: "It can help, as part of its investigatory function, to evaluate the

---

50. U. S. Congress, Senate, Committee on Foreign Relations, *United States Security Agreements and Commitments Abroad: The Republic of the Philippines, Hearings* before the Subcommittee on the United States Security Agreements and Commitments Abroad of the Committee on Foreign Relations, Senate, 91st Cong., 1st sess., 1969, pp. 17, 18.
51. Robert A. Dahl, *Congress and Foreign Policy* (New York: W. W. Norton, 1964), p. 151.
52. *Ibid.*, p. 111. Dahl says this revenge may take the form of harassing "the executive by investigations, by using the appropriations process to weaken the organization or to secure policy changes, by legislating certain personnel out of office, and if need be by modifying the statute itself."

performance of the executive on a selective basis."[53] In this functioning Congress plays a role comparable to that of "Her Majesty's Loyal Opposition" in the British system.[54] By adroit questioning of administration witnesses the Congressional Committee can sometimes force the President to make up his own mind on an issue; former Defense Secretary McElroy termed this to "hold an administrator's feet in the fire."[55]

Hearings of this sort quickly become controversial, and it becomes difficult or impossible to present the sort of national unity that is often sought in American foreign policy. Senator Fulbright believes this price is worth paying, as his activities in the late 1960s so eloquently demonstrate, and as early as 1956 Fulbright decried the stifling of debate that he believed was inherent in the much-heralded "bipartisan" foreign policy.[56]

Some advocate the use of hearings, since they are milder than such other actions as Resolutions, denial of funds, and impeachment. In addition hearings do not reduce the authority of the President. This point was expressed in a *Christian Science Monitor* editorial that was reprinted in the *Congressional Record:*

> But the Senate can best boost its influence by convening competent committee hearings eliciting able testimony, by holding influential debates on the floor, and by showing its own ability to respond to crises with clarity and dispatch. Congress will not improve matters by curtailing the freedom of the executive—by restricting the President's preeminence in foreign policy and his ability to act speedily in tune with fast-moving events.[57]

Hearings have been especially effective as a technique for bringing to light the details of military spending.[58] They can also,

53. *What Is Wrong With Our Foreign Policy, Hearing*, p. 6.
54. *The Formulation and Administration of United States Foreign Policy*, p. 24.
55. Ernest S. Griffith, *Congress: Its Contemporary Role* (New York: New York University Press, 1967), p. 193.
56. Quoted in *ibid.*, p. 194.
57. "Martha Rountree's Press Conference."
58. *Christian Science Monitor*, Mary 20, 1969, reprinted in *Congressional Record*, 115, No. 102, p. S 6914.

if they are promptly used, discourage the use of the *fait acçompli*. Merlo Pusey points out that hearings may be inhibited, as they were in August of 1964 over the Gulf of Tonkin incidents, by a fear on the part of members of Congress that they would appear "unpatriotic."[59] If hearings are to become effective, such reluctance must be overcome, but in the light of political realities and the pressures on members of Congress this is not highly likely.

For the hearings process to be effective, Congress needs to have a better information-gathering system. In some cases the need for hearings might be lessened if Congress had access to more information from the Executive than it gets at present. Former Vice-President Humphrey put the matter this way:

> Well, the reason they don't get full information is because they don't have a system to get it. You can't be running around like you are trying to peddle shoes or underwear, going from one committee to another. What you have happen is the Secretary of Defense goes to the Armed Services Committee, he gives them a lot of information, then he is called over to the Foreign Relations Committee and there is maybe a degree of hostility there; they feel there that they have to drag the information out of him. Then he finally gets over to the Joint Committee on Atomic Energy where it is very secret and closed and he gives them all the information. The same thing is true of the President, he doesn't know where to go. I happen to believe that Congress must be brought in more and more into foreign policy decisions, but in order to get in you have to be able to find the road. You have to have a vehicle, a path or a conduit and today we simply do not have it.[60]

To get genuinely effective information, as has been mentioned above, a fuller degree of executive cooperation is needed.

Hearings can also serve as an important means for Congress to educate and influence the public on foreign policy. That public opinion lags behind the needed level of public understanding

59. Edward A. Kolodoziej, "Congressional Responsibility for the Common Defense: The Money Problem," *Western Political Quarterly* 16 (March 1963): 154.
60. Merlo J. Pusey, *The Way We Go to War* (Boston: Houghton Mifflin Company, 1969), p. 170.

has long been recognized.[61] Some leaders have expressed the thought that on occasion Congress has "feared the people."[62] Senator Fulbright has argued that the biggest obstacle to a re-evaluation of our China policy is "the fear of many government officials, *undoubtedly well-founded,* that even the suggestion of new policies toward China and Vietnam would provoke a vehement public outcry."[63] Roger Hilsman, however, concludes that Senators face relatively little pressure on foreign policy as compared to organized pressures they receive on domestic issues.[64] On the other hand, the public has come to look to the President for foreign-policy information and leadership.[65] Senator Fulbright has sought to involve the public in the foreign-policy-making process through the efforts of his Committee on Foreign Relations.[66] In 1966 at the time of the Vietnam hearings he expressed his objectives this way:

> In recent weeks the Senate Committee on Foreign Relations has engaged in an experiment in public education. With results thus far that seem to me highly satisfactory, the Committee has made itself available as a forum for the meeting of politicians and professors and, more broadly, as a forum through which recognized experts and scholars can help increase Congressional and public understanding of the problems associated with our involvement in Vietnam and our relations with Communist China.[67]

Naturally this "educational" function was on Fulbright's terms and under his control. Through these efforts he sought to restore

---

61. Interview with Hubert H. Humphrey.
62. *The Formulation and Administration of United States Foreign Policy,* p. 2.
63. Senator Frank Lausche quoted in *What Is Wrong With Our Foreign Policy, Hearings,* p. 21.
64. Quoted in Archibald T. Steele, *The American People and China* (New York: Published for the Council on Foreign Relations by McGraw Hill, 1966), pp. 213–14.
65. Roger Hilsman, "Congressional-Executive Relations and the Foreign Policy Consensus," *American Political Science Review* 52 (September 1958): 727, 728.
66. Stanley Hoffman, *Gulliver's Troubles, Or the Setting of American Foreign Policy* (New York: McGraw-Hill Book Company, 1968), p. 229.
67. *Hearings* before the Subcommittee on Separation of Powers, p. 52.

the Senate to the "creative leader" status that the Brookings study set as an objective.[68] One observer, Henry Steele Commager, sees the goal of such efforts as ridding ourselves as a nation of "our delusions of universalism and our obsession with communism and other ideological threats."[69]

A step beyond hearings is the passage of resolutions, such as the National Commitments Resolution. Through resolutions Congress can take a stronger and more specific position than it can with hearings. Resolutions also can express the specific sense of the Senate or House, or both. In this respect they are more authoritative than committee reports or hearings, for they may include the strongest statements possible. Hearings may air the views of nonmembers of Congress, and these may contain logic or carry prestige, but they lack authority. Even a single committee represents a limited group, not the majority view of the chamber that constitutes it. Some regard the ultimate force of even a resolution as small, since the President can ignore it, justifying actions contrary to it by reference to some treaty or some "vital interest."[70]

While a single resolution has only limited effect, the totality of the resolutions from which Presidents have gained authority for foreign-policy actions is substantial. By late 1969 and 1970 Senators Charles McC. Mathias and Mike Mansfield with several colleagues were attempting to seek a resolution to repeal the four resolutions under which Presidents have been conducting numerous actions: The Formosa Straits Resolution of 1955, The Middle East Resolution of 1957, The Cuban Resolution of 1962, and the Tonkin Gulf Resolution of 1964.[71] The proposed new resolution in addition to these repeals would also terminate the state of national emergency proclaimed by President Truman on December 16, 1950, which still remains in effect.[72] By March of

68. "Higher Education and the Crisis in Asia."
69. *The Formulation and Administration of United States Foreign Policy,* p. 23.
70. Henry Steele Commager, "Can We Limit Presidential Power?," *New Republic* (April 6, 1968), p. 18.
71. *Ibid.,* p. 17.
72. *Congressional Record,* 115, No. 203, pp. S 16017, S 16028. See Appendix A.

1970 the State Department was reported as stating that "we neither advocate nor oppose Congressional action" on the repeal resolution.[73] Senator Mansfield and Senator Fulbright praised this "neutral" and conciliatory position by the administration.[74] On May 1, 1970, after review by the Senate Foreign Relations Committee, the resolution was revised and resubmitted as a Concurrent Resolution, but its new form repealed only the Middle East and the Gulf of Tonkin Resolutions.[75]

Declarations of war are often regarded as obsolete and undesirable.[76] This is due, at least in part, to the commitment to "total victory," even through use of nuclear weapons, which is thought to be implied in a declaration of war. Senator Fulbright in 1957, however, when nuclear weapons were well developed, did not feel that this was a necessary restraint. He made this statement with respect to the Korean War and those who criticized President Truman for failing to seek a declaration:

> There were those who insisted that the President should have sought a declaration of war by the Congress, or some other ratification of his action. Hindsight tells me, speaking personally, that this probably would have been wise. But it also tells me that a Congress truly interested in preserving its prerogatives, itself could have asserted its undenied power to declare that a state of war existed, or for those who felt like it, that it did not exist.[77]

In early May of 1970, in response to the invasion of Cambodia, Senators McGovern, Hatfield, Goodell, and Hughes advocated either a declaration of war in Indochina or a veto of the conflict. The *Washington Post* editorialized that the real purpose of this

73. *Congressional Record*, 115, No. 203, pp. S. 16027–30. Also see U. S. Congress, Senate, Senator Charles McC. Mathias, "American Foreign Policy," speech delivered at St. John's College, Annapolis, Maryland, January 14, 1970 printed in 91st Cong., 2d sess., January 29, 1970 *Congressional Record*, 116, No. 10, pp. S 852, S 853.
74. *The Kansas City Times*, March 14, 1970, p. 18A.
75. *Ibid.*
76. Senate Concurrent Resolution 64; 91st Cong., 2d sess.; Calendar No. 838, May 1, 1970. See Appendix A.
77. "Notes," *Harvard Law Review*, p. 1802.

action was not to declare war, which the writer said would be "akin to madness," but to bring public attention to the alternative of vetoing the war.[78]

The power of the purse is perhaps the ultimate constitutional power short of impeachment for Congress to exercise, and the way in which it is exercised can have important foreign-policy implications. All spending must pass the approval of Congress and must be submitted by Congress to the test of economic feasibility.[79] This involves the weighing of such priorities as defense versus nondefense spending.

Former Vice-President Humphrey pointed out that while the President has the power to start an action of which Congress may disapprove, the appropriations power may later be used to restrict him: "Now, you can cut off money, that's true, you can do that, but basically the initial decision will be his."[80] Senator Fulbright has been an advocate of controlling the executive by regulating spending more carefully:

> When we finally get down to it, this is about the only really effective power Congress has—that is, the power of the purse. We can talk, we can give advice, we can do all of that sort of thing, but they do not have to abide by it. The only thing they can abide by is this power.[81]

However, there are practical limitations to this power. One vivid example is the continuation of financial support by even the strongest opponents of the war in Vietnam to American military operations in that country. Once troops are committed, the power to withhold financial support has been traditionally believed to be unusable.

Until recently the withholding of appropriations for specific actions already taken were considered at best divisive of a united front and at worst unpatriotic. During May 1970 an almost un-

---

78. *Congressional Record,* 103, Part 2, p. 1856.
79. Editorial, *Washington Post,* May 5, 1970, p. A16.
80. Kolodoziej, p. 155.
81. Interview with Hubert H. Humphrey.

precedented attempt led by Senators John Sherman Cooper and Frank Church sought to prevent the President from continuing to deploy troops in Cambodia through restricting his use of funds in that nation.[82] Senator Fulbright gave endorsement to the Church-Cooper amendment to an authorization bill. Troops had been ordered to Cambodia at the end of the previous month, April, so the reaction was swift. There had been an earlier restriction on the power to utilize funds for ground forces in Laos and Thailand. The earlier amendment had overlooked Cambodia because it was a neutral state. Fulbright made this comment:

. . . by the votes we hope to demonstrate to the President the extent of the opposition to the continuation of the war in Southeast Asia, that it is not in the interest of this nation, and that this could cause him as a responsible public servant to reconsider his views and his method of trying to end the war.[83]

Congress can lead and educate the public. It can also do a better job of educating itself.[84] A systematic method of briefing all members on foreign-policy matters should be instituted by Congress itself. The sheer problems of time and numbers restrict the extent to which the executive branch can consult with the legislative. More detailed briefings to House and Senate members respectively can be given by the chairmen or other members of the House Foreign Affairs Committee and the Senate Foreign Relations Committee.

Congress might also attempt to work out an institutionalized system for getting better briefings and fuller information from the Administration. One way to attain this objective would be for staff members of congressional committees working in the foreign-policy field to be assigned to executive agencies involved in processing information in crises. They would have full access to all information, and they would sit in on all major discussions. They

82. *Congressional Record*, 115, No. 132, p. S 9205.
83. *Kansas City Star*, May 19, 1970, p. 18A.
84. *Ibid.*, May 10, 1970, p. 18A.

would not take part in the decisions, but would merely listen and observe. Had such persons seen the telegrams that actually came in from the field at the time of the Gulf of Tonkin action, Congress would have had much better guidance than they actually got from President Johnson. Care would need to be taken, however, that such staff members retain their independence from their assigned agencies. It would also be necessary to insure that giving Congress access to "classified" information that was already available in the press would not be used to prevent open discussion on the ground that security regulations were breached. Still another potential problem with this proposal would be that it would produce merely another layer in the bureaucratic structure, and one that could inhibit independent congressional thought and action.[85] Despite these potential problems, the critical need for fuller foreign-policy information for Congress makes careful consideration of this proposal desirable.

Numerous proposals to improve the organizational aspects of the Congress's functioning in foreign relations have been presented. Fairly basic is the point that the budget and staff of the Senate Committee on Foreign Relations be increased.[86] As the executive departments, especially Defense, gain constantly increasing resources, the Senate cannot hope to play a meaningful role itself if the financial means to do so are not present. Existing resources could be applied more effectively if the present committees, such as Armed Services, Foreign Relations, and Atomic Energy, worked more closely together. At present, as Hubert Humphrey said, there is a "separatism" and "fragmentation" that allows the Executive "to play off one group against another."[87] If Congress allows itself to be used in this way

---

85. *The Formulation and Administration of United States Foreign Policy*, p. 32.
86. Joseph C. Goulden, "The Imperfect Line," *Vista*, March–April, 1970, pp. 31–35.
87. Bruce M. Sapin, *The Making of United States Foreign Policy* (Washington, D. C.: Published for the Brookings Institution by Frederick A. Praeger, 1966), pp. 61, 62. Also see *The Formulation and Administration of United States Foreign Policy*, pp. 32–34 and 37, 38.

because of the features of its own organization, it invites such executive action.

In a similar way closer cooperation between the Senate and the House of Representatives could be introduced.[88] This cuts out duplication that in some cases is unnecessary.[89] It could also lead, if successful, to more Joint Resolutions, which would carry more weight than Senate Resolutions.[90] The success of such a course is greatly reduced if, as was apparently true in the late 1960s and early 1970s, a majority in the House of Representatives did support such presidential action as the war in Southeast Asia more than did the Senate.

The process for making committee assignments often produces choices that do not utilize talent in an optimal way. One famous example of this was the fact that it was a foregone conclusion in 1949 when John Foster Dulles was appointed to the Senate by Governor Dewey that he would not be appointed to the Foreign Relations Committee despite his distinguished record in the foreign-relations field.[91] The executive branch may have gained some of its extra power in the 1940s and the 1950s, because of the highly advanced age of most of the Chairmen of the Senate Committee on Foreign Relations; this is, of course, a product of the seniority system. It can be argued that a body that appoints and promotes on the basis of seniority rather than merit does not deserve a policy-making voice. Here again the Congress itself can choose or reject a course that would build itself more influence. It is true that seniority can build experience that can have value. Senator Fulbright would not have his present influence without the skill and experience gained in over a decade of service as Committee Chairman. An improved system would have to include a careful blend of experience as a criterion along with other indicators of merit, such as nonsenatorial background gained in executive departments, or academic work.

Senator Fulbright is one of the few congressional leaders who

---

88. Interview with Hubert H. Humphrey.
89. "Notes," *Harvard Law Review*, pp. 1799, 1800.
90. Sapin, pp. 61–63.
91. Dahl, p. 133.

even mention impeachment, a remedy available to the Congress to remove a President who has gone beyond his constitutional limits in foreign policy. In a 1957 speech he referred to impeachment as Congress's "ultimate alternative."[92] During the very brief 1964 debate on the Gulf of Tonkin Resolution, Fulbright considered the possibility of impeachment:

> I realize that we all have our apprehensions about what may happen in Vietnam or elsewhere. But fundamentally, under our system, it is the President, as our representative in these activities, who must necessarily have the dominant role, however jealous we may be of our own privileges—and we rightly should be in many areas. But in dealing with the Nation's security or with threatened warfare, we must rely to a great extent on the decisions of the Executive. We always have reserve power, when we see that the President has made a mistake. We can always later impeach him, if we like, if we believe that he has so far departed from the sense of duty that he has betrayed the interests of our country.[93]

In 1970 Senator Fulbright further commented on impeachment, although he emphasized the problem associated with it:

> Presidents, if they are determined to do so can easily go beyond the Constitution and there is no real good sanction for it. You can always say you can impeach him, but this is too drastic a remedy. It's like a lot of criminal statutes; when the remedy is too drastic, it's never used. If there was some lesser way, you might have a chance of doing it. But it's not a very good sanction to impeach a President. Party matters come in and all sorts of other things come in to prevent it. There's not much prospect of anybody being impeached even though they go far beyond their proper authority under the Constitution.[94]

Impeachment is not popular, and generally is not a usable

---

92. *Ibid.*, p. 144. The committee is difficult to get on because of its popularity and prestige.
93. *Congressional Record*, 103, Part 2, p. 1855.
94. U. S. Congress, Senate, Debate and Vote on the Gulf of Tonkin Resolution, S. J. Res. 189 and H. J. Res. 1145, 88th Cong., 2d sess., August 7, 1964, *Congressional Record*, 110, Part 14, p. 18462.

tool. It is available, however, and if it is exercised against a Supreme Court Justice, as it has been in the past and may be again, it is conceivable that the practice might be extended to the President under extreme circumstances.

The prospect of a new "grand debate" on foreign policy has been raised by scholar Charles Gati. Within the framework of Morgenthau's concept of "realism" other writers, such as Walter Lippman, George Kennan, and Morgenthau, together with political practitioners such as Fulbright and Eugene McCarthy, have charged that the Executive in the 1960s made major errors. This group, which Gati terms the "limitationists," has charged that the United States has "disregarded the principle of solvency and the rule of priorities and discrimination in the use of national power."[95] The "limitationists" demand a change from the "globalism" of the Johnson era.

If such changes take place, they will reflect the work of Senator J. William Fulbright as much as that of any single individual. He has occupied a post that Dahl regards as one of those in Congress most likely to confer political power on its occupant.[96] By April 24, 1970, Fulbright had occupied the position of Chairman of the Committee on Foreign Relations for a longer time period than any other man. Fulbright occupied this post during his prime years, and he became familiar with the "intricate design" in the "tapestry of infinite complexity" that is foreign policy.[97]

Through this intensely practical process of experience, Fulbright has continued to argue against being doctrinaire, and it is his adaptive approach to the question of the proper relationship between the Congress and the President in the determination of American foreign policy that is his major contribution. It is possible and proper to disagree with many specific policy positions that Senator Fulbright has taken. He has contended that there should be active discussion of foreign-policy issues between

95. Interview with J. William Fulbright.
96. Charles Gati, "Another Grand Debate? The Limitationist Critique of American Foreign Policy," *World Politics* 21 (October 1968): 141.
97. Dahl, p. 146.

the executive and legislative branches, and this should take place before and after the fact of decision. As this study is being concluded, the need for such discussion was shown as an acute one, for the President sent troops to Cambodia without consulting any congressional leaders. The implications of such presidential power were commented on as follows by Tom Wicker in the *New York Times* on May 5, 1970:

> It will mean that one man, and one man alone, however narrowly elected and for whatever reasons, holds in the world's oldest democracy the absolute power of war and peace, life and death, perhaps even survival and extinction.
> If that is indeed the pragmatic fact, it is repugnant to the Constitution, to democratic theory, and to American ideals; and if that is indeed what "the system" has come to, it ought to be changed.[98]

In essence this is the point Senator Fulbright has been emphasizing almost consistently since 1965. Fulbright, however, has stated that if we merely use our constitutional system fully, we are less likely to pursue policies that will be unsatisfactory. In his public statements Senator Fulbright has often stressed the constitutional power of the whole Congress to declare war and to authorize military spending. These are the minimum rights that Congress can unquestionably demand. It seems clear, however, that what Fulbright would really prefer to the simple exercise of these rights is a participative role in foreign-policy decision-making, especially as it would be granted to the Senate Foreign Relations Committee. Such a role goes beyond minimum constitutional rights, but it broadens the base of deliberation and would permit the introduction of some additional viewpoints.

Additional viewpoints are genuinely needed because of the intellectual isolation in which the President exists. One scholar thinks that effective machinery to challenge executive policies does not exist within the Administration.[99] George Reedy, Press

---

98. Gabriel Almond, quoted by Fulbright in "Public Opinion and Foreign Policy."
99. *New York Times,* May 5, 1970, p. 44.

Secretary to President Johnson, has put the matter even more pointedly. He states that information flowing to the President is designed to support and reinforce the ideas the President is known to hold. There is simply no one around who will say directly to the President, "That's a stupid idea."[100] It is likely that full and challenging debate will result in more productive policy. The President would be wise to consider any policy decision arrived at with limited discussion and quick agreement as suspect and in need of further investigation.

The Senate Committee on Foreign Relations should play the Devil's Advocate, since too often the President's advisers seem to be incapable or unwilling to do so. The Committee's independence from the President can give it special value to him. The President should accept these challenges and be willing to reconsider policies as well as to justify them.

Such consultations would probably answer some objections raised to American policy in the 1960s and 1970s, and one can speculate that it could have produced policies that would have had the more general support that much of earlier American foreign policy enjoyed. Senator Fulbright, however, recognizes that the day may return when foreign policy deteriorates in terms of its breadth of public support, even with extensive Senatorial participation. At that point the reassertion of presidential initiative, or other means, should be employed to remedy the situation. At such a time the most responsible proposal for a Senator to make might be to advocate a minimum of exercise of power by the Senate in foreign policy. It should be noted that Senator Fulbright has emphasized the participation by the Senate more than he has participation by the whole Congress. He has stressed the unique role of the Senate and especially the Committee on Foreign Relations. It is quite possible that his effectiveness will be limited by his inability to include the House of Representatives in his proposals. The markedly different positions of the House and Senate in the 1960s and 1970s with respect

100. Joseph H. de Rivera, *The Psychological Dimension of Foreign Policy* (Columbus, Ohio: Charles E. Merrill Publishing Company, 1968), pp. 103, 104.

to the war in Indochina may account for his position. If there is no reasonable likelihood of influencing the House, he could merely be wasting time and dissipating his energy by trying to do so.

Essentially, Senator Fulbright maintains that if the existing power balance between the Senate and the President is producing successful results, it should not be disturbed. If it is not producing successful results, then the various means available to change the balance should be called into action. The basic problem, of course, comes in determining when the results are in fact successful. The tensions of the 1970s in many ways reflect the magnitude of public feeling and may provide a clue. The whole 1965–1970 period is one in which numerous responsible observers in political and academic circles voiced enough questions about the wisdom of American foreign policy to raise doubts about its success. Perhaps "success" in foreign policy can only be defined in Justice Stewart's words about what constitutes "hard-core pornography":

> I shall not attempt to further define the kinds of materials I understand to be embraced within that shorthand definition; and perhaps I could never succeed in intelligently doing so. But I know it when I see it.[101]

In the deeper sense, however, the ultimate problem in foreign policy is that the rightness of a policy really cannot be determined on sight. Rather, the judgment rests with history, and even then the open season on debate never ends.

In general no procedural arrangement or system can be counted on to give the proper results for all times. Instead, human judgment must be employed by each generation as it faces the problems that confront it. Senator Fulbright's lesson is that such judgment is not perfect, but it is the best guide we have as a nation.

The trend in recent years has been for the President to gain more and more power in the formulation of foreign policy. It must be concluded then that this trend has not resulted in an unqualified success, even if we judge merely on the basis of the

101. "A House Divided," NBC telecast, May 10, 1970.

domestic repercussions of foreign policy. There is nothing sacrosanct about this trend, and the time has come to reverse it and to require the Executive to accept a more balanced role, with Congress assuming a more active advisory role in which the legislative branch regains its constitutional war-making powers.

The President tends to become insulated from exposure to a diversity of viewpoints. This situation exists not only because of an intellectual isolation, but because of the great breadth of his responsibilities, the large volume of his workload, and the sheer magnitude of the decisions he must make. For these reasons congressional participation is useful. This is not to say that Congress should make foreign policy, but merely that congressional views, in all their diversity, should be an input that enters into the decision-making process. Since all questions concerning foreign policy come before the Senate only after discussion by the Foreign Relations Committee, this body should occupy a special consultative position. Senator Fulbright has been at the forefront of those expressing these views, and their correctness or incorrectness will be known only with the unfolding of the events that he has affected and that he will influence.

APPENDIX A

Significant Resolutions and Proclamations

Proclamation 2914: Proclaiming the Existence of a National Emergency. *December 16, 1950**

By the President of the United States of America a Proclamation

WHEREAS recent events in Korea and elsewhere constitute a grave threat to the peace of the world and imperil the efforts of this country and those of the United Nations to prevent aggression and armed conflict; and

WHEREAS world conquest by communist imperialism is the goal of the forces of aggression that have been loosed upon the world; and

WHEREAS, if the goal of communist imperialism were to be achieved, the people of this country would no longer enjoy the full and rich life they have with God's help built for themselves and their children; they would no longer enjoy the blessings of the freedom of worshipping as they severally choose, the freedom of reading and listening to what they choose, the right of free speech including the right to criticize their Government, the right to choose those who conduct their Government, the right to engage freely in collective bargaining, the right to engage freely in their own business enterprises, and the many other freedoms and rights which are a part of our way of life; and

WHEREAS the increasing menace of the forces of communist aggression requires that the national defense of the United States be strengthened as speedily as possible:

* Source: *Public Papers of the Presidents of the United States: Truman, 1950* (Washington: U. S. Government Printing Office, 1960), pp. 746, 747.

Now, THEREFORE, I, HARRY S. TRUMAN, President of the United States of America, do proclaim the existence of a national emergency, which requires that the military, naval, air, and civilian defenses of this country be strengthened as speedily as possible to the end that we may be able to repel any and all threats against our national security and to fulfill our responsibilities in the efforts being made through the United Nations and otherwise to bring about lasting peace.

I summon all citizens to make a united effort for the security and well-being of our beloved country and to place its needs foremost in thought and action that the full moral and material strength of the Nation may be readied for the dangers which threaten us.

I summon our farmers, our workers in industry, and our businessmen to make a mighty production effort to meet the defense requirements of the Nation and to this end to eliminate all waste and inefficiency and to subordinate all lesser interests to the common good.

I summon every person and every community to make, with a spirit of neighborliness, whatever sacrifices are necessary for the welfare of the Nation.

I summon all State and local leaders and officials to cooperate fully with the military and civilian defense agencies of the United States in the national defense program.

I summon all citizens to be loyal to the principles upon which our Nation is founded, to keep faith with our friends and allies, and to be firm in our devotion to the peaceful purposes for which the United Nations was founded.

I am confident that we will meet the dangers that confront us with courage and determination, strong in the faith that we can thereby "secure the Blessings of Liberty to ourselves and our Posterity."

IN WITNESS WHEREOF, I have hereunto set my hand and caused the Seal of the United States of America to be affixed.

DONE at the City of Washington this sixteenth day of December in the year of our Lord nineteen hundred and fifty, and of the Independence of the United States of America the one hundred and seventy-fifth.

HARRY S. TRUMAN

By the President:
  DEAN ACHESON
    Secretary of State

Joint Resolution *

Authorizing the President to employ the Armed Forces of the
  United States for protecting the security of Formosa, the
  Pescadores and related positions and territories of that area.
Whereas the primary purpose of the United States, in its relations
  with all other nations, is to develop and sustain a just and en-
  during peace for all; and
Whereas certain territories in the West Pacific under the jurisdiction of the Republic of China are now under armed attack,
  and threats and declarations have been and are being made
  by the Chinese Communists that such armed attack is in aid
  of and in preparation for armed attack on Formosa and the
  Pescadores,
Whereas such armed attack if continued would gravely endanger
  the peace and security of the West Pacific Area and particularly
  of Formosa and the Pescadores; and
Whereas the secure possession by friendly governments of the
  Western Pacific Island chain, of which Formosa is a part, is
  essential to the vital interests of the United States and all
  friendly nations in or bordering upon the Pacific Ocean; and
Whereas the President of the United States on January 6, 1955,
  submitted to the Senate for its advice and consent to ratification
  a Mutual Defense Treaty between the United States of America
  and the Republic of China, which recognizes that an armed
  attack in the West Pacific area directed against territories,
  therein described, in the region of Formosa and the Pescadores,
  would be dangerous to the peace and safety of the parties to
  the treaty: Therefore be it
*Resolved by the Senate and House of Representatives of the
United States of America in Congress assembled,* That the President of the United States be and he hereby is authorized to em-

* Source: U. S. *Statutes at Large,* Vol. LXIX, 84th Cong., 1st sess.,
1955, 7.

ploy the Armed Forces of the United States as he deems necessary for the specific purpose of securing and protecting Formosa and the Pescadores against armed attack, this authority to include the securing and protection of such related positions and territories of that area now in friendly hands and the taking of such other measures as he judges to be required or appropriate in assuring the defense of Formosa and the Pescadores.

This resolution shall expire when the President shall determine that the peace and security of the area is reasonably assured by international conditions created by action of the United Nations or otherwise, and shall so report to the Congress.

Approved January 29, 1955, 8:42 a.m.

*Joint Resolution**

To promote peace and stability in the Middle East

Resolved by the Senate and House of Representatives of the United States of America in Congress assembled, That the President be and hereby is authorized to cooperate with and assist any nation or group of nations in the general area of the Middle East desiring such assistance in the development of economic strength dedicated to the maintenance of national independence.

SEC. 2. The President is authorized to undertake, in the general area of the Middle East, military assistance programs which any nation or group of nations of that area desiring such assistance. Furthermore, the United States regards as vital to the national interest and world peace the preservation of the independence and integrity of the nations of the Middle East. To this end, if the President determines the necessity thereof, the United States is prepared to use armed forces to assist any such nation or group of such nations requesting assistance against armed aggression from any country controlled by international communism: *Provided,* That such employment shall be consonant with the treaty obligations of the United States and with the Constitution of the United States.

SEC. 3. The President is hereby authorized to use during the

---

* Source: U. S. *Statutes at Large,* Vol. LXXI, 85th Cong., 1st sess., 1957, pp. 5, 6.

balance of fiscal year 1957 for economic and military assistance under this joint resolution not to exceed $200,000,000 from any appropriation now available for carrying out the provisions of the Mutual Security Act of 1954, as amended, in accord with the provisions of such Act: *Provided*, That, whenever the President determines it to be important to the security of the United States, such use may be under the authority of section 401 (a) of the Mutual Security Act of 1954, as amended (except that the provisions of section 105 (a) thereof shall not be waived), and without regard to the provisions of section 105 of the Mutual Security Appropriation Act, 1957: *Provided further*, That obligations incurred in carrying out the purpose of the first sentence of section 2 of this joint resolution shall be paid only out of appropriations for military assistance, and obligations incurred in carrying out the purposes of the first section of this joint resolution shall be paid only out of appropriations other than those for military assistance. This authorization is in addition to other existing authorizations with respect to the use of such appropriations. None of the additional authorization contained in this section shall be used until fifteen days after the Committee on Foreign Relations of the Senate, the Committee on Foreign Affairs of the House of Representatives, the Committees on Appropriations of the Senate and the House of Representatives and, when military assistance is involved, the Committees on Armed Services of the Senate and the House of Representatives have been furnished a report showing the object of the proposed use, the country for the benefit of which such use is intended, and the particular appropriation or appropriations for carrying out the provisions of the Mutual Security Act of 1954, as amended, from which the funds are proposed to be derived: *Provided*, That funds available under this section during the balance of fiscal year 1957 shall, in the case of any such report submitted during the last fifteen days of the fiscal year, remain available for use under this section for the purposes stated in such report for a period of twenty days following the date of submission of such report. Nothing contained in this joint resolution shall be construed as itself authorizing the appropriation of additional funds for the purpose of carrying out the provisions of the first section or of the first sentence of section 2 of this joint resolution.

SEC. 4. The President should continue to furnish facilities and military assistance, within the provisions of applicable law and established policies, to the United Nations Emergency Force in the Middle East, with a view to maintaining the truce in that region.

SEC. 5. The President shall within the months of January and July of each year report to the Congress his action hereunder.

SEC. 6. This joint resolution shall expire when the President shall determine that the peace and security of the nations in the general area of the Middle East are reasonably assured by international conditions created by action of the United Nations or otherwise except that it may be terminated earlier by a concurrent resolution of the two Houses of Congress.

Approved March 9, 1957.

*Joint Resolution**

Expressing the determination of the United States with respect to the situation in Cuba

Whereas President James Monroe, announcing the Monroe Doctrine in 1823, declared that the United States would consider any attempt on the part of European powers "to extend their system to any portion of this hemisphere as dangerous to our peace and safety"; and

Whereas in the Rio Treaty of 1947 the parties agreed that "an armed attack by any State against an American State shall be considered as an attack against all the American States, and, consequently, each one of the said contracting parties undertakes to assist in meeting the attack in the exercise of the inherent right of individual or collective self-defense recognized by article 51 of the Charter of the United Nations"; and

Whereas the Foreign Ministers of the Organization of American States at Punta del Este in January 1962 declared: "The present Government of Cuba has identified itself with the principles of Marxist-Leninist ideology, has established a political, economic, and social system based on that doctrine,

---

*Source: U. S. *Statutes at Large,* Vol. LXXVI, 87th Cong., 2d sess., 1962, p. 697.

and accepts military assistance from extracontinental Communist powers, including even the threat of military intervention in America on the part of the Soviet Union"; and
Whereas the international Communist movement has increasingly extended into Cuba its political, economic, and military sphere of influence; Now, therefore, be it *Resolved by the Senate and House of Representatives of the United States of America in Congress assembled,* That the United States is determined—

(a) to prevent by whatever means may be necessary including the use of arms, the Marxist-Leninist regime in Cuba from extending, by force or the threat of force, its aggressive or subversive activities to any part of this hemisphere;

(b) to prevent in Cuba the creation or use of an externally supported military capability endangering the security of the United States; and

(c) to work with the Organization of American States and with freedom-loving Cubans to support the aspirations of the Cuban people for self-determination. Approved October 3, 1962.

Joint Resolution *
To promote the maintenance of international peace and security in southeast Asia

Whereas naval units of the Communist regime in Vietnam, in violation of the principles of the Charter of the United Nations and of international law, have deliberately and repeatedly attacked United States naval vessels lawfully present in international waters, and have thereby created a serious threat to international peace; and
Whereas these attacks are part of a deliberate and systematic campaign of aggression that the Communist regime in North Vietnam has been waging against its neighbors and the nations joined with them in the collective defense of their freedom; and
Whereas the United States is assisting the peoples of southeast Asia to protect their freedom and has no territorial, military or political ambitions in that area, but desires only that these

---

* Source: *U. S. Statutes at Large,* Vol. LXXVIII, 88th Cong., 2d sess., 1964, p. 384.

peoples should be left in peace to work out their own destinies in their own way: Now therefore, be it

Resolved by the Senate and House of Representatives of the United States of America in Congress assembled, That the Congress approve and supports the determination of the President, as Commander in Chief, to take all necessary measures to repel any armed attack against the forces of the United States and to prevent further aggression.

SEC. 2. The United States regards as vital to its national interest and to world peace the maintenance of international peace and security in southeast Asia. Consonant with the Constitution of the United States and the Charter of the United Nations and in accordance with its obligations under the Southeast Asia Collective Defense Treaty, United States is, therefore, prepared, as the President determines to take all necessary steps, including the use of armed force, to assist a member or protocol state of the Southeast Asia Collective Defense Treaty requesting assistance in defense of its freedom.

SEC. 3. This resolution shall expire when the President shall determine that the peace and security of the area is reasonably assured by international conditons created by action of the United Nations otherwise, except that it may be terminated earlier by concurrent resolution of the Congress.

Approved August 10, 1964.

*National Commitments**

Senate Resolution 85

Whereas accurate definition of the term "national commitment" in recent years has become obscured: Now, therefore, be it

Resolved, That it is the sense of the Senate that a national commitment by the United States to a foreign power necessarily and exclusively results from affirmative action taken by the executive and legislative branches of the United States Government through means of a treaty, convention, or other legislative instrumentality specifically intended to give effect to such a commitment.

---

* Source: U. S. Congress, Senate, Committee on Foreign Relations, *National Commitments,* S. Rept. 91–129, 91st sess., 1st sess., April 16, 1969.

Senate Concurrent Resolution 64*

To terminate certain joint resolutions authorizing the use of the Armed Forces of the United States in certain areas outside the United States.

Resolved by the Senate (the House of Representatives concurring), That (a) under the authority of section 6 of the joint resolution entitled "Joint resolution to promote peace and stability in the Middle East", approved March 9, 1957 (71 Stat. 5; Public Law 85–7), as amended, such joint resolution is terminated effective upon the day that the second session of the Ninety-first Congress is adjourned.

(b) Under the authority of section 3 of the joint resolution entitled "Joint resolution to promote the maintenance of international peace and security in Southeast Asia", approved August 10, 1964 (78 Stat. 384; Public Law 88–408), such joint resolution is terminated effective upon the day that the second session of the Ninety-first Congress is adjourned.

---

* Source: Senate Concurrent Resolution 64, 91st Cong., 2d sess., Calendar No. 838, May 1, 1970.

APPENDIX B

National Commitments (S. Res. 85) was passed with 70 yeas, 16 nays, and 14 not voting.*

Yeas 70

Aiken	Dole	Magnasun	Percy
Allen	Eagleton	Mansfield	Prouty
Anderson	Eastland	Mathias	Proxmire
Baker	Ellender	McCarthy	Randolph
Bible	Ervin	McClellan	Saxbe
Boggs	Fulbright	McGovern	Schweiker
Brooke	Gravel	McIntyre	Scott
Burdick	Harris	Metcalf	Spong
Byrd, Va.	Hartke	Miller	Stennis
Byrd, W. Va.	Hatfield	Mondale	Stevens
Cannon	Holland	Montoya	Symington
Case	Hruska	Mundt	Talmadge
Church	Inouye	Muskie	Williams, Del.
Cook	Javits	Nelson	Yarborough
Cooper	Jordon, N. C.	Packwood	Young, N. Dak.
Cotton	Jordon, Idaho	Pastore	Young, Ohio
Cranston	Kennedy	Pearson	
Curtis	Long	Pell	

Nays

Allott	Dodd	Griffin	McGee
Bellmon	Dominick	Gurney	Smith
Bennett	Fannin	Hansen	Thurmond
Dirksen	Goldwater	Jackson	Tower

---

*Source: U. S. Congress, Senate, Vote on National Commitments, S. Res. 85, 91st Cong., 1st sess., June 25, 1969, *Congressional Record,* 115, No. 105, p. S7153.

Not Voting

Bayh	Hart	Murphy	Tydings
Fong	Hollings	Ribicoff	Williams, N. J.
Goodell	Hughes	Russell	
Gore	Moss	Sparkman	

Gore, Hart, Hughes, Ribicoff, Russell, and Sparkman if present and voting, would each vote "yea." Senator Murphy would vote "nay."

BIBLIOGRAPHICAL NOTE

To examine the nature of Senator Fulbright's views and to analyze the changes in, reasons for, and implications of these views a variety of source materials were employed in this study. Published materials furnished both useful background information and valuable specific data. General works on American foreign policy provided the setting for the issues. Various works on United States history were also used to add another perspective. Studies of both the presidency and the Congress gave insights. Biographies of Senator Fulbright offer important information about his career and the experiences that have shaped his thought. The Senator himself is a prolific writer, and his works have been valuable source materials.

The scholarly journals were important sources on the various issues encountered in this study. Popular magazines, too, were useful, especially those which Senator Fulbright has used as a platform for expounding his views. Academic people writing about Fulbright have found a forum in the popular press. Newspapers, particularly the *New York Times,* were highly useful sources.

Various government documents were major sources of data and information. The *Congressional Record* is one such source. Despite the fact that the statements in the *Congressional Record* sometimes do not reveal important matters of expression, inflection, and tone of voice, and are subject to pre-publication editing by Congressional speakers, the source is generally reliable and highly informative. Congressional Committee hearings and Senate

Reports and Documents were among other sources that this study employed extensively. Court cases were also used.

Radio and television interviews, both printed and tape recorded, often gave data of importance. Senator Fulbright furnished hundreds of speeches, and other documents in his files in his Washington, D. C. office provided extremely valuable concepts. At this point the authors would like to acknowledge with deep appreciation the cooperation and assistance that Senator Fulbright and his Washington staff furnished in making these speeches and other papers available. Senator Fulbright's voting record was studied with the aid of information obtained from the *Congressional Quarterly.*

Questions for which written sources could not provide answers necessitated interviews with several national leaders, which yielded invaluable information. Most important was the interview with Senator Fulbright himself. Senator Fulbright's full, frank and open answers to questions and his willingness to provide additional materials were very helpful.* Former Vice-President Hubert H. Humphrey was also gracious in granting a full interview to present his viewpoint and insights in matters related to this study. Senators Mike Mansfield and Albert Gore also gave helpful information in interviews. All of the interviews not only furnished important data and concepts that would not otherwise have been available, but also made it possible to submit propositions to these leaders for their testing and reactions.

Most students who have considered the growth of presidential power would agree with Edgar E. Robinson's statement that it is presidential power that is the power of first importance in United States foreign policy.[1] Johnson and Walker also assert that "The President's primary function is to formulate and direct the basic

---

* The authors acknowledge with gratitude the help of Senator James Pearson of Kansas in arranging the interview with Senator Fulbright and with Senator Mansfield.

1. Edgar E. Robinson, "Presidential Power in the Nuclear Age," in Edgar E. Robinson and others, *Powers of the President in Foreign Affairs, 1945–1965* (San Francisco: A Research Study Commissioned by the Commonwealth Club of California, published by Lederer, Street and Zenz, 1966), p. 245.

foreign policy of the nation."[2] Dawson in 1962 pointed out that the legislative branch had long been weak in overseeing the national defense policies initiated in executive departments.[3] In 1968 Stanley Hoffman referred to talk of "abdication" of responsibility by Congress.[4]

Admittedly, public support of such presidential leadership is important. Lerche, in his 1966 book, stated that President Lyndon B. Johnson's power was augmented in 1965 by broad public support for his Vietnam policy.[5]

Few writers question the fact of the existence of the President's supremacy in foreign-policy formulation. In 1952 Cheever and Haviland were able to state that the President did not have the power to control foreign policy without regard to Congress.[6] Corwin points to the historically cyclical character of Presidential power.[7] He also points out that different Presidents operate in different ways; where Franklin D. Roosevelt used a "personalized" approach, President Eisenhower developed an "institutionalized" presidency.[8] Neustadt also shows that temperament is a greater separator of different Presidents.[9] Regardless of these points, the greater evidence suggests that presidential power has grown, and this growth, like other great changes, has come like the tide.[10]

2. Donald Bruce Johnson and Jack L. Walker, eds., *The Dynamics of the American Presidency* (New York: John Wiley & Sons, 1964), p. 297.

3. Raymond H. Dawson, "Congressional Innovation and Intervention in Defense Policy: Legislative Authorization of Weapons Systems," *American Political Science Review*, 56 (March, 1952), p. 42.

4. Stanley Hoffman, *Gulliver's Troubles, Or the Setting of American Foreign Policy* (New York: McGraw-Hill Book Company, 1968), p. 254.

5. Charles O. Lerche, *Foreign Policy of the American People* (Englewood Cliffs, New Jersey: Prentice-Hall, Inc., 1967), p. 38.

6. Daniel S. Cheever and H. Field Haviland, *American Foreign Policy and the Separation of Powers* (Cambridge: Harvard University Press, 1952), p. 11.

7. Edward S. Corwin, *The President: Office and Powers 1787–1957* (New York: New York University Press, 1957), p. 309.

8. Corwin, p. 313.

9. Richard E. Neustadt, *Presidential Power* (New York: John Wiley and Sons, 1962), p. 182. Neustadt quoted Justice Holmes as describing Franklin Roosevelt as "a second-rate intellect but a first-rate temperament."

10. Osgood uses this figure of speech to describe the United States shift from a national to a world view. Robert Endicott Osgood, *Ideals and Self-Interest in America's Foreign Policy* (Chicago: the University of Chicago Press, 1953), p. 429.

If there is a fairly general agreement among recent writers that presidential power in foreign relations has grown, there is less agreement about the desirability of the President's holding the power that he does.

One of the strongest statements in defense of strong presidential power is that of historian Clinton Rossiter. Speaking against those who would allow Congress to reduce this authority, he says this:

> Their cause, I am bound to say, is ill-considered because any major reduction now in the powers of the President would leave us naked to our enemies, to the invisible forces of boom and bust at home and to the visible forces of unrest and aggression abroad.[11]

Dahl points out that periods of congressional leadership in governmental affairs usually have occurred when "nonentities" have occupied the White House.[12] In his famous exposition of the comparative amounts of knowledge and discretion possessed by various groups, Dahl also shows that Congress has a wider range of discretion than the President, but the President has more detailed knowledge than does Congress.[13]

More numerous are the authorities who point out the danger of congressional interference than are those who extol the virtues of presidential power. Heller states that Congress constantly tries to gain control over areas in which the President "clearly dominates."[14] Waltz sees the prerogative of the President to formulate and carry out foreign policy as one that frustrates Congress, and he characterizes the interference of Congress as "worrisome."[15] In the view of some authorities the influence in foreign policy that Congress has exerted has not been desirable.

11. Clinton Rossiter, *The American Presidency* (New York: Published as a Mentor Book by arrangement with Harcourt, Brace and Company, 1960), p. 150.
12. Robert A. Dahl, *Congress and Foreign Policy* (New York: W. W. Norton & Company, 1964), p. 170.
13. Dahl, p. 143.
14. Francis H. Heller, *The Presidency: A Modern Perspective* (New York: Random House, 1960), p. 68.
15. Kenneth N. Waltz, *Foreign Policy and Democratic Politics* (Boston: Little, Brown and Company, 1967), pp. 100, 196.

Radway points out the "coolness" of Congress to friendly nations (as to Britain in 1940), the nationalistic attitude of Congress, and the "hard-nosed" perspective of the legislative branch.[16] Dahl cites the congressionally sponsored neutrality legislation of the 1930s as evidence of the "rigid" nature of the sort of foreign policy that Congress would stress.[17] Perhaps one of the major events of modern history that led to the questioning by social scientists of the propriety of the Congressional exercise of initiative in foreign policy was the proposal of the Bricker Amendment. This proposal never had large public support, but it became a major and drawn-out issue.[18]

Another body of writers, and one that appears to be increasing in numbers, argues that the President's power has become excessive. Small states that the power of the President has increased to the point that the whole governmental system is generally out of balance.[19] Henry Steele Commager also urges a reconsideration of the "drift" to presidential supremacy, which he believes to be a danger.[20] Among leading newspapers the *New York Times* has editorialized that the trend toward total erosion of the power of Congress must be avoided.[21] Hans Morgenthau advocates that the Senate adopt its own foreign policy as an alternative to that of the President.[22] Sapin proposes that what is needed is a sharing of major functions by both the Congress and the President.[23] Hoffman pointed out in 1968 that Congress has retreated from a

---

16. Laurence I. Radway, *The Liberal Democracy in World Affairs: Foreign Policy and National Defense* (Glennview, Ill.: Scott, Foresman and Company, 1969), p. 109.
17. Dahl, p. 172.
18. Malcolm E. Jewell, *Senatorial Politics & Foreign Policy* (Lexington: University of Kentucky Press, 1962), p. 182.
19. Melvin Small, "Democracy and Foreign Policy," *Journal of Conflict Resolution*, 12 (June, 1968), p. 249.
20. U. S. Congress, Senate, Committee on Foreign Relations, *Changing American Attitudes Toward Foreign Policy, Hearing* before the Committee on Foreign Relations, Senate, 90th Cong., 1st sess., February 20, 1967, p. 20.
21. Editorial, *New York Times,* May 9, 1965, p. 12.
22. Hans J. Morgenthau, "Senator Fulbright's New Foreign Policy," *Commentary,* 37 (May, 1964), p. 68.
23. Sapin, p. 36.

policy of harassing the President and now occupies only "the temperate zone of surveillance."[24]

Wolfgang Friedman, writing in the *Political Science Quarterly* for June 1968, shows how a group that he characterizes as "humanitarian liberals" have changed their views on foreign-policy matters since 1917. In particular this group supported worldwide alliances and the use of force against Fascist aggression in the 1940s. They were less anxious to use regional alliances, such as OAS and SEATO, against recent Communist expansion, which many saw as a danger far smaller than that posed earlier by the Nazis.[25]

Small points out how the position of "internationalists" and "isolationists" have changed since 1950.[26] Schlesinger shows how "liberals" in foreign-policy formulation traditionally supported a strong President, while "conservatives" tended to support a strong Congress. Since the escalation of the Vietnam War there are signs that these positions may be exchanged for one another in a shift of such historic proportions as that which took place from 1800 to 1814 between Jeffersonians and the Federalists.[27] Brown explains this change of viewpoint by stating that at some point—he estimates that it was during the Eisenhower years— United States policy shifted away from being primarily a defensive one relative to the Soviet Union to one that was more concerned with the "third world."[28] Policies adopted toward the less-developed nations contained elements that were regarded by some as aggressive rather than purely defensive. This shift in the

---

24. Hoffman, p. 221.
25. Wolfgang Friedman, "Interventionism, Liberalism, and Power Politics: The Unfinished Revolution in International Thinking," *Political Science Quarterly*, 83 (June, 1968), pp. 176, 179, also see pp. 182, 185. Morgenthau whose advocacy of an independent foreign policy by the Senate has been cited, disagrees that the nature of U. S. relations with Communist nations has changed. Morgenthau, p. 68.
26. Small, p. 253.
27. Arthur M. Schlesinger, Jr., and Alfred de Grazia *Congress and the Presidency: Their Role in Modern Times* (Washington, D. C.: American Enterprise Institute for Public Policy Research, 1967), p. 28.
28. Seyom Brown, *The Faces of Power* (New York: Columbia University Press, 1968), p. 366.

views of various interested and informed Americans is important, and analysis of the views of Senator Fulbright will shed more light on this matter. We need a better basis for understanding how the views of social scientists are formed, for these views may be influential, even when they are wrong.[29] Not only are the utterances of Senator Fulbright influencing social scientists, but the views of these scholars and writers are being read and digested by the Senator.

---

29. Dahl points out that in 1939 a study showed that only half of social scientists thought that the armed forces of the United States should be increased in size, while 75 per cent of the general public approved this increase. Dahl, p. 84.

BIBLIOGRAPHY

Congressional Record

U. S. Congress. House. Vote on Fulbright Resolution. C. Res. 25, 78th Cong., 1st sess., September 21, 1943. *Congressional Record*, 89, Part 6, pp. 7728, 7729.

U. S. Congress. Senate. Senator Fulbright speaking on "American Foreign Policy—International Organization for World Security." 79th Cong., 1st sess., March 28, 1945. *Congressional Record*, 91, Part 3, pp. 2896–2900.

U. S. Congress. Senate. Senator Watkins speaking about Truman's action in Korea. 81st Cong., 2d sess., June 27, 1950. *Congressional Record*, 96, Part 7, pp. 9229–33.

U. S. Congress. Senate. Senator Taft speaking against Truman's action in Korea. 82d Cong., 1st sess., January 5, 1951. *Congressional Record*, 97, Part 1, p. 37.

U. S. Congress. Senate. Vote on sending troops to Europe. S. Res. 99, 82d Cong., 1st sess., April 4, 1951. *Congressional Record*, 97, Part 3, p. 3282.

U. S. Congress. Senate. Senator McCarran introducing the Bricker Amendment for debate. S. J. Res. 1, 83d Cong., 2d sess., January 20, 1954. *Congressional Record*, 100, Part 1, pp. 478–86.

U. S. Congress. Senate. Senator Fulbright speaking on the Bricker Amendment. S. J. Res. 1, 83d Cong., 2d sess., January 28, 1954. *Congressional Record*, 100, Part 1, pp. 939, 940, 943.

U. S. Congress. Senate. Senator Fulbright speaking against the Bricker Amendment. S. J. Res. 1, 83d Cong., 2d sess., February 2, 1954. *Congressional Record*, 100, Part 1, pp. 1105, 1106.

U. S. Congress. Senate. Senator Fulbright speaking against the Bricker Amendment. S. J. Res. 1, 83d Cong., 2d sess., February 25, 1954. *Congressional Record*, 100, Part 2. pp. 2260, 2261.

U. S. Congress. Senate. Senator Morse speaking against Presidential authority to use Armed Forces to protect Formosa and the Pescadores. H. J. Res. 159, 84th Cong., 1st sess., January 24, 1955. *Congressional Record*, 101, Part 1, p. 766.

U. S. Congress. Senate. Senator Fulbright speaking on "The Administration's Middle East Proposal." S. J. Res. 19, 85th Cong., 1st sess., February 11, 1957. *Congressional Record*, 103, Part 2, pp. 1855–70.

U. S. Congress. Senate. Vote on Middle East Resolution. H. J. Res. 17, 85th Cong., 1st sess., March 5, 1957. *Congressional Record*, 103, Part 3, p. 3104.

U. S. Congress. Senate. Senator Fulbright discussing the Middle East situation. 85th Cong., 2d sess., June 16, 1958. *Congressional Record*, 104, Part 11, pp. 13907, 13908.

U. S. Congress. Senator Fulbright, speech "On the Brink of Disaster." 85th Cong., 2d sess., August 6, 1958. *Congressional Record*, 104, Part 13, pp. 16317–20.

U. S. Congress. Senate. Senator Fulbright, speech "The Character of Present-Day American Life." 85th Cong., 2d sess., August 21, 1958. *Congressional Record*, 104, Part 15, pp. 18903–5.

U. S. Congress. Senate. Senator Fulbright, speech "The Position of the United States in the Berlin Crisis." 86th Cong., 1st sess., March 16, 1959. *Congressional Record*, 105, Part 3, pp. 4231, 4232.

U. S. Congress. Senate. Senator Fulbright speaking on the Mutual Security Act of 1959. S. 1451, 86th Cong., 1st sess., June 30, 1959. *Congressional Record*, 105, Part 9, pp. 12273–76.

U. S. Congress. Senate. Senator Fulbright, speech "The Ugly American." 86th Cong., 1st sess., September 7, 1959. *Congressional Record*, 105, Part 14, pp. 18332–35.

U. S. Congress. Senate. Senator Fulbright speaking on the Mutual Security Act of 1960. S. 3058, 86th Cong., 2d sess., April 27, 1960. *Congressional Record*, 106, Part 7, pp. 8744–47.

U. S. Congress. Senate. Senator Fulbright discussing his recent trip to the Middle East. 86th Cong., 2d sess., June 15, 1960. *Congressional Record*, 106, Part 10, pp. 12616–21.

U. S. Congress. Senate. Senator Fulbright speaking about events related to the Summit Conference. S. Rept. 1761, 86th Cong.,

2d sess., June 28, 1960. *Congressional Record*, 106, Part 11, pp. 14733–37.

U. S. Congress. Senate. Senator Fulbright speaking on behalf of the "Mutual Educational and Cultural Exchange Act of 1961. S. 1154, 87th Cong., 1st sess., June 27, 1961. *Congressional Record*, 107, Part 9, pp. 11399, 11403.

U. S. Congress. Senate. Senator Fulbright, speech "Some Reflections Upon Recent Events and Continuing Problems." 87th Cong., 1st sess., June 29, 1961. *Congressional Record*, 107, Part 9, pp. 11702–05.

U. S. Congress. Senate. Senator Fulbright discussing propaganda activities of military personnel. 87th Cong., 1st sess., August 2, 1961. *Congressional Record*, 107, Part 11, pp. 14433–39.

U. S. Congress. Senate. Senator Fulbright, speech "European Unity and Atlantic Partnership." 88th Cong., 1st sess., January 24, 1963. *Congressional Record*, 109, Part 1, pp. 925, 926.

U. S. Congress. Senate. Senator Fulbright, speech "Liberalism and Coexistence." 88th Cong., 1st sess., August 2, 1963. *Congressional Record*, 109, Part 10, pp. 13960, 13961.

U. S. Congress. Senate. Senator Fulbright speaking on the Foreign Assistance Act of 1963. H. R. 7885, 88th Cong., 1st sess., October 28, 1963. *Congressional Record*, 109, Part 15, pp. 20337–39.

U. S. Congress. Senate. Senator Fulbright, speech "Foreign Policy —Old Myths and New Realities." 88th Cong., 2d sess., March 25, 1964. *Congressional Record*, 110, Part 5, pp. 6227–32.

U. S. Congress. Senate. Editorial comments on "Foreign Policy— Old Myths and New Realities." 88th Cong., 2d sess., April 20, 1964. *Congressional Record*, 110, Part 6, pp. 8466, 8467.

U. S. Congress. Senate. Senator Fulbright speaking on the Foreign Assistance Act of 1964. H. R. 11380, 88th Cong., 2d sess., August 1, 1964. *Congressional Record*, 110, Part 3, pp. 17717–20.

U. S. Congress. Senate. Introduction and Debate on Gulf of Tonkin Resolution. S. J. Res. 189, 88th Cong., 2d sess., August 5, 1964. *Congressional Record*, 110, Part 14, pp. 18132–39.

U. S. Congress. Senate. Debate and Vote on Gulf of Tonkin

Resolution. S. J. Res. 189 and H. J. Res. 1145, 88th Cong., 2d sess., August 7, 1964. *Congressional Record*, 110, Part 14, pp. 18461–71.

U. S. Congress. Senate. Senator Fulbright, speech "The Conservation of a Conservative," 88th Cong., 2d sess., August 15, 1964. *Congressional Record*, 110, Part 15, pp. 19785–88.

U. S. Congress. Senate. Senator Fulbright, speech "The Basic Issue in Foreign Affairs." 88th Cong., 2d sess., September 8, 1964. *Congressional Record*, 110, Part 16, pp. 21675–77.

U. S. Congress. Senate. Senator Fulbright, speech "Ideology and the Politics of Survival." 88th Cong., 2d sess., September 10, 1964. *Congressional Record*, 110, Part 17, pp. 21916–18.

U. S. Congress. Senate. Senator Fulbright discussing the Foreign Assistance Act of 1961. S. 1367, 89th Cong., 1st sess., March 4, 1965. *Congressional Record*, 111, Part 3, pp. 4188–92.

U. S. Congress. Senate. Debate on treaty amending the United Nations Charter. 89th Cong., 1st sess., June 3, 1965. *Congressional Record*, 111, Part 9, pp. 12557–59.

U. S. Congress. Senate. Senator Fulbright and others discussing the Foreign Assistance Act of 1965. H. R. 7750, 89th Cong., 1st sess., June 4, 1965. *Congressional Record*, 111, Part 9, pp. 12608–13.

U. S. Congress. Senate. Senator Fulbright, speech "The War in Vietnam." 89th Cong., 1st sess., June 15, 1965. *Congressional Record*, 111, Part 10, pp. 13656–58.

U. S. Congress. Senate. Senator Fulbright, speech "Public and Private Responsibility in the Conduct of Foreign Relations." 89th Cong., 1st sess., July 26, 1965. *Congressional Record*, 111, Part 13, p. 18226.

U. S. Congress. Senate. Senator Fulbright and others discussing the Dominican crisis. 89th Cong., 1st sess., September 30, 1965. *Congressional Record*, 111, Part 19, pp. 25622, 25623.

U. S. Congress. Senate. Editorial comments on Senator Fulbright's Dominican Republic speech. 89th Cong., 1st sess., October 7, 1965. *Congressional Record*, 111, Part 19, pp. 26237–39.

U. S. Congress. Senate. Senator Fulbright, speech "The Situation in the Dominican Republic," reprint of speech of September 15, 1965 and editorial comments on the speech. 89th Cong., 1st sess., October 22, 1965. *Congressional Record*, 111, Part 21, pp. 28372–406.

U. S. Congress. Senate. Senator Fulbright speaking on "Military Supplemental Fiscal Year 1966." S. 2791, 89th Cong., 2d sess., March 1, 1966. *Congressional Record*, 112, Part 6, pp. 4379–85.

U. S. Congress. Senate. Senator Fulbright, speech "The United States and China." 89th Cong., 2d sess., March 7, 1966. *Congressional Record*, 112, Part 4, pp. 5145–48.

U. S. Congress. Senate. Senator Fulbright suggesting basic changes in the foreign aid program. 89th Cong., 2d sess., April 1, 1966. *Congressional Record*, 112, Part 6, pp. 7464–68.

U. S. Congress. Senate. Senator Fulbright speaking on the Foreign Assistance Act of 1966. S. 3584, 89th Cong., 2d sess., July 18, 1966. *Congressional Record*, 112, Part 12, pp. 16020–23.

U. S. Congress. Senate. Senator Fulbright speaking on "The Asian Doctrine." 89th Cong., 2d sess., July 22, 1966. *Congressional Record*, 112, Part 13, p. 16808.

U. S. Congress. Senate. Senator Fulbright speaking on the Foreign Assistance Act of 1966. H. R. 15750, 89th Cong., 2d sess., July 26, 1966. *Congressional Record*, 112, Part 13, pp. 17065–68.

U. S. Congress. Senate. Senator Fulbright, speech "A New Concept in Foreign Aid." 89th Cong., 2d sess., July 26, 1966. *Congressional Record*, 112, Part 13, pp. 17065–67.

U. S. Congress. Senate. Senator Fulbright speaking on the political atmosphere in the United States. 89th Cong., 2d sess., August 22, 1966. *Congressional Record*, 112, Part 15, p. 20185.

U. S. Congress. Senate. Senator Fulbright, speech "The Building Up In Thailand." 89th Cong., 2d sess., October 3, 1966. *Congressional Record*, 112, Part 18, pp. 24776–78.

U. S. Congress. Senate. Senator Fulbright speaking on the "Consular Convention with the Soviet Union." 90th Cong., 1st sess., March 7, 1967. *Congressional Record*, 113, Part 5, pp. 5697–99.

U. S. Congress. Senate. Senator Fulbright and others discussing U. S. Commitments to Foreign Powers. S. Res. 151, 90th Cong., 1st sess., July 31, 1967. *Congressional Record*, 113, Part 15, pp. 20702–19.

U. S. Congress. Senate. Senators Hatfield and Fulbright discussing the extension of the war in Southeast Asia. S. Con. Res.

63, 90th Cong., 2d sess., February 28, 1968. *Congressional Record*, 114, Part 4, pp. 4545, 4546.

U. S. Congress. Senate. Senator Fulbright and others discussing the buildup of American Forces in Vietnam. 90th Cong., 2d sess., March 7, 1968. *Congressional Record*, 114, Part 5, pp. 5644–77.

U. S. Congress. Senate. Senator Fulbright speaking on the Gulf of Tonkin incidents. 90th Cong., 2d sess., March 27, 1968. *Congressional Record*, 114, Part 6, pp. 7837, 7838.

U. S. Congress. Senate. Senator Fulbright and others discussing needed clarification on the extent of the present cessation of bombing in North Vietnam. 90th Cong., 2d sess., April 2, 1968. *Congressional Record*, 114, Part 7, pp. 8569–77.

U. S. Congress. Senate. Senator Fulbright and others discussing authorization for Military Procurement, 1969. S. 3293, 90th Cong., 2d sess., April 18, 1968. *Congressional Record*, 114, Part 6, pp. 9980–87.

U. S. Congress. Senate. Senator Fulbright and others debating the rules of the Senate. 91st Cong., 1st sess., January 28, 1969. *Congressional Record*, 115, No. 18, pp. S 958–60.

U. S. Congress. Senate. Senator Fulbright speaking on classification of statistics on the Vietnam War. 91st Cong., 1st sess., May 12, 1969. *Congressional Record*, 115, No. 76, S 4884, S 4885.

U. S. Congress. Senate. Senator Fulbright and others speaking on behalf of National Commitments. S. Res. 85, 91st Cong., 1st sess., June 19, 1969. *Congressional Record*, 115, No. 101, pp. S 6828–41.

U. S. Congress. Senate. Senator Church speaking on behalf of National Commitments. S. Res. 85, 91st Cong., 1st sess., June 20, 1969. *Congressional Record*, 115, No. 102, pp. S 6878–914.

U. S. Congress. Senate. Debate on National Commitments. S. Res. 85, 91st Cong., 1st sess., June 24, 1969. *Congressional Record*, 115, No. 104, pp. S 7078–84.

U. S. Congress. Senate. Debate on National Commitments. S. Res. 85, 91st Cong., 1st sess., June 25, 1969. *Congressional Record*, 115, No. 105, pp. S 7122–53.

U. S. Congress. Senate. Senator Fulbright speaking on behalf of National Commitments. S. Res. 85, 91st Cong., 1st sess.,

June 26, 1969. *Congressional Record*, 115, No. 106, pp. S 7248–50.

U. S. Congress. Senate. Senator Fulbright commenting on a statement by Senator Proxmire. 91st Cong., 1st sess., June 29, 1969. *Congressional Record*, 115, No. 106, p. S 7230.

U. S. Congress. Senate. Senator Fulbright and others speaking against ABM. S. 2546, 91st Cong., 1st sess., July 25, 1969. *Congressional Record*, 115, No. 125, pp. S 8599–614.

U. S. Congress. Senate. Senator Fulbright and others speaking against ABM. S. 2546. 91st Cong., 1st sess., August 5, 1969. *Congressional Record*, 115, No. 132, pp. S 9196–211.

U. S. Congress. Senate. Senator Fullbright speaking on privileges and prerogatives of the Senate. 91st Cong., 1st sess., August 8, 1969. *Congressional Record*, 115, No. 135, pp. S 9503, S 9504.

U. S. Congress. Senate. Senator Fulbright, speech "Let's Put Space to Earthly Uses." 91st Cong., 1st sess., August 11, 1969. *Congressional Record*, 115, No. 136, pp. S 9631–34.

U. S. Congress. Senate. Senators Mathias and Mansfield speaking on behalf of a resolution which would rescind four Congressional actions giving emergency powers to the Executive. S. J. Res. 166, 91st Cong., 2d sess., December 8, 1969. *Congressional Record*, 115, No. 203, pp. S 16027–30.

U. S. Congress. Senate. Debate on the Department of Defense Appropriations, 1970. H. R. 15090, 91st Cong., 1st sess., December 15, 1969. *Congressional Record*, 115, No. 208, pp. S 16751–70.

U. S. Congress. Senate. Senator Fulbright speaking on Defense Appropriation Bill, 1970. H. R. 15090, 91st Cong., 1st sess., December 18, 1969. *Congressional Record*, 115, No. 211, pp. S 17181–87.

U. S. Congress. Senate. Senator Mathias, speech "American Foreign Policy," delivered at St. John's College, Annapolis, Maryland, January 14, 1970. Printed in 91st Cong., 2d sess., January 29, 1970. *Congressional Record*, 116, No. 10, pp. S 852, S 853.

U. S. Congress. Senate. Senator Fulbright speaking on "Hearing on Vietnam—1970." 91st Cong., 2d sess., February 6, 1970. *Congressional Record*, 116, No. 16, pp. S 1369, S 1370.

U. S. Congress. Senate. Senator Young of Ohio speaking about

Walter Cronkite's television interview with former President Lyndon B. Johnson. 91st Cong., 2d sess., February 10, 1970. *Congressional Record*, 116, No. 18, pp. S 1514–16.

U. S. Congress. Senate. Senator Fulbright, speech "What is the National Interest of the United States in Laos?" 91st Cong., 2d sess., March 3, 1970. *Congressional Record*, 116, No. 31, pp. S 2818–20.

U. S. Congress. Senate. Senator Fulbright's submission of a resolution to express the sense of the Senate on Armed Forces in Laos. S. Res. 368, 91st Cong., 2d sess., March 11, 1970. *Congressional Record*, 116, No. 37, pp. S 3506, S 3507.

U. S. Congress. Senate. Senator Fulbright, speech "Old Myths and New Realities—I." 91st Cong., 2d sess., April 2, 1970. *Congressional Record*, 116, No. 51, pp. S 4928–36.

Senate Reports and Committee Prints and Documents

U. S. Congress. Senate. Committee on Foreign Relations. *A Decade of American Foreign Policy, Basic Documents 1941–1949*. Sen. Doc. 123, 81st Cong., 1st sess., 1950.

U. S. Congress. Senate. Committee on Appropriations. *Department of Defense Appropriations Bill, 1970*. S. Rept. 91–607, 91st Cong., 1st sess., 1969.

U. S. Congress. Senate. Committee on Foreign Relations. *Background Information Relating to the Dominican Republic*. Committee Print, 89th Cong., 1st sess., July, 1965.

U. S. Congress. Senate. Committee on Foreign Relations. *Background Information on the Committee on Foreign Relations, United States Senate*. Committee Print, 90th Cong., 2d sess., February, 1968.

U. S. Congress. Senate. Committee on Foreign Relations. *Background Information Relating to Southeast Asia and Vietnam*. Committee Print, 91st Cong., 1st sess., March, 1969.

U. S. Congress. Senate. Committee on Foreign Relations. *The Formulation and Administration of United States Foreign Policy*. Study prepared at the Request of the Committee on Foreign Relations, Senate, by the Brookings Institution Pursuant to S. Res. 336, 85th Cong., and S. Res. 31, 86th Cong., No. 9. Committee Print, 86th Cong., 2d sess., January 13, 1960.

U. S. Congress. Senate. Committee on Foreign Relations. *The*

BIBLIOGRAPHY   **195**

Gulf of Tonkin, The 1964 Incidents, Part 11. Committee Print, 90th Cong., 2d sess., December 16, 1968.

U. S. Congress. Senate. Committee on Foreign Relations. *National Commitments.* S. Rept. 797, 90th Cong., 1st sess., 1967.

U. S. Congress. Senate. Committee on Foreign Relations. *National Commitments.* S. Rept. 91–129, 91st Cong., 1st sess., 1969.

U. S. Congress. Senate. Committee on Foreign Relations. *Perspective on Asia: The New U. S. Doctrine and Southeast Asia.* Committee Print, 91st Cong., 1st sess., 1969.

U. S. Congress. Senate. Committee on Foreign Relations. *A Select Chronology and Background Documents Relating to the Middle East* (First revised editions). Committee Print, 91st Cong., 1st sess., May, 1969.

U. S. Congress. Senate. Committees on Foreign Relations and Armed Services. *To Promote Peace and Stability in the Middle East.* S. Rept. 70, 85th Cong., 1st sess., 1957.

U. S. Congress. Senate. Committee on the Judiciary. Report of the Committee on the Judiciary made by its Subcommittee on Separation of Powers. *Separation of Powers.* S. Rept. 91–549, 90th Cong., 1st sess., 1967.

Senate Hearings

U. S. Congress. Senate. Committee on Foreign Relations. *Ambassadorial Appointments. Hearing* before the Committee on Foreign Relations, Senate, 85th Cong., 1st sess., August 1, 1957.

U. S. Congress. Senate. Committee on Foreign Relations. *Briefing by Secretary of State William P. Rogers. Hearing* before the Committee on Foreign Relations, Senate, 91st Cong., 1st sess., March 27, 1969.

U. S. Congress. Senate. Committee on Foreign Relations. *Briefing on Vietnam. Hearings* before the Committee on Foreign Relations, Senate, 91st Cong., 1st sess., November, 1969.

U. S. Congress. Senate. Committee on Foreign Relations. *Changing American Attitudes Toward Foreign Policy. Hearing* before the Committee on Foreign Relations, Senate, 90th Cong., 1st sess., February 20, 1967.

U. S. Congress. Senate. Committee on Foreign Relations. *Defense Department Sponsored Foreign Affairs Research. Hearing* before the Committee on Foreign Relations, Senate, 90th Cong., 2d sess., May 9, 1968.

U. S. Congress. Senate. Committee on Foreign Relations. *Events Incident to the Summit Conference. Hearings* before the Committee on Foreign Relations, Senate, 86th Cong., 2d sess., May, June, 1960.

U. S. Congress. Committee on Foreign Relations. *Foreign Assistance, 1964. Hearings* before the Committee on Foreign Relations, on S. 2659, S. 2660, S. 2662 and H. R. 11380, 88th Cong., 2d sess., March–June, 1964.

U. S. Congress. Senate. Committee on Foreign Relations. *Foreign Assistance, 1965. Hearings* before the Committee on Foreign Relations, Senate, 89th Cong., 1st sess., March, April, 1965.

U. S. Congress. Senate. Committee on Foreign Relations. *Foreign Assistance, 1966.* Hearings before the Committee on Foreign Relations, Senate, on S. 2859 and S. 2861, 89th Cong., 2d sess., April, May, 1966.

U. S. Congress. Senate. Committee on Foreign Relations. *Foreign Assistance Act of 1968, Part 1—Vietnam. Hearings* before the Committee on Foreign Relations, Senate, on S. 3091, 90th Cong., 2d sess., March, 1968.

U. S. Congress. Senate. Committee on Foreign Relations. *Foreign Assistance Act of 1968, Part 2. Hearings* before the Committee on Foreign Relations, Senate, on S. 3091, 90th Cong., 2d sess., March, May, 1968.

U. S. Congress. Senate. Committee on Foreign Relations. *The Gulf of Tonkin, The 1964 Incidents. Hearing* before the Committee on Foreign Relations, Senate, 90th Cong., 2d sess., February 20, 1968.

U. S. Congress. Senate. Committee on Foreign Relations. *Harrison E. Salisbury's Trip to North Vietnam. Hearing* before the Committee on Foreign Relations, 90th Cong., 1st sess., February 2, 1967.

U. S. Congress. Senate. Committee on Foreign Relations. *Intelligence and the ABM. Hearing* before the Committee on Foreign Relations, 91st Cong., 1st sess., June 23, 1969.

U. S. Congress. Senate. Committee on Foreign Relations. *Chemical and Biological Warfare. Hearing* before the Committee on Foreign Relations, 91st Cong., 1st sess., April 30, 1969.

U. S. Congress. Senate. Committee on Foreign Relations. *Nomination of Maxwell H. Gluck. Hearing* before the Committee on Foreign Relations, Senate, 85th Cong., 1st sess., July 2, 1957.

J. S. Congress. Senate. Committee on Foreign Relations. *Nonproliferation Treaty.* *Hearing* before the Committee on Foreign Relations, Senate, on Executive H, 90th Cong., 2d sess., February, 1969.

J. S. Congress. Senate. Committee on Foreign Relations. *North Atlantic Treaty.* *Hearings* before the Committee on Foreign Relations, Senate, on Executive L, 81st Cong., 1st sess., April, May, 1949.

J. S. Congress. Senate. Committee on Foreign Relations. *Nuclear Test Ban Treaty.* *Hearings* before the Committee on Foreign Relations, Senate, on Executive M, 88th Cong., 1st sess., August, 1963.

J. S. Congress. Senate. Committee on Foreign Relations. *Present Situation in Vietnam.* *Hearing* before the Committee on Foreign Relations, Senate, 90th Cong., 2d sess., March 20, 1968.

J. S. Congress. Senate. Committee on Foreign Relations. *Presidential Determination on Countries Receiving Loans and Technical Assistance.* *Hearing* before the Committee on Foreign Relations, Senate, 90th Cong., 1st sess., January 25, 1967.

J. S. Congress. Senate. Committee on Foreign Relations. *Psychological Aspects of Foreign Policy.* *Hearings* before the Committee on Foreign Relations, Senate, 91st Cong., 1st sess., June, 1969.

J. S. Congress. Senate. Committee on Foreign Relations. *Strategic and Foreign Policy Implications of ABM Systems.* *Hearings* before the Subcommittee on International Organization and Disarmament of the Committee on Foreign Relations, Senate, 91st Cong., 1st sess., May, 1969.

J. S. Congress. Senate. Committee on Foreign Relations. *Submission of the Vietnam Conflict to the United Nations.* *Hearings* before the Committee on Foreign Relations, Senate, on S. Con. Res. 44, 90th Cong., 1st sess., 1967.

J. S. Congress. Senate. Committee on Foreign Relations. *Supplemental Foreign Assistance, Fiscal Year 1966—Vietnam.* *Hearings* before the Committee on Foreign Relations, Senate, on S. 2793, 89th Cong., 2d sess., January, February, 1966.

J. S. Congress. Senate. Committee on Foreign Relations. *U. S.*

Commitments to Foreign Powers. Hearings before the Committee on Foreign Relations, Senate, on S. Res. 151, 90th Cong., 1st sess., August, September, 1967.

U. S. Congress. Senate. Committee on Foreign Relations. *United States Foreign Policy. Hearings* before the Committee on Foreign Relations, Senate, Studies pursuant to S. Res. 336, 85th Cong., S. Res. 31, 86th Cong., and S. Res. 41, 87th Cong. 1st sess., January–March, 1961.

U. S. Congress. Senate. Committee on Foreign Relations. *U. S Policy with Respect to Mainland China. Hearings* before the Committee on Foreign Relations, Senate, 89th Cong. 2d sess., March, 1966.

U. S. Congress. Senate. Committee on Foreign Relations. *United States Security Agreements and Commitments Abroad. The Republic of the Philippines. Hearings* before the Subcommittee on the United States Security Agreements and Commitments Abroad of the Committee on Foreign Relations, Senate, 91st Cong., 1st sess., 1969.

U. S. Congress. Senate. Committee on Foreign Relations. *What Is Wrong with our Foreign Policy. Hearing* before the Committee on Foreign Relations, Senate, 86th Cong., 1st sess. April 15, 1959.

U. S. Congress. Senate. Committees on Foreign Relations and Armed Services. *Assignment of Ground Forces of the United States to Duty in the European Area. Hearings* before the Committee on Foreign Relations and the Committee or Armed Services, Senate, on S. Con. Res. 8, 82nd Cong., 1st sess., February, 1951.

U. S. Congress. Senate. Committees on Foreign Relations and Armed Services. *Military Situation in the Far East. Hearings* before the Committee on Foreign Relations and the Committee on Armed Services, Senate, 82nd Cong., 1st sess. May, 1951.

U. S. Congress. Senate. Committees on Foreign Relations and Armed Services. *The President's Proposal on the Middle East. Hearings* before the Committee on Foreign Relations and the Committee on Armed Services, Senate, on S. J. Res 19 and H. J. Res. 117, 85th Cong., 1st sess., January, February, 1957.

U. S. Congress. Senate. Committee on the Judiciary. *Separation of Powers,* Part 1. *Hearings* before the Subcommittee or

Separation of Powers of the Committee on the Judiciary, Senate, 90th Cong., 1st sess., July–September, 1967.

Articles and Newspapers

Blaisdell, Donald C. "Pressure Groups, Foreign Policies and International Politics." *Annals of the American Academy of Political and Social Science* 319 (September 1958): 149–57.

Broder, David S. "Consensus Politics: End of an Experiment." *Atlantic*, October, 1966, pp. 60–65.

Brower, Brock. "The Roots of the Arkansas Questioner." *Life*, May 13, 1966, pp. 92–94 ff.

Brown, MacAlister. "The Demise of State Department Public Opinion Polls: A Study in Legislative Oversight." *Midwest Journal of Political Science* 5 (February 1961): 1–17.

Buchanan, William and Eulau, Heinz, Ferguson, LeRoy C., and Wahlke, John C. "The Legislator as Specialist." *Western Political Quarterly* 13 (September 1960): 636–51.

Campbell, Alex. "Fulbright on Camera." *New Republic*, May 21, 1966, pp. 19–22.

Cannon, Clarence. "Congressional Responsibilities." *American Political Science Review* 42 (April 1948): 307–16.

Cimbala, Stephen J. "Foreign Policy as an Issue Area: A Roll Call Analysis." *American Political Science Review* 63 (March 1969): 148–56.

Coffin, Tristram. "Congress: Its Lost Sacred Powers." *Bulletin of the Atomic Scientist* 23 (December 1967): 35–37.

Coffin, Tristram. "Senator Fulbright." *Holiday*. September 1964, pp. 35–37, *passim.*

Colegrove, Kenneth W. "The Role of Congress and Public Opinion in Formulating Foreign Policy." *American Political Science Review* 38 (October 1944): 956–69.

Commager, Henry Steele. "Can We Limit Presidential Power?" *New Republic*, April 6, 1963, pp. 15–18.

"Congress and Foreign Relations." *Annals of the American Academy of Political and Social Science* 289 (September 1953), entire issue.

Connery, Robert H. and David, Paul T. "The Mutual Defense Assistance Program." *American Political Science Review* 45 (June 1951): 321–47.

Dawson, Raymond H. "Congressional Innovation and Intervention in Defense Policy: Legislative Authorization of Weapons Systems." *American Political Science Review* 56 (March 1962): 42–57.

Draper, Theodore. "The Dominican Crisis: A Case Study in American Policy." *Commentary*, December, 1965, pp. 33–68.

———. "Senator Fulbright's Cuban Options." *New Leader*, April 27, 1964, pp. 3–9.

Driggs, D. W. "President as Chief Educator on Foreign Affairs." *Western Political Quarterly* 11 (December 1958): 813–19.

"Enter Fulbright." *Time*, August 7, 1944, p. 19.

Evans, Rowland, Jr. "Louisiana's Passman: The Scourge of Foreign Aid." *Harpers*, January, 1962, pp. 78–83.

Fenno, Richard F. "The House Appropriations Committee as a Political System: The Problem of Integration." *American Political Science Review* 56 (June 1962): 310–24.

"Foreign Policy Critic," *U. S. News and World Report*, February 8, 1957, p. 18.

Friedmann, Wolfgang. "Interventionism, Liberalism, and Power Politics: The Unfinished Revolution in International Thinking." *Political Science Quarterly* 83 (June 1968): 169–89.

Fulbright, J. William. "The American Agenda." *Saturday Review*, July 20, 1963, pp. 15–17, 62, 63.

———. "American Foreign Policy in the 20th Century Under an 18th-Century Constitution." *Cornell Law Quarterly* 47 (Fall 1961): 1–13.

———. "Bipartisanship is a Two-Way Street." *Reporter*, December 16, 1954, pp. 8–11.

———. "Challenge to Our Complacency." *New York Times Magazine*, September 14, 1958, pp. 244.

———. "A Concert of Free Nations." *International Organization* 17 (Summer 1963): 787–803.

———. "Criticism and Praise for Dulles's Views." *U. S. News and World Report*, March 9, 1956, pp. 111–13.

———. "Dangerous Delusions." *Saturday Review*, October 24, 1964, pp. 24, 25+.

———. "The Fatal Arrogance of Power." *New York Times Magazine*, May 15, 1966, pp. 27, 28+.

———. "For a Concert of Free Nations." *Foreign Affairs* 40 (October 1961): 1–18.

————. "Foreign Aid? Yes, But with a New Approach." *New York Times Magazine,* March 21, 1965, pp. 27, *passim.*

————. "Foreign Policy Implications of the ABM Debate." *Bulletin of the Atomic Scientists* 25 (June 1969): 20–23.

————. "Let's Talk Sense about Cuba." *Saturday Evening Post,* May 16, 1964, pp. 8, 10.

————. "Open Doors Not Iron Curtains." *New York Times Magazine,* August 5, 1959, pp. 18, *passim.*

————. "Vietnam: The Crucial Issue." *The Progressive,* February, 1970, pp. 16–18.

————. "Views of J. William Fulbright." *Foreign Policy Bulletin* 38 (September 15, 1958): 5, 6.

————. "The Wars in Your Future." *Look,* December 2, 1969, pp. 82–88.

————. "We Must Negotiate Peace in Vietnam." *Saturday Evening Post,* April 9, 1966, pp. 10, 12, 14.

————. "We Must Not Fight Fire with Fire." *New York Times Magazine,* April 23, 1967, pp. 27, *passim.*

————. "Vietnam: Where Do We Go From Here." *Saturday Evening Post,* February 8, 1969, pp. 24, 25, 49.

————. "Fulbright Criticizes Foreign Policy." *Christian Century,* April 8, 1964, pp. 452, 453.

"Fulbright: 'Mistaken Policies' Behind U. S. Troubles in World." *U. S. News and World Report,* August 15, 1958, p. 86.

"Fulbright's Pilgrimage." *Economist,* June 4, 1966, pp. 1081, 1082.

"Fulbright's Progress." *Nation,* April 13, 1964, pp. 357, 358.

Frye, Alton. "Gobble'uns and Foreign Policy: A Review." *Journal of Conflict Resolution* 8 (September 1964): 314–321.

Gati, Charles. "Another Grand Debate? The Limitationist Critique of American Foreign Policy." *World Politics* 21 (October 1968): 133–51.

Goldbloom, Maurice. "The Fulbright Revolt." *Commentary,* September, 1966, pp. 63–69.

Gould, James W. "The Origins of the Senate Committee on Foreign Relations." *Western Political Quarterly* 12 (September 1959): 670–82.

Goulden, Joseph C. "The Imperfect Link." *Vista,* March–April, 1970, pp. 30–35.

Graff, Henry F. "Thinking Aloud: Participatory Foreign Policy." *New Leader,* March 2, 1970, pp. 11–15.

Gray, Charles H. "A Scale Analysis of the Voting Records of Senators Kennedy, Johnson and Goldwater, 1957–1960." *American Political Science Review* 59 (September 1965): 615–21.

Griffith, Ernest. "The Place of Congress in Foreign Relations." *Annals of the American Academy of Political and Social Science* 289 (September 1953): 11–21.

Grundy, Kenneth W. "The Apprenticeship of J. William Fulbright." *Virginia Quarterly Review* 43 (Summer 1967): 382–99.

Hardin, Charles M. "Congressional Farm Policies and Economic Foreign Policy." *Annals of the American Academy of Political and Social Science* 331 (September 1960): 98–102.

Henkin, Louis. "Vietnam in the Courts of the United States: Political Questions." *American Journal of International Law* 63 (April 1969): 284–89.

Hilsman, Roger. "Congressional-Executive Relations and the Foreign Policy Consensus." *American Political Science Review* 52 (September 1958): 725–44.

Hitchens, Harold L. "Influences on the Congressional Decision to Pass the Marshall Plan." *Western Political Quarterly* 21 (March 1968): 51–68.

Hughes, Thomas L. "Foreign Policy on Capital Hill." *Reporter*, April 30, 1959, pp. 28–31.

Huitt, Ralph K. "Democratic Party Leadership in the Senate." *American Political Science Review* 55 (June 1961): 333–44.

Humphrey, Hubert H. "The Senate in Foreign Policy." *Foreign Affairs* 37 (July 1959): pp. 525–36.

Hyman, Sidney. "The Advice and Consent of J. William Fulbright." *Reporter*, September 17, 1959, pp. 23–25.

———. "Fulbright: The Wedding of Arkansas and the World." *New Republic*, May 14, 1962, pp. 19–26.

Jahnige, Thomas P. "The Congressional Committee System and the Oversight Process: Congress and NASA." *Journal of Conflict Resolution* 21 (June 1968): 227–39.

Javits, Jacob K. "The Congressional Record in Foreign Relations." *Foreign Affairs* 48 (January 1970): 221–234.

Jones, Charles O. "Representation in Congress: The Case of the House Agriculture Committee." *American Political Science Review* 55 (June 1961): 358–67.

Kansas City Star, 1969, 1970.

Kansas City Times, 1969, 1970.

Kaplan, Norton A. "Old Realities and New Myths." *World Politics* 17 (January 1965): 334–67.

Katzenbach, Edward L. "How Congress Strains at Gnats, Then Swallows Military Budgets." *Reporter,* July 20, 1954, pp. 31–35.

Katzenbach, Nicholas. "Comparative Roles of the President and the Congress in Foreign Affairs." *Department of State Bulletin* 47 (September 11, 1967): 333–36.

Kenworthy, E. W. "Fulbright Becomes a National Issue." *New York Times Magazine,* October 1, 1961, pp. 21, *passim.*

————. "The Fulbright Idea of Foreign Policy." *New York Times Magazine,* May 10, 1959, pp. 10, 11, *passim.*

Keown, Stuart S. "The President, the Congress, and the Power to Declare War." *Kansas Law Review* 16 (November 1967): 82–97.

Kessleman, Mark. "Presidential Leadership in Congress on Foreign Policy." *Midwest Journal of Political Science* 5 (August 1961): 284–89.

Kolodoziej, Edward A. "Congressional Responsibility for the Common Defense: The Money Problem." *Western Political Quarterly* 16 (March 1963): 149–60.

Kopkind, Andrew. "The Speechmaker." *New Republic,* October 2, 1965, pp. 15–19.

"The Legislative-Executive Foreign Policy Relationship in the 90th Congress." *Congressional Digest* 47 (October 1968), entire issue.

Lindley, Ernest K. "Kefauver and Fulbright." *Newsweek,* April 2, 1951, p. 25.

Lippman, Walter. "A Senator Speaks Out." *Newsweek,* April 13, 1964, p. 19.

Marcy, Carl. "Depending on Where One Sits." *Foreign Service Journal* 42 (January 1965): 43–50.

Martin, Kingsley. "With Fulbright in Little Rock." *New Statesman,* November 17, 1961, pp. 730, 732.

Meeker, Leonard C. "The Legality of United States Participation in the Defense of Viet Nam." *Department of State Bulletin* 54 (March 28, 1966): 474–89.

Mellor, Norman. "Legislative Behavior Research." *Western Political Quarterly* 13 (March 1960): 131–53.

Meyer, Karl E. "Fulbright of Arkansas." *Progressive,* September, 1962, pp. 26–30.

————. "Mr. Fulbright's Heresy." *New Statesman,* April 3, 1964, p. 513.

Morgenthau, Hans J. "Senator Fulbright's New Foreign Policy." *Commentary,* May, 1964, pp. 70–71.

————. "Time for a Change." *New York Review of Books,* April 6, 1967, pp. 18–22.

Nelson, Randall H. "Legislative Participation in the Treaty and Agreement Making Process." *Western Political Quarterly* 13 (March 1960): pp. 154–72.

New York Times. 1943–1970.

Nigro, Felix A. "Senate Confirmation and Foreign Policy." *Journal of Politics* 14 (May 1952): 281–90.

"Notes: Congress, the President and the Power to Commit Forces to Combat." *Harvard Law Review* 81 (June 1968): 1771–805.

Oberdorfer, Don. "Common Noun Spelled f-u-l-b-r-i-g-h-t." *New York Times Magazine,* April 4, 1965, pp. 79, 80, *passim.*

Patterson, Samuel C. "Legislative Leadership and Political Ideology." *Public Opinion Quarterly* 27 (Fall 1963): 399–410.

Polsby, Nelson W. "Foreign Policy and Congressional Activity." *World Politics* 15 (January 1963): 354–59.

Reston, James B. "Rethinking the Unthinkable." *Reporter,* September 21, 1967, pp. 14, 15.

Reston, Richard. "Fulbright Pro and Con." *Atlantic,* October, 1966, pp. 10–12.

Riker, William H. and Niemi, Donald. "The Stability of Coalitions on Roll Calls in the House of Representatives." *American Political Science Review* 56 (March 1962): 58–65.

Ripley, Randall B. "Power in the Post World War II Senate." *Journal of Politics* 31 (May 1969): 465–92.

Sanford, David. "A Talk with Senator Fulbright." *New Republic,* March 9, 1968, pp. 19, 20.

"Secret Agreements." *New Republic,* July 26, 1969, pp. 5, 6.

Seib, Charles B. and Otten, Alan L. "Fulbright: Arkansas Paradox." *Harpers,* June, 1956, pp. 60–66.

Senate Committee on Foreign Relations. "Pro: Should Resolution 187 Concerning the Power of the Executive in Foreign Relations Be Adopted?" *Congressional Digest*, October, 1968, p. 236.

"Senate's 1968 Defense Debate Ranked Among Longest." *Congressional Quarterly Weekly Report* 27 (September 26, 1969): 1817–19.

"Senate's Scholarly Dissenter." *Business Week*, April 4, 1964, pp. 28, 29.

"Senator Fulbright Hits at Ike's Summit Views." *U. S. News and World Report*, June 15, 1959, p. 24.

Sevareid, Eric. "Why Our Foreign Policy Is Failing: An Exclusive Interview with Senator Fulbright." *Look*, May 3, 1966, pp. 23–31.

Small, Melvin. "Democracy and Foreign Policy." *Journal of Conflict Resolution* 12 (June 1968): 249–57.

Smith, Beverly. "Egghead from the Ozarks." *Saturday Evening Post*, May 2, 1959, pp. 31, 115–18.

Steel, Ronald. "The Case for Retrenchment." *New Leader*, February 17, 1969, pp. 9–13.

Stone, I. F. "Fulbright: From Hawk to Dove, (Part 2)." *New York Review of Books*, January 12, 1967, pp. 8, 10, 12.

———. "Fulbright of Arkansas, (Part 1)." *New York Review of Books*, December 29, 1966, pp. 5, 6.

———. "Fulbright: The Timid Opposition." *New York Review of Books*. January 26, 1967, pp. 10, 12, 13.

Tansill, Charles C. "War Powers of the President of the United States with Special Reference to the Beginning of Hostilities." *Political Science Quarterly* 45 (March 1930): 1–55.

"The Question of U. S. Foreign Military Commitments: Pro & Con." *Congressional Digest*, August–September, 1969, entire issue.

Unna, Warren. "CIA: Who Watches the Watchman?" *Harpers*, April, 1958, pp. 46–53.

Vile, M. J. C. "Formulation and Execution of Policy in the United States." *Political Quarterly* 33 (April 1962): 162–71.

Washington Post. March 26, 1945. Fulbright File, Washington, D. C.

———. 1969, 1970.

Wildasvsky, Aaron. "The Two Presidencies: Presidential Power is Greatest When Directing Military and Foreign Policy," *Transaction*, December, 1966, pp. 7–14.

Williams, Benjamin H. "Bipartisanship in American Foreign Policy." *Annals of the American Academy of Social and Political Science* 259 (September 1948): 136–43.

Wolfinger, Raymond E. and Heifetz, Joan. "Safe Seats, Seniority, and Power in Congress." *American Political Science Review* 59 (June 1965): 337–49.

Books

Acheson, Dean. *Present at the Creation.* New York: W. W. Norton & Company, 1969.

———. *Sketches from Life of Men I Have Known.* London: Hamish Hamilton, 1961.

Bailey, Stephen K. *The New Congress.* New York: St. Martin's Press, 1966.

Bailey, Thomas A. *A Diplomatic History of the American People.* New York: Appleton-Century Crofts, 1969.

Bartlett, Ruhl J., ed. *The Record of American Diplomacy.* New York: Alfred A. Knopf, 1954.

Bauer, Raymond A., Ithiel de Sola Pool, and Dexter, Lewis Anthony. *American Business and Public Policy: The Politics of Foreign Trade.* New York: Atherton Press, 1963.

Beloff, Max. *Foreign Policy and the Democratic Process.* Baltimore: John Hopkins Press, 1955.

Bibby, John and Davidson, Roger. *On Capital Hill: Studies in the Legislative Process.* New York: Holt, Rinehart and Winston, 1967.

Bolling, Richard. *House Out of Order.* New York: E. P. Dutton, 1965.

Brown, Seyom. *The Faces of Power.* New York: Columbia University Press, 1968.

Burns, James MacGregor. *The Deadlock of Democracy: Four-Party Politics in America.* Englewood Cliffs, New Jersey: Prentice-Hall, 1963.

Campbell, John T. and the Research Staff of the Council on Foreign Relations. *The United States in World Affairs 1945–1947.* New York: Published for the Council on Foreign Relations by Harper & Brothers, 1947.

Cheever, Daniel S. and Haviland, H. Field. *American Foreign Policy and the Separation of Powers.* Cambridge: Harvard University Press, 1952.

Clapp, Charles E. *The Congressman: His Work As He Sees It.* Washington, D. C.: The Brookings Institution, 1963.

Cerf, Jay H. and Pozens, Walter, eds. *Strategy for the 60's.* New York: Frederick A. Praeger, 1960.

Coffin, Tristram. *Senator Fulbright: Portrait of a Public Philosopher.* New York: E. P. Dutton & Company, 1966.

Cohen, Bernard Cecil, ed. *Foreign Policy in American Government.* Boston: Little, Brown, 1965.

Congressional Quarterly Almanac. Vols. 12–24. Washington, D. C.: Congressional Quarterly Service, 1956–1968.

Corwin, Edward S. *The President: Office and Powers 1787–1957.* New York: New York University Press, 1957.

Crabb, Cecil V. *Bipartisan Foreign Policy: Myth or Reality?* Evanston, Ill.: Row, Peterson and Company, 1957.

Dahl, Robert A. *Congress and Foreign Policy.* New York: W. W. Norton, 1964.

Dangerfield, Royden J. *In Defense of the Senate: A Study of Treaty Making.* Norman, Okla.: University of Oklahoma Press, 1933.

Dean, Vera. *Foreign Policy Without Fear.* New York: McGraw-Hill, 1953.

de Rivera, Joseph H. *The Psychological Dimension of Foreign Policy.* Columbus, Ohio: Charles E. Merrill Publishing Company, 1968.

De Tocqueville, Alexis. *Democracy in America.* Vol. 1. New York: Alfred A. Knopf, 1945.

Donham, Philip and Fahey, Robert J. *Congress Needs Help.* New York: Random House, 1966.

Egger, Rowland. *The President of the United States.* New York: McGraw-Hill, 1967.

Eisenhower, Dwight David. *Mandate for Change 1953–1956.* Garden City, New York: Doubleday & Company, 1963.

Ellsberg, Daniel. *Papers On the War.* New York: Simon and Schuster, 1972.

Farnsworth, David N. *The Senate Committee on Foreign Relations.* Urbana: University of Illinois Press, 1961.

Farrand, Max., ed. *The Records of the Federal Convention of 1787.* Vol. 2. New Haven: Yale University Press, 1966.

Ferrell, Robert H. *Peace In Their Time.* New Haven: Yale University Press, 1952.

Finer, Herman. *Dulles Over Suez.* Chicago: Quadrangle Books, 1964.

————. *The Presidency: Crisis and Regeneration.* Chicago: The University of Chicago Press, 1960.

Froman, Lewis A. *The Congressional Process: Strategies, Rules, and Procedures.* Boston: Little, Brown and Company, 1967.

Fulbright, J. William. *The Arrogance of Power.* New York: Vintage Books, 1966.

————. *Old Myths and New Realities.* New York: Random House, 1964.

Gerberding, William P. *United States Foreign Policy: Perspectives and Analysis.* New York: McGraw-Hill, 1966.

Graebner, Norman A. *The New Isolationism.* New York: The Ronald Press, 1956.

Griffith, Ernest S. *Congress: Its Contemporary Role.* New York: New York University Press, 1967.

Hamilton, Alexander. *The Papers of Alexander Hamilton.* Edited by Harold C. Syrett. Vol. 15. New York: Columbia University Press, 1969.

————, Madison, James, and Jay, John. *Selections from the Federalist.* Edited by Henry Steele Commager. New York: Appleton-Century Crofts, 1949.

Harris, Joseph P. *Congress and the Legislative Process.* New York: McGraw-Hill, 1967.

Heller, Francis H. *The Presidency: A Modern Perspective.* New York: Random House, 1960.

Hilsman, Roger. *To Move A Nation.* Garden City, New York: Doubleday, 1967.

Hoffmann, Stanley. *Gulliver's Troubles, Or the Setting of American Foreign Policy.* New York: McGraw-Hill Book Company, 1968.

Jewell, Malcolm E. *Senatorial Politics & Foreign Policy.* Lexington: University of Kentucky Press, 1962.

Johnson, Claudius O. *Borah of Idaho.* New York: Longmans, Green and Company, 1936.

Johnson, Donald Bruce and Walker, Jack L., eds. *The Dynamics of the American Presidency.* New York: John Wiley & Sons, 1964.

Johnson, Haynes and Bernard M. Gwertzman. *Fulbright: The Dissenter.* New York: Doubleday and Company, 1968.

Kefauver, Estes and Levin, Jack. *A Twentieth-Century Congress.* New York: Greenwood Press, 1959.

Kennedy, Robert F. *Thirteen Days: A Memoir of the Cuban Missile Crisis.* New York: W. W. Norton and Company, 1969.

Lerche, Charles O. *Foreign Policy of the American People.* Englewood Cliffs, N. J.: Prentice-Hall, 1967.

Lincoln, Abraham. *The Collected Works of Abraham Lincoln.* Edited by Roy P. Basler. Vol. 1. New Brunswick: Rutgers University Press, 1953.

Lippman, Walter. *Men of Destiny.* New York: The Macmillan Company, 1928.

McCamy, James. *Conduct of the New Diplomacy.* New York: Harper & Row, 1964.

McCarthy, Eugene J. *The Limits of Power.* New York: Holt, Rinehart and Winston, 1967.

McGee, Gale W. *The Responsibilities of World Power.* Washington, D. C.: The National Press, Inc., 1968.

Madison, James. *The Writings of James Madison.* Edited by Gaillard Hunt. Vol. 6. New York: G. P. Putnam's Sons, 1906.

Mathews, Donald R. *U. S. Senators & Their World.* Chapel Hill: University of North Carolina, 1960.

Meyer, Karl E., ed. *Senator Fulbright.* New York: McFadden-Bartell, 1964.

Morison, Samuel Eliot. *The Oxford History of the American People.* New York: Oxford University Press, 1965.

Neustadt, Richard E. *Presidential Power.* New York: John Wiley & Sons, 1962.

Osgood, Robert Endicott. *Ideals and Self-Interest in America's Foreign Policy.* Chicago: The University of Chicago Press, 1953.

Pettit, Lawrence K. and Keynes, Edward, eds. *The Legislative Process in the U. S. Senate.* Chicago: Rand McNally & Company, 1969.

Paolucci, Henry. *War, Peace, and the Presidency.* New York: McGraw-Hill Book Company, 1968.

Polsby, Nelson W. *Congress and the Presidency.* Englewood Cliffs, N. J.: Prentice-Hall, 1964.

Pressman, Jeffrey L. *House vs. Senate.* New Haven: Yale University Press, 1966.

Public Papers of the Presidents of the United States: Eisenhower, 1954. Washington, D. C.: Government Printing Office, 1960.

Public Papers of the Presidents of the United States: Truman, 1950. Washington, D. C.: Government Printing Office, 1965.

Pusey, Merlo J. *The Way We Go to War.* Boston: Houghton Mifflin Company, 1969.

Radway, Laurence I. *The Liberal Democracy in World Affairs: Foreign Policy and National Defense.* Glenview, Ill.: Scott, Foresman and Company, 1969.

Rieselbach, Leroy N. *The Roots of Isolationism.* Indiana: The Bobbs-Merrill Company, 1966.

Ripley, Randall B. *Power in the Senate.* New York: St. Martin's Press, 1969.

Robinson, Edgar E. and others. *Powers of the President in Foreign Affairs, 1945-1965.* San Francisco: A Research Study Commissioned by the Commonwealth Club of California, published by Lederer, Street and Zeuz, 1966.

Robinson, James A. *Congress and Foreign Policy-Making.* Homewood, Ill.: The Dorsey Press, 1967.

Rosenau, James N. *National Leadership and Foreign Policy.* Princeton, N. J.: Princeton University Press, 1963.

Rossiter, Clinton. *The American Presidency.* New York: Harcourt, Brace and Company, 1956.

Sapin, Bruce M. *The Making of United States Foreign Policy.* Washington, D. C.: Published for the Brookings Institution by Frederick A. Praeger, 1966.

Schlesinger, Arthur M., Jr. *A Thousand Days.* Boston: Houghton Mifflin, 1965.

————, and Alfred de Grazia. *Congress and the Presidency: Their Role in Modern Times.* Washington, D. C.: American Enterprise Institute for Public Policy Research, 1967.

Seabury, Paul. *Power, Freedom and Diplomacy.* New York: Random House, 1963.

Sorenson, Theodore C. *Decision-Making in the White House:*

The Olive Branch or the Arrows. New York: Columbia University Press, 1963.

———. *Kennedy.* New York: Harper and Row, 1965.

Stebbins, Richard P. and the Research Staff of the Council on Foreign Relations. *The United States in World Affairs 1951.* New York: Published for the Council on Foreign Relations by Harper & Brothers, 1952.

Steele, Archibald T. *The American People and China.* New York: Published for the Council on Foreign Relations by McGraw-Hill, 1966.

Taft, Robert A. *A Foreign Policy for Americans.* New York: Doubleday and Company, 1951.

Truman, David. *The Governmental Process.* New York: Alfred A. Knopf, 1951.

———, ed. *The Congress and America's Future.* Englewood Cliffs, N. J.: Prentice-Hall, 1965.

Tugwell, Roxford G. *The Enlargement of the Presidency.* Garden City, N. Y.: Doubleday and Company, 1960.

U. S. Congress, Joint Committee on Printing. *Compilation of Messages and Papers of the Presidents.* Vol. 1. Edited by James D. Richardson. New York: Bureau of National Literature, 1897.

Waltz, Kenneth M. *Foreign Policy and Democratic Politics.* Boston: Little, Brown and Company, 1967.

Warren, Sidney. *The President as World Leader.* Philadelphia: J. B. Lippincott Company, 1964.

Weintal, Edward and Charles Bartlett. *Facing the Brink.* New York: Charles Scribner's Sons, 1967.

Westerfield, H. Bradford. *The Instruments of America's Foreign Policy.* New York: Thomas Y. Crowell, 1963.

Wilson, Woodrow. *The Political Thought of Woodrow Wilson.* Edited by E. David Cronon. New York: Bobbs-Merrill Company, 1965.

———. *Congressional Government.* Boston: Houghton Mifflin Company, 1913.

Speeches

Fulbright, J. William. "Approaches to International Community." Speech at Pennsylvania State University, University Park,

Pennsylvania, March 6, 1965. Fulbright files, Washington, D. C.

———. "Atlantic Partnership." Speech before the Association for the Study of Foreign Affairs, Munich, Federal Republic of Germany, November 19, 1964. Fulbright files, Washington, D. C.

———. "Atlantic Partnership and the Defense of Freedom." Speech before the Italian Society for International Organizations, Rome, November 21, 1962. Fulbright files, Washington, D. C.

———. "Atlantic Partnership and its World Responsibilities." Speech at Festakt, Aula, University of Bonn, Germany, November 19, 1962. Fulbright files, Washington, D. C.

———. "Bridges East and West." Speech at Southern Methodist University, Dallas, Texas, December 8, 1964. Fulbright files, Washington, D. C.

———. "The Cold War in American Life." Speech at the University of North Carolina 1965 Symposium "Arms and the Man: National Security and the Aims of a Free Society," April 5, 1964. Fulbright files, Washington, D. C.

———. "The Commonwealth and the United States in Eastern Asia." Speech at the Eleventh Commonwealth Parliamentary Conference, Wellington, New Zealand, December 8, 1965. Fulbright files, Washington, D. C.

———. "A Creative War." Speech before the Commission to Study the Organization of Peace, New York City, February 26, 1943. Fulbright files, Washington, D. C.

———. "Current Affairs." Speech at the University of Maryland, March 25, 1957. Fulbright files, Washington, D. C.

———. "The Debate on Vietnam and its Meaning for the Class of 1966." Speech at the University of Arkansas Commencement, Fayetteville, Arkansas, June 4, 1966. Fulbright files, Washington, D. C.

———. "Education for a New Kind of International Relations." Speech at the Annual Meeting of the Swedish Institute for Cultural Relations, Stockholm, Sweden, December 5, 1966. Fulbright files, Washington, D. C.

———. "Higher Education and the Crisis in Asia." Speech before the 21st National Conference on Higher Education, Chicago, March 14, 1966. Fulbright files, Washington, D. C.

———. "Human Needs and World Politics." Speech at California State College at Long Beach, June 12, 1964. Fulbright files, Washington, D. C.

———. "Ideology and Foreign Policy." The George Huntington Williams Memorial Lecture, Johns Hopkins University, Baltimore, Maryland, March 12, 1965. Fulbright files, Washington, D. C.

———. "The Legislator." Speech at the University of Chicago, February 19, 1946. Fulbright files, Washington, D. C.

———. "Lighting the Lamps of Europe." Speech before the Austrian Foreign Policy Association on the 600th Anniversary of the University of Vienna, Vienna, Austria, May 11, 1965. Fulbright files, Washington, D. C.

———. "Militarism and American Democracy." Owens-Corning Lecture, Denison University, Granville, Ohio, April 18, 1969. Fulbright files, Washington, D. C.

———. "A New Era in International Relations." Speech at the annual dinner of the regional office of the Institute of International Education, Denver, Colorado, April 27, 1957. Fulbright files, Washington, D. C.

———. "On Relations Between the Most Powerful Country and the Most Populous Country in the World." Speech at the Center for Study of Democratic Institutions, Santa Barbara, California, January 24, 1969. Fulbright files, Washington, D. C.

———. "Our Complex Government." Speech at Agnes Scott College, December 3, 1958. Fulbright files, Washington, D. C.

———. "Our Foreign Policy." Speech before a joint meeting of the American Academy of Arts and Letters and the National Institute of Arts, New York City, May 17, 1946. Fulbright files, Washington, D. C.

———. "Our Responsibilities in World Affairs." Gabriel Silver Lecture on International Understanding, Columbia University, May 7, 1959. Fulbright files, Washington, D. C.

———. "Political Semantics." Speech before the American Society of Newspaper Editors, Washington, D. C., April 17, 1968. Fulbright files, Washington, D. C.

———. "Prospects for Peace with Freedom." Speech before Rhodes Scholar Reunion, Swarthmore College, Swarthmore, Pennsylvania, June 19, 1965. Fulbright files, Washington, D. C.

————. "Public Opinion and Foreign Policy." Speech at Bowling Green State University, Bowling Green, Ohio, March 9, 1963. Fulbright files, Washington, D. C.

————. "Public Policy and Military Responsibility." Speech delivered at the Opening Session of the National War College and the Industrial College of the Armed Forces, Washington, D. C., August 21, 1961. Fulbright files, Washington, D. C.

————. "Putting Our Own House in Order." Speech at Virginia Polytechnic Institute, Blacksburg, Virginia, April 3, 1965. Fulbright files, Washington, D. C.

————. "Russia and the West." William L. Clayton Lecture, The Fletcher School of Law and Diplomacy, Tufts University, April 29, 1963. Fulbright files, Washington, D. C.

————. "Some Aspects of American Foreign Policy." Speech before the American Bar Association, Washington, D. C., September 1, 1960. Fulbright files, Washington, D. C.

————. "Some Aspects of Foreign Relations." Speech at the University of Indiana, March 10, 1961. Fulbright files, Washington, D. C.

————. "The Two Americas." Brian McMahon Lecture at the University of Connecticut, printed in the *Congressional Record*, 112, Part 5, pp. 6749–6753.

————. "The United Nations in World Politics." Speech before the United Nations Association of Greater Phoenix, Phoenix, Arizona, October 24, 1964. Fulbright files, Washington, D. C.

————. Untitled speech before the American Society of Newspaper Editors, Washington, D. C., April 18, 1959. Fulbright files, Washington, D. C.

————. Untitled speech before the Arkansas Chamber of Commerce, November 8, 1961. Fulbright files, Washington, D. C.

————. Untitled speech before the Bond Club, New York City, December 11, 1944. Fulbright files, Washington, D. C.

————. Untitled speech before the Consultative Assembly of the Council of Europe, Strasbourg, France, May 4, 1965. Fulbright files, Washington, D. C.

————. Untitled speech before the Los Angeles World Affairs Council, October 31, 1960. Fulbright files, Washington, D .C.

————. Untitled speech at Pine Bluff, Arkansas, December 17, 1958. Fulbright files, Washington, D. C.

————. "The Vietnam Fallout." Speech before the Bureau of

Advertising of the American Newspaper Publishers Association, New York City, April 28, 1966. Fulbright files, Washington, D. C.

———. "What Kind of a Country Do You Want America to Be." Speech at Kansas State University, Manhattan, Kansas, May 5, 1967. Fulbright files, Washington, D. C.

———. "What Makes U. S. Foreign Policy?" Speech at the tenth anniversary banquet of the *Reporter* magazine, Overseas Press Club, New York City, April 15, 1959. Fulbright files, Washington, D. C.

Interviews

Senator J. William Fulbright, Washington, D. C., January 26, 1970.

Senator Albert Gore, Washington, D. C., January 27, 1970.

Former Vice-President Hubert H. Humphrey, Manhattan, Kansas, January 9, 1970.

Senator Mike Mansfield, Washington, D. C., January 27, 1970.

Parker Westbrook, Washington, D. C., January 27–February 1, 1970.

Miscellaneous

Correspondence between Senator J. William Fulbright and officials of the Department of State and the New York *Herald Tribune,* September 17, 1960–October 19, 1960. Fulbright files, Washington, D. C.

Fulbright, J. William. "Foreign Aid, Vietnam and American Objectives." Statement at the Hearings on S. 3091, Committee on Foreign Relations. Press release, March 11, 1968. Fulbright files, Washington, D. C.

———. "France and the Western Alliance." Press release, undated. Fulbright files, Washington, D. C.

———. Letter to The Editor, *Washington Post,* March 26, 1945. Fulbright files, Washington, D. C.

———. Memorandum to the Department of Defense, 1961. Fulbright files, Washington, D. C.

———. "Political and Economic Reconstruction in South Vietnam." Press release, undated. Fulbright files, Washington, D. C.

————. Remarks before the Senate regarding Senate action on the Development Loan Fund. Press release, undated. Fulbright files, Washington, D. C.

————. "Repeal of the Connally Amendment." Memorandum, February 22, 1961. Fulbright files, Washington, D. C.

————. Statement concerning the selection of Ambassadorial appointments, May 12, 1959. Fulbright files, Washington, D. C.

————. Statement correcting Vice-President Nixon's campaign speech concerning the American use of a veto in the United Nations. Press release, October 23, 1960. Fulbright files, Washington, D. C.

————. Statement relating to a memorandum submitted by him to the Department of Defense, 1961. Fulbright files, Washington, D. C.

————. Statement in response to Vice-President Nixon's campaign statements about Quemoy and Matsu. Press release, October 15, 1960. Fulbright files, Washington, D. C.

————. "Vietnam: A Proposal for the Democratic Party in 1968." Statement to the Platform Committee of the Democratic National Committee, August 20, 1968. Fulbright files, Washington, D. C.

Glad, Betty. "The Significance of Role Personality For Role Performance As Chairman of the Senate Foreign Relations Committee: A Comparison of Borah and Fulbright." Paper delivered at the American Political Science Association Meeting, September 3, 1969.

Mock, Lucille. "Truman and Fulbright: The Controversial Proposal for Resignation." Unpublished Graduate Seminar Paper, Central Missouri State University, 1970.

Perry, Bruce. Senator J. William Fulbright on European and Atlantic Unity. Ph.D. dissertation, University of Pennsylvania, 1968.

Radio and Television Programs

N.B.C. Radio, November 23, 1945. Fulbright files, Washington, D. C.

"Advice and Dissent." C.B.S. Special Report, telecast, February 1, 1966. Printed in Congressional Record, 112, Part 2, pp. 1941–1943.

"Face the Nation." C.B.S. telecast, January 27, 1957. Fulbright files, Washington, D. C.

"A House Divided." N.B.C. telecast, May 10, 1970.

"Martha Rountree's Press Conference." A.B.C. telecast, December 30, 1956. Fulbright files, Washington, D. C.

"Meet the Press." N.B.C. telecast, June 7, 1959. Fulbright files, Washington, D. C.

————. N.B.C. telecast, August 6, 1961. Fulbright files, Washington, D. C.

————. N.B.C. telecast, March 14, 1965. Fulbright files, Washington, D. C.

————. N.B.C. telecast, January 22, 1967. Fulbright files, Washington, D. C.

Court Cases, Public Laws, and Resolutions

Mora v. *McNamara*, 389 U. S. 934 (1967).

Myers v. *United States*, 272 U. S. 293 (1926).

United States v. *Belmont*, 301 U. S. 324 1937).

United States v. *Curtiss-Wright Export Corporation*, 299 U. S. 304 (1936).

United States v. *Pink*, 315 U. S. 203 (1942).

Youngstown Sheet and Tube Company v. *Sawyer*, 343 U. S. 579 (1952).

U. S. *Statutes at Large*. Vol. LXIX. 84th Cong., 1st sess., 1955, 7.

U. S. *Statutes at Large*. Vol. LXXI. 85th Cong., 1st sess., 1957, 5, 6.

U. S. *Statutes at Large*. Vol. LXXVI. 87th Cong., 2d sess., 1962, 697.

U. S. *Statutes at Large*. Vol. LXXVIII. 88th Cong., 2d sess., 1964, 384.

Senate Concurrent Resolution 64. 91st Cong., 2d sess., Calendar No. 838, May 1, 1970.

INDEX